D0538775

PREVENTION'S
Quick and Healthy
LOW-FAT COOKING

FEATURING
PASTA AND OTHER
ITALIAN FAVORITES

EDITED BY JEAN ROGERS, FOOD EDITOR, **PREVENTION** MAGAZINE HEALTH BOOKS

RODALE PRESS, INC.
EMMAUS, PENNSYLVANIA

This book is simultaneously being published by Rodale Press as *Prevention's Low-Fat Italian Favorites.*

Copyright ©1996 by Rodale Press, Inc.
Illustrations copyright ©1996 by Tad Ware & Company, Inc.
Photographs copyright ©1996 by Rodale Press, Inc.

Front Cover: Braised Peppers on Pasta (page 66)

Cover Photography: Tad Ware & Company, Inc.

Library of Congress Cataloging-in-Publication Data

Prevention's quick and healthy low-fat cooking: featuring pasta and other Italian
    favorites / edited by Jean Rogers.
            p.   cm.
    Includes index.
    ISBN 0–87596–305–6 hardcover
    1. Cookery, Italian.   2. Low-fat diet—Recipes.   I. Rogers, Jean,
date.   II. Prevention (Emmaus, Pa.)
TX723.P76 1995
641.5'638—dc20   95–24994

        2   4   6   8   10   9   7   5   3   1   hardcover

─── OUR MISSION ───

We publish books that empower people's lives.

─── RODALE 🌱 BOOKS ───

Prevention's Quick and Healthy Low-Fat Cooking

Editorial Staff

Editor: Jean Rogers
Contributing Writer: Beth Dooley
Book and Cover Designer: Debra Sfetsios
Studio Manager: Joe Golden
Book Layout: Tad Ware & Company, Inc.
Illustrator: Tad Ware & Company, Inc.
Photographer: Tad Ware Photography
Food Stylist: Robin Krause
Assistant Food Stylist: Genie Zarling
Recipe Development and Coordination: Beth Dooley
Recipe Development: Laura Tiffany, Genie Zarling
Recipe Testing: Joanna Jacox, Nicole Strandlund
Nutritional Consultant: Linda Yoakam, M.S., R.D.
Production Manager: Helen Clogston
Manufacturing Coordinator: Melinda B. Rizzo
Editor, **Prevention** *Magazine:* Mark Bricklin

Prevention *Magazine Health Books*

Vice-President and Editorial Director: Debora T. Yost
Art Director: Jane Colby Knutila
Research Manager: Ann Gossy Yermish
Copy Manager: Lisa D. Andruscavage

Contents

Introduction

*W*hen you look at the overall healthfulness of the Italian lifestyle, you must take more into consideration than just the food. Yes, the type of recipes and ingredients found in this book go a long way toward imbuing Italians with the robust health they enjoy. But the story goes deeper than that. Consider these other factors that contribute to the Italians' overall well-being.

"In many areas of Italy, people spend the evening walking back and forth in the town center, visiting and chatting," says anthropologist Peter Brown, Ph.D., of Emory University in Atlanta. "It's a pleasant way to get exercise while they see their friends."

"In Italy, the roads are small, narrow and clogged," says food writer Judith Olney, a cookbook author and restaurant critic of *The Washington Times*, who's visited Italy several times and savored the easy, graceful ways of the Italian lifestyle. "So people walk a lot. They have strong legs. Even very elderly people haul wheeled baskets around town to shop."

When it does come to food, Italian versions of dishes often differ from what's served in America under the same name. Take pizza. Fulvia Castelli, a Milanese philosophy student now living in Los Angeles, explains that "A real Italian pizza fits inside your dinner plate. It's dotted with a little tomato, basil and oil. It's not loaded with lots of toppings, and usually has less cheese."

A typical Italian dessert is fruit rather than something like ice cream, which is a staple in American freezers. "We don't usually keep a big pack of ice cream in the freezer," says Fulvia. "If we want gelato (the Italian version of ice cream), we have to go out for it. Compared with the United States, you get a tiny serving."

All of this gives you some clues why, as a nation, Italians are slimmer and healthier than Americans. If you'd like to tap into some of that good health, consider taking to heart the tips above as well as those in the text chapters and recipes that follow.

Jean Rogers

JEAN ROGERS
Food Editor, *Prevention* Magazine Health Books

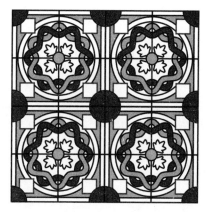

CHAPTER 1

LIFELONG
CHANGES FOR A
HEALTHIER YOU

LIVING HEALTHY– THE ITALIAN WAY

Ask an Italian the best place to eat and most likely he will direct you to his mother's table. Here you'll find platters of roasted vegetables, bowls of steaming pasta with fresh herbs and crusty hot bread. Enter her kitchen with its ropes of garlic and baskets of brilliant red and yellow peppers and fat tomatoes. Just outside, a hedge of rosemary and a bush of basil cast their scents on the soft breeze. With its terra-cotta tiles, bread stone, trestle table and open hearth, it has changed very little since the farmhouse was built in the 1700s, yet it is very much a kitchen of today.

Italian cooking is home cooking. It is nourishing and balanced, healthy and sublime. It is spontaneous, relying on fresh and seasonal foods. And it is classic, using traditional cooking methods and the complex flavors of aged ingredients such as balsamic vinegar and Parmesan cheese.

Italian cooking calls to all of our senses with the aroma of a simmering marinara sauce, the quiet rhythm of kneading pizza dough, the beauty of bright peppers on pasta. Dating back to the mid-1600s, this homey, honest, natural food spans centuries of remembered history, yet it is timeless and contemporary.

LIVING SIMPLY IN A COMPLEX WORLD

Recently, medical experts have confirmed what generations of Italians who have lived off the bounty of their land and sea have known for centuries —the Italian diet is not only delicious but extremely healthy. Italians suffer far fewer heart attacks, and their sound eating habits put them at lower risk for high blood pressure, diabetes, cancer, arthritis and intestinal problems than their American and northern European counterparts. Those who enjoy a healthful diet and active life not only live longer, but are slimmer and have beautiful skin, shiny hair and agile bodies.

The healthy Italian diet is high in grains, legumes, fruits, vegetables and fish, with very small amounts of lean meat and poultry. Fat comes largely in the monounsaturated form from foods such as olive oil, nuts and olives. There is very little saturated fat (the fat that raises blood cholesterol levels) from red meat, eggs and dairy products. Italians use unsaturated oils in place of artery-clogging butters and other fats found in packaged foods and fast foods. Potato chips, French fries, doughnuts, candy bars and other processed temptations have no place in the typical Italian diet.

Food prepared outside the home in bakeries and *trattorias*, even the "street food," is made with natural, unprocessed ingredients. The local baker sells fresh, wholesome bread made with just a little olive oil; street vendors offer *granità* (icy sorbet), *gelato* (fresh ice cream without stabilizers and processed fats) and paper cones of dried fruit and roasted nuts.

"I remember watching my mother's sister, Aunt Buliti, dancing the twist with her girlfriends without a care in the world, while munching on slices of Pizza Marguerita from the bakery down the street. When Aunt Buliti took Mario and me to the public gardens, we always stopped for la Brioscia con Gelato (a fresh roll with handmade ice cream)," writes Nick Stellino, in his book, *Cucina Amore*.

In addition, Italians enjoy active lives. They walk or ride bikes to work, walk to the piazza for espresso, walk to market and to visit friends, logging several miles in the course of a day. Most Italians enjoy the physical work of tending their own lush gardens and orchards. They play soccer and bocci and hike through the glorious hillside. This healthy lifestyle is neither trendy nor new but passed down through generations as so much family wisdom.

Perhaps for all of us, the challenge of dealing with the stresses and temptations of our high-speed, high-tech world is in learning to slow down and step back in time. Instead of watching TV after a long day at the computer, we need to walk around the block, weed the garden or shovel snow. Instead of reaching for the microwave macaroni and cheese dinner, we'd do well to make a quick dish of angel hair pasta and braised sweet peppers. These changes are simple and subtle, but they make a huge difference in the course of a lifetime.

HEALTHFUL AND HEALING

We are just now beginning to appreciate the benefits of a diet focused on grains, vegetables and fruit, understanding that these foods not only promote good health but prevent disease and speed recovery. Here's how:

Antioxidants: These natural chemicals found in fruits and vegetables help keep low-density-lipoprotein (LDL) cholesterol from clinging to arterial walls. Foods high in vitamin C (tomatoes, oranges, grapefruit) and beta-carotene (carrots, sweet potatoes, winter squashes) are loaded with these natural heart protectors.

Antioxidants may also help reduce the risk of cancer by protecting genetic materials from becoming damaged and growing out of control into cancerous cells. In addition, phytochemicals—compounds in vegetables such as broccoli, carrots, fennel, tomatoes—help the body resist cancer.

Monounsaturated fats: Olive oil, canola oil, peanut oil and avocado oil—all *mono* or single fat oils—actually bring down the levels of harmful LDL cholesterol without lowering the protective HDL cholesterol. These oils are also a good source of vitamin E, found to lower the risk of heart disease, cancer and other serious diseases.

The benefits of fish oil (omega-3 fatty acids) are many and varied. It inhibits blood clots that lead to strokes, increases HDL, prevents some cancers and soothes tender arthritic joints ("True Fish Tales," page 87).

High fiber: A diet high in fruits, vegetables and grains is also naturally high in dietary fiber. Soluble fiber (very prominent in beans, for instance) is shown to help reduce LDLs. Insoluble fiber (such as wheat bran) helps reduce the risk of colon, breast and prostate cancers.

FOOD PYRAMIDS:
SIMPLE GUIDELINES FOR HEALTHY EATING

To illustrate the healthy diet, researchers and dietitians have created "food pyramids" to depict the nutritional priority of different foods. The USDA Food Guide Pyramid and the Traditional Healthy Mediterranean Diet Pyramid are shown below. At first glance they present a dramatic contrast to the old "four food group" theory that lumped together meat, poultry and fish as "protein" and gave it the same weight as bread and grains, eggs and dairy, and vegetables and fruit.

The first pyramid was released in 1992 by the U.S. Department of Agriculture. With its emphasis on grains, breads, fruits and vegetables, it dismisses the notion of a "square meal." It provides specific recommendations for the number of servings of breads, vegetables, fruit, dairy products and proteins American should eat daily, while limiting the fat intake to 30 percent of the total diet. Sweets are used sparingly.

In 1994, the Traditional Healthy Mediterranean Diet Pyramid, a culinary and scientific rejoinder to the USDA matrix, was published through the joint efforts of the Harvard School of Public Health, the European office of the World Health Organization and Oldways Preservation & Exchange Trust, a Boston-based "food think tank." It is more restrictive than the USDA pyramid in the amount of red meat, poultry, eggs, fish and cheese it recommends people consume daily. It also allows for up to 35 percent of the day's calories from fat but mostly limits those fat calories to monounsaturated fats such as olive oil. Perhaps the most controversial aspect of the diet is its recommendation that wine be consumed daily in moderation. It draws on research that shows those who imbibe two drinks a day have a lower rate of heart disease, stroke and premature death.

The differences in these two pyramids are subtle but important. The USDA pyramid presents all protein foods—fish, beans, nuts and eggs—on the same level and ignores the huge difference between saturated and unsaturated fat. It recommends two to three servings from the "meat" category per day, which could be interpreted as nine ounces of hamburger, more than a healthful diet should allow.

The Mediterranean pyramid, on the other hand, separates vegetable proteins (beans and nuts) from animal proteins and recommends fish and poultry over meat. Unlike the USDA model, it makes no allowances for butter or margarine and encourages the use of olive oil for those not concerned about calories.

The pyramids are not meant as rigid prescriptions but general guidelines. Key to both pyramids is variety: carbohydrates, dried beans and other legumes, vegetables, fruit and a sparing use of fats and sweets.

There are no tricks or hints or complicated schemes that identify the "Italian diet." In fact, the term "diet" may be misleading. This is rather a model for enjoying fresh, natural food, thoughtfully prepared and beautifully presented. It has nothing in common with strict regimes of artless, tasteless "diet" fare. It is tuned to the seasons, in step with the body's rhythms.

THE ITALIAN TABLE

The word "diet" itself derives from Greek *diaita*, meaning "way of life." This Italian diet, or way of life, embraces moderation. The basic tenets are few and easy to follow. They leave lots of room for a cook's imagination and creativity. Enjoy pasta, risotto or polenta but use little butter, oil or cream. Experiment with lower-fat cheeses (such as part-skim mozzarella and nonfat ricotta). Steam vegetables and serve them with a little oil or a light vinaigrette, or braise them in stock. Reduce oil or butter to a minimum in all dishes and never, ever deep-fat fry. Use meat sparingly. Grill or quickly broil meat, fish and poultry, using as little fat as possible, and serve them without sauce. Season with fresh and dried herbs and flavor with lemon, wine, garlic and vegetable purees.

Here is what a typical Italian day might look like:

Breakfast *(Prima Colazione)*: Most Italians enjoy a small "continental" breakfast of juice or fruit, coffee and an Italian or sourdough roll, without jam or butter.

Lunch *(Colazione)*: The midday meal is considered very important, is often social and is always taken at leisure. It is never rushed or eaten at one's desk or in the car. It might start with a light pasta dish with vegetables or a cup of *minestra* (a "little" or light soup). A small frittata would then be served with bread or focaccia, followed by a light tossed salad. The meal would end with espresso, cheese or fruit.

Dinner *(Pranzo)*: This is the evening meal for the entire family. It most often begins with a *primo piatto*, a light soup or some pasta served with a light sauce. Then comes the *secondi piatti*, the second or main course, served with bread or focaccia. Often this is a small portion of fish or poultry or, on special occasions, meat. Vegetables are served along with this course; a light salad often follows. The meal ends with *dolci*, the cheese or fruit course, served with a strong cup of espresso. Baked desserts and sweets are reserved for special occasions.

The midday meal is often followed by a short rest. Stores close, businessmen return home, housewives sit a spell, and everyone catches their collective breaths, returning to their chores relaxed and refreshed. The quantities served at midday are not large but substantial and satisfying enough that most people last comfortably through the afternoon to a relatively late dinner, served around eight o'clock. It is considered wise to eat lightly at night, even though there may be more courses than at midday.

Italians do not snack the way Americans do. Street merchants sell dried fruits and nuts, roasted chestnuts and pumpkin seeds, toasted fava beans and chick-peas. Children often buy paper cones of roasted nuts to eat on their way home from school. Adults pause late in the day for an espresso with a small piece of *biscotti* (a dry cookie) or a slice of plain bread or *focaccia*.

Eating this way, calories are spread throughout the day, the most effective way to speed the metabolism, minimize fat storage and dampen the appetite. It's long been observed that missing meals, especially early in the day, is hazardous to the waistline. "Skipping breakfast, eating a moderate lunch and having a huge dinner is the most common pattern for people with weight problems," notes James J. Kenney, Ph.D., R.D., nutrition research specialist at the Pritikin Longevity Center in Santa Monica, California. By-passing breakfast or lunch can leave you starving for dinner. The result, as most of us know, is overeating and a slower metabolism. "We found that people who skipped breakfast, or breakfast and lunch, burned about 25 percent fewer calories than people who were eating three meals a day or more," says obesity expert C. Wayne Callaway, M.D., associate clinical professor of medicine, George Washington University in Washington, D.C.

This pattern also affects production of the hormone insulin, which encourages fat production and storage, says Dr. Kenney. Large meals cause the body to release more insulin. The time of day seems to make a difference, too. "In the evening, the body responds better to insulin," says Dr. Kenney. "That means it stores fat more efficiently at dinnertime."

Eating smaller, more frequent meals not only reduces insulin but boosts the metabolism, burning more calories as well. The best plan is to eat about 25 percent of the daily calories at breakfast, another 25 percent at lunch, then 20 percent to 25 percent on a substantial afternoon snack. Dinner should be moderate with about the same number of calories as earlier meals. Any snacks eaten after dinner should be light and low-fat.

LIGHT ITALIAN HOME COOKING

Over the past 50 years in Italy, the trend has been to lighten home cooking. Known as *cucina magra*, this slimming, healthful cuisine is simple and elegant, inspired by the world-famous health spas of Tuscany. Light Italian cuisine is not rigid or complicated; it relies on the best and the freshest ingredients for its success.

Here are a few hints for converting your favorite recipes into healthful dishes:

■ Skim fat from all soups and stews. You can do that while they cook if you place half of the pot over a hot flame. As the liquid boils, it will push the scum and fat to the other side of the pot, where it is cooler. Using a wide large spoon, scoop off the scum and fat. An alternate method is to allow the hot soup or stew to cool to room temperature then place it in the refrigerator for at least an hour, or until it is cool and a fatty film has formed on top. Scrape off the fat with a wide spoon.

■ Instead of sautéing vegetables in oil or butter, braise them in a little stock, wine or water with fresh herbs. Put the vegetables in a no-stick frying pan set over high heat and add half an inch of liquid. Cover and cook about two or three minutes, or until the vegetables are just tender. Remove the lid and continue cooking another minute until the liquid is reduced.

■ Use canned fish such as tuna, salmon and sardines packed in water, not oil.

■ Remove fish skin after the fish has cooked.

■ Reduce the amount of meat called for in a recipe to no more than three ounces of red meat per serving and no more than four ounces of poultry per serving.

■ Trim fat from meat or poultry before cooking. Remove poultry skin before eating.

■ For broiling, baking and braising meat, fish and poultry, use chicken or beef stock and wine to reduce the amounts of butter and oil.

■ Be sure to drain any fat from browned meat before adding it to a dish or before adding vegetables to the frying pan.

■ Reduce the amount of oil for stir-frying and sautéing to no more than one tablespoon per four servings and use a no-stick frying pan.

■ No-stick sprays are useful. You can make your own healthy "spray" by filling a plant-spritzing water bottle with olive oil. A few squirts will coat the pan with less than one teaspoon of oil.

■ Liberally use lemon juice and herbs for flavoring.

■ Salt food only after it has cooked or at the end of a recipe.

■ Substitute skim and evaporated skim milk for whole milk and cream.

■ Use nonfat plain yogurt or nonfat Yogurt Cheese (page 28) instead of sour cream and cream cheese.

■ Reduce the oil in salad dressings by replacing one-quarter of the amount with chicken stock, tomato juice, fruit juice or nonfat plain yogurt.

■ Substitute extra egg whites for some yolks. If making scrambled eggs, for instance, use one whole egg and four egg whites instead of three whole eggs.

■ Cut the amount of nuts in a recipe by half and toast them first for the most flavor.

■ Cut the amount of sugar in a recipe by 25 percent.

LIGHT ITALIAN DINING OUT

Of all the ethnic restaurants, Italian is the most popular in the United States. Up until several years ago, most "Italian-style" restaurants featured Americanized versions of Italian food: spaghetti loaded with golf ball-size meatballs, heavily breaded veal, pizza with congealed cheese that, on the first bite, slid off the crust in a slab. No wonder Italian food had a bad rap.

Today's restaurants offer more authentic menus. Chefs are making good use of the wealth of fresh ingredients. Thankfully, eating at an Italian restaurant is no longer a gut-busting proposition. Still, an understanding of what the different Italian dishes are and how they are prepared can help the smart diner navigate a safe course through the sea of choices—some healthy, some disastrous.

Here are a few suggestions:

Here is a guide to a traditional Italian menu:

The antipasto or appetizer course may offer a selection of meats such as prosciutto and salami, cheeses, olives and marinated vegetables. Stick with the vegetables. Or order a tossed salad with vinaigrette, oil and vinegar or lemon juice on the side. Look for salads of radicchio, arugula, endive, tomatoes, broccoli, spinach, peppers and other raw vegetables. Avoid Caesar salads with their eggs, grated cheese, anchovies and oily dressing.

The primo or first course may include soup, pasta, risotto or polenta. Stick with a light soup, a pasta with tomato sauce or vegetables, or maybe a light tossed salad.

Pasta is simply wheat with a little protein, risotto is rice, and polenta is cornmeal. All are low in fat and calories by themselves; it's what goes with them that can be disastrous to a diet. Look for sauces and toppings that focus on vegetables: marinara (tomato) sauce, primavera (sautéed vegetables) or red and white clam sauce. Avoid high-fat cheese, sausage, cream, bacon and other fattening toppings. Pesto, made of crushed basil, olive oil, Parmesan cheese and pine nuts, is delicious but fattening. It may be ordered on the side.

Steer clear of stuffed pastas such as tortellini, ravioli, cannelloni, manicotti, agnolotti and lasagna. These are loaded with cheese and egg mixtures.

Although pasta, risotto and polenta are often offered as first courses, they may be ordered as an entrée.

The secondo, the second course or entrée, includes meat, poultry or fish, usually served with a vegetable. Fish or poultry is often your best bet, served simply grilled or with a tomato or vegetable sauce. Veal dishes are often breaded and pan-fried, and not a wise choice if you're watching cholesterol and calories.

You may choose pasta, polenta or risotto for your entrée. The waiter may offer an entrée-sized portion, but an appetizer portion is usually plenty, especially if the meal includes an antipasto and salad.

The insalada, the salad course, might be a tossed salad, or sliced tomatoes with sliced mozzarella cheese or cooked vegetables dressed in vinaigrette. In Italy, the salad usually follows the entrée, but you may order it as a first course or an entrée.

■ Remember, you are the patron and can design your own meal, regardless of the way the menu reads.

■ Share and share alike. The fun of eating out is in experiencing new foods and different flavors. Often just a bit or two of something rich is all one really wants. Better to have a taste than to feel deprived and in need of some ice cream once you are home.

■ Skip the bread if it is drenched in butter and garlic. Indulge if it is a truly wonderful focaccia or hearth-style country loaf.

In Italy, most Italians end a meal with a strong cup of espresso—no fat, no cholesterol, few calories and, when caffeinated, no sleep. Try decaf espresso or a decaf skim-milk cappuccino (frothed skim milk with decaf espresso). If feeling an urge to splurge, you may always share a spumoni, cannoli, tortoni or tiramisu (layers of brandy-and-espresso-drenched ladyfingers, creamy mascarpone, zabaglione and whipped cream). After a good meal, just one or two bites is plenty, and helps stave off the feeling of being deprived. Fat-free *granità*, fruit sorbet or a simple dish of fresh strawberries or raspberries makes a delicious, sensible choice, too.

Pizza is perhaps the most popular "Italian" food of all, far more popular here than in Italy, where it is considered American. It is the mainstay of several fast-food chain restaurants, the top choice for home-delivered foods and the darling of upscale wine bars and pasta places.

The biggest problem with pizza, nutritionally speaking, is not its crust but what gets piled on top. Today, thanks to the push by nutrition advocates, even the least expensive chains offer more vegetable selections. Think of ordering mushrooms, peppers, onions, tomato slices, artichokes, broccoli—whatever vegetables are available—in lieu of pepperoni, anchovies, meatballs, sausage and extra cheese (or any cheese).

It's too easy to eat more pizza than you really need or even want. Decide on how may slices you'll have and stick to that. Start with a big salad of fresh greens tossed in a little vinaigrette.

The next chapter is a guide to Italian ingredients, the tools of healthy Italian cooking. It is deliciously easy to embrace these sunny flavors, this simple way of cooking and eating. Try it; you'll like it.

CHAPTER 2

STOCKING
the ITALIAN
KITCHEN

SAVOR THE FLAVOR

In Italy, there is no such thing as "Italian cuisine," only Bolognese, Venetian, Roman, Milanese, Tuscan, Florentine, Genoese, Piedmontese, Sicilian and Neapolitan cuisine, as well as that of the other ten regions in this small yet very diverse nation. Until 1861, these regions were part of sovereign and often hostile states that shared few cultural traditions and no common spoken language. Even today, native idioms vary so greatly that a Venetian may not understand a Neapolitan's slang nor recognize some items on the Neapolitan table.

In Naples and southern Italy, the flavors are distinctly Mediterranean: pasta dressed with the tomatoes, garlic, eggplant, olives and basil that grow so abundantly there. In Venice, the food is delicate and colorful, often compared to the mosaics and tinted marbles of that exotic city, ancient hub of the spice trade. Here one might lunch on a light saffron risotto with peas and artichokes, followed with sliced cantaloupe steeped in honey and cinnamon.

Italy is a country of diverging landscapes and extreme climates, of alpine mountains and bountiful seas. The land itself is rich and varied: Olive trees grow on rugged hillsides, wheat grows in fertile fields, and cattle graze the lush grasslands. The bountiful sea yields a harvest of fish and shellfish—tuna, halibut, swordfish, striped bass, sole, flounder, mackerel, anchovies, sardines, shrimp, mussels, clams and squid. Trout and catfish swim the clear streams. Climate, tradition, the land and the sea have greatly shaped regional cooking. Hearty soups and warming stews abound to the north, and various seafood salads and marinated vegetables are prominent in the south.

The one culinary thread that binds Italian cooks is a consuming passion for the freshest fare and the finest ingredients. The Italians take food very seriously. The making of vinegar, olive oil and cheese is an art that requires years of study. Fresh fruit and herbs are abundant; what isn't grown in one's garden is available at the open-air market. The shellfish and fish are harvested daily. All Italians know and trust their town or neighborhood butcher.

Freshness and quality, important in any well-made dish, are critical in low-fat cooking. There are no cream and butter sauces or thick, sweet toppings to mask inferior ingredients. This cooking relies on clean, true flavors; it focuses on the natural goodness of the food itself. The ingredients must be worthy of such attention.

While healthful, light and quick Italian fare is simple and easy, it also relies on the good judgment and discipline of the committed cook. It means avoiding the processed foods of our culture and dispensing with frozen dinners, packaged snacks and artificial desserts. It means reading labels, recognizing sugar, fat and sodium in their many guises and knowing that "light" doesn't necessarily mean nutritious. It means returning to an older, simpler style of cooking that may take some getting used to. This kind of effort deserves to be recognized and rewarded. Why not spend a little more on those brilliant, thick-fleshed sweet red peppers? Why not splurge on that beautiful bottle of rich-tasting balsamic vinegar? The little more spent on the best ingredients may make a huge difference in the success of these recipes, of a low-fat diet and ultimately of a healthy and energetic lifestyle.

THE FUNDAMENTALS

These are ingredients you will come to rely on. Standard items in the Italian pantry, they are used in a variety of different recipes throughout this book. (They are presented here alphabetically, not in order of importance.)

BALSAMIC VINEGAR

Balsamic vinegar has been made for the past thousand years in the Italian province of Modena, north of Bologna. It is made from the sweet juice of white grapes, boiled down into a heady concentrate, then aged for decades in a succession of barrels, each of a different wood. The very finest balsamic vinegars, according to noted food writer Lynne Rossetto Kasper, "are luscious enough to be sipped like liqueurs. The taste resembles a mixture of old port and a full-flavored brown sauce." Authentic balsamic vinegars are put up in containers that resemble perfume bottles and carry the officially established appellation *Aceto Balsamico Tradizionale di Modena*. These are used sparingly: Only a small spoonful is needed to season a simple pasta, finish grilled vegetables or make a simple dish of strawberries taste exotic.

Commercial balsamic vinegars from Modena and Reggio, the vinegars most readily available, are used throughout this book. The best of these are a blend of fine-quality wine vinegars, young balsamic vinegars and caramel; they're aged for a short time in balsamic barrels. They offer a balanced blend of acidity and sweetness to sauces, dressings and marinades. Poor balsamic vinegars are rough and pungent.

Once opened, balsamic vinegar is best kept refrigerated and used within a year.

BEANS

Dried beans and lentils are used in many Italian dishes, especially in the regions of Tuscany, Abruzzi, Umbria and Latium. Tuscans favor *cannellini* or white kidney beans. Chick-peas (*ceci*), fava beans, cranberry beans and "Scotch" beans, as well as the quick-cooking lentils, are used throughout the country. Many beans are used fresh for short times throughout the year, but in the U.S., they are hard to come by.

In this collection, canned beans are interchangeable with soaked and cooked dried beans in most recipes (unless otherwise noted). Canned beans tend not to be as firm as home-cooked beans and may need to be rinsed if the manufacturer has processed them with too much salt. A number of organic varieties that have been canned without salt are now available commercially. The information box

("Beans, Beans, Beans," page 20) gives quick-soaking and overnight-soaking instructions for dried beans.

Store dried beans in an airtight container. "Dry" does not mean "immortal," so try to use them within a year. The older they are, the longer they need to soak and to cook.

BREAD

Italian breads are varied and wholesome. Big, chewy, rustic loaves; flat, herbed focaccia; thin, crusty breadsticks—all play a huge role in the healthy Italian menu. Besides these fragrant loaves (many now available in local bakeries throughout the U.S.), leftover and stale breads are widely used by creative Italian cooks. *Bruschetta* is sliced toasted bread lightly brushed with oil and garlic; *crostini* is the classic Italian crouton, cut into one-inch cubes or served as larger toasts. Both are served as is or topped with any number of spreads or vegetables and served alongside soup and salad.

Bread crumbs made from good-quality, low-fat, low-salt, rustic Italian bread can help thicken a soup, give body to a stuffing, enrich a pasta sauce and use up those odds and ends of stale loaves. They are most often used dry. To make fresh bread crumbs, put the bread in a food processor fitted with the steel blade; process until very fine. To dry, spread the crumbs on a baking sheet and toast at 375° for 10 to 15 minutes, or until very dry. Store the crumbs in an airtight container at room temperature for a week or freeze in plastic bags.

CHEESE

From the famous, well-aged *Parmigiano-Reggiano* to delicate fresh ricotta, Italian cheeses are among the finest, most interesting in the world. Many are now available in low-fat or nonfat forms that add interest to low-fat fare. Here is a brief description of those most often called for in the recipes ahead.

Asiago cheese is a semifirm, rich-tasting cheese that is somewhat softer and milder than Parmesan. It is made from part-skim cow's milk and is delicious grated in dishes that might be dominated by Parmesan.

Mozzarella in Italy is made from buffalo's milk. Available in the U.S. in specialty cheese shops, fresh mozzarella is pure white and has a very mild, almost sweet flavor and a very tender texture. It is most often served with sliced tomatoes and basil with a splash of balsamic vinegar and a touch of extra-virgin olive oil.

The recipes in this book call for the part-skim mozzarella available commercially. It tastes best if bought in chunks and shredded right before use.

Parmesan is the name we Americans often use for any cheese grated over pasta or pizza. The true Parmesan—*Parmigiano-Reggiano*—is rich, full-bodied and melts beautifully into the ingredients it joins. A certified Parmesan, made using the same process for the past 700 years, is created from the partly skimmed milk of cows raised within the provinces of Parma and Reggio and aged at least 18 months.

Buy real Parmesan from a reliable source and have it cut from a larger wheel. Once cut or shredded, the cheese begins to lose moisture and acquires a sharp taste. Good Parmesan should have a smooth, nutty flavor and be mildly salty but never harsh or pungent. The packaged grated Parmesan, though convenient, does not have nearly the flavor or texture of the real thing. When you use truly fresh grated Parmesan, just a little will go a long way.

Ricotta literally means "recooked," describing the process of making this cheese by cooking whey (watery residue) left from making another cheese. In Italy, ricotta is made from a combination of ewe's milk and skimmed cow's milk. Very soft, granular and mild-tasting, it is used in spreads, with vegetables, as a stuffing, in sauces and in desserts. Look for the nonfat varieties now readily available. They taste good and work well in baked foods.

FRUIT

Fresh fruit is plentiful in the lush growing areas of southern Italy. Citrus fruits—especially oranges and lemons—flavor chicken, seafood and pasta dishes, as well as numerous desserts and pastries. Pears, peaches, apricots, melons and all sorts of berries are served as dessert, sometimes with cheese or syrup but often as themselves in all their natural glory.

GARLIC

Garlic, of all the Italian ingredients, may be the one most associated with Italian cooking. Roasted chicken, grilled mushrooms, soups, stews, fricassees, pasta sauces and the beloved pesto all rely on its presence. For thousands of years, garlic was prized for its healing properties. It was used to sterilize wounds, relieve coughs and treat snake bites. Today, it is believed that garlic may "thin" the blood and lower cholesterol.

When prepared for Italian cooking, the cloves are always peeled, then mashed, sliced thin or minced. In many recipes, the garlic is sautéed (often with other ingredients) to soften its flavor before the liquid is added to the frying pan. In good Italian cooking, the garlic should never be too strong, and it should never be allowed to burn.

Beware of garlic presses and the pureed garlic paste sold in jars. The press releases too many of the garlic's oils that create a bitter or pungent flavor in a dish; jarred garlic often tastes bitter and flat.

When buying garlic, look for large-cloved heads that are firm when pressed and show no sign of yellowing or drying out. The heavier a head of garlic feels, the fresher it is. Do not peel the garlic cloves until ready to chop and do not chop too far ahead of using. Store garlic with onions in an open basket or container at room temperature and out of the light. It should keep about two weeks.

HERBS AND SPICES

Fresh and dried herbs add tremendous flavor to low-fat, low-salt food. The herbs most used in Italy are basil, bay leaves, marjoram, oregano, rosemary, sage and thyme. These recipes most often call for fresh herbs, but one-third the amount of dried may be substituted for fresh. Bay leaves, oregano, rosemary, sage and thyme are as flavorful in their dried form as they are in their fresh, and all release their flavors through long cooking.

Basil is always best fresh and should not be added to a dish until the dish is cooked. Heat destroys its delicate fragrance. Marjoram, too, is better if used fresh, not dried, and added toward the end of cooking, though it is sturdier than basil.

Ancient spice traders introduced a variety of Asian and Middle Eastern flavors to Italian food. Nutmeg and black pepper were once literally considered "worth their weight in gold." They are most often used in ricotta and spinach fillings. Anise, saffron, ginger, cloves, cumin, coriander, cinnamon and turmeric, too, will season a risotto, sauce, sausage or dessert.

OLIVE OIL

Italian master chefs will agree that olive oil is the most frequently used fat in Italian cooking; they will disagree on the grades of oil cooks should use for different dishes. Some insist on using extra-virgin olive oils for everything (sautés, salad dressings and pastas). Others reserve this premium oil for seasoning pasta, dressing salads and vegetables. Here is a definition of the most common olive oils.

Extra-virgin olive oils are premium oils, produced by machines that crush ("cold press") the fruit and the pit without the use of heat or chemical solvents. The varying degrees of "virginity" are determined by the percentage of oleic acid. Extra-virgin may contain no more than 1 percent oleic acid.

The colors of extra-virgin olive oil range from gold to deep green, according to where and with which fruit the oil is made. One color is not better than the other, and oils vary greatly in style and flavor. Price is no indication of quality; it's best to find an oil you like and stick with it. A fine extra-virgin olive oil is not bland. It should not taste flat or bitter, nor leave a fatty feeling on the tongue. Good oils may be delicate, flowery, fruity or olive-tasting; some even taste peppery. Store olive oil in a dark place (cupboard, pantry, closet). Unopened, it keeps for a year. Once opened, use within three months. Sniff before using; if it is "off," it will have a rancid odor and tinny, pungent taste.

In this book, many of the recipes call for extra-virgin olive oil, even in sautés, because so little is used, and the flavor is important to the dish. Other oils may be used instead, but the results will vary.

Virgin olive oil cannot exceed 1.5 percent acidity, and it too is processed without the use of heat or chemicals. It has a subtler flavor than extra-virgin, and many cooks prefer it over extra-virgin in sautés and on pasta. You may use this oil in place of extra-virgin olive oil if you prefer.

Olive oil has an acidity under 4 percent and is a refined oil, treated with heat and solvents, then blended with virgin olive oil to give it color and flavor.

Light olive oil is an American marketing title that describes an oil with little flavor or character (it tastes like any vegetable oil). It contains the same number of calories as the extra-virgin, virgin and olive oils; there is no reason to use it.

PASTA

Pasta is a low-fat, high-carbohydrate food that is great for a healthy diet. Too often it is laden with heavy sauces and cheese. Tossed with lots of fresh vegetables and light sauces, it is deliciously low in fat and calories.

Italian pasta may be dried or fresh. Dried factory-made pasta contains golden semolina flour and water; homemade fresh pasta is made with eggs and flour and remains somewhat pliant before being cooked.

The most familiar dried pasta is spaghetti, along with fusilli, penne, rigatoni and others with whimsical names. Good-quality factory pasta should have a faintly rough surface and compact body. It swells considerably in cooking and is well-suited to heavier sauces. The stuffed pastas and those for baking, such as tortellini and lasagna, are usually shaped from soft homemade doughs. More delicate and tender, home-made pasta will absorb the flavors of a light and fragrant sauce.

STOCK

Stock made of poultry, vegetables or meat bones is used in cooking risotto, creating soup, braising meats and making polenta. Homemade stocks are light-bodied but flavorful. Two stock recipes appear in the soup chapter. These are not only easy to make but may be kept frozen. The canned varieties of reduced-sodium, defatted stocks now on the market make very good substitutions. Read the labels; many canned stocks are overly salty. Many of the sauces in this book are made by "reducing" the stock, simmering it down into a more concentrated liquid. The stock must taste right for the sauce to be successful.

VEGETABLES

The Italians grow many of their own vegetables. Even city dwellers have big pots of tomatoes and lettuces growing on their patios; the markets offer a daily garden of delights to choose from. Although tomatoes have always grown in the "new world," they did not become a popular food item until the 1900s when Italian immigrants introduced the varieties they had cultivated for cooking, and myriad ways of using them. They also introduced broccoli and broccoli rabe to their new home (in fact, Americans now eat more broccoli than the Italians).

Fennel: This anise-scented bulb resembles celery with delicate fronds. It may be eaten raw and chopped into fresh salads or sautéed, braised or baked. It makes its appearance in the spring and summer.

Mushrooms, cultivated and wild varieties, are becoming increasingly familiar in grocery stores throughout America. They add wonderful, rich dark flavor to sautés and sauces. Grilled or roasted, they have an almost meaty flavor and texture.

Cremini mushrooms look like white button mushrooms but are mustard or brown in color. They may be substituted for button mushrooms and will add a richer flavor.

Portobello mushrooms look like big, domestic button mushrooms but with flatter heads and thicker stems. They're actually the giant form of cremini mushrooms. They are dark and meaty and great for grilling or roasting with just a little oil and garlic.

Porcini mushrooms are rarely sold fresh but are available dried. Drying concentrates that musky, earthy flavor that can do wonders for a low-fat soup, stew or sauce. The dried are sold in small transparent packets and will keep indefinitely. Another name for porcinis is *cèpes*.

Before using dried porcini mushrooms, they must be reconstituted. Pour 2 cups warm water over 1 ounce of porcini mushrooms and allow to soak for 30 minutes. Lift the mushrooms out, squeezing out the water, and rinse under cold running water. Dry with paper towels. Strain the soaking water and save it to enrich soups and stews.

Radicchio has become more popular in American gardens recently. This pretty, bright, beet-colored member of the chicory family is delicious shredded into green salads or lightly braised with a touch of oil. It is at its sweetest in late summer.

Tomatoes (and tomato products) play a huge role in Italian cooking. Italian, plum or roma tomatoes are used most often, though the other fresh varieties may also be used in any dish calling for tomatoes. The plum tomatoes tend to have thicker skin and fewer seeds than other varieties. They hold their shape better when stuffed and baked or cooked in sauces and stews. If fresh are not available, no-salt canned tomatoes, well-drained, may be substituted, except in fresh salads. Look for the canned organic varieties; they seem to have more flavor.

Sun-dried tomatoes are dried plum tomato halves that look something like deep-red apricots. They need to be reconstituted first in boiling water or stock, then drained before using. They have a deep tomato flavor that is a bit sweet.

This list is partial and excludes many Italian ingredients that are particularly high in fat and sodium. Many specialties such as anchovies, sardines, prosciutto, pancetta and Italian cheeses such as fontina, Gorgonzola and mascarpone are certainly delicious and worthy of a splurge once in a while but are not the foods to be eaten every day.

There are several new products that, while not Italian in origin, work quite well as substitutes for some of the higher-calorie, higher-fat foods. Nonfat sour cream, nonfat cream cheese and nonfat half-and-half will help the cook create rich-tasting sauces and desserts traditionally made with cream, butter and cheese.

The recipes ahead express the colors, aromas and tastes of Italian food and attempt to share the authentic flavors of this bountiful land. Adapted for today's health-wise kitchen, they are true in spirit to a rich and generous Italian table. *Buon appetito!*

BEANS, BEANS, BEANS

D ried beans, *fagioli*, are a low-fat source of protein in the healthful Italian diet, especially when combined with pasta, risotto and polenta. Most beans require soaking to soften them up before they are cooked.

Many beans are available canned, a great help to the busy cook. The canned tend to be softer than home-cooked beans and are best added to a soup or stew toward the end of the cooking time. They need only to be warmed up a bit. If there's a lot of sodium in the beans (check the label), rinse and drain them well before using to remove some of the excess.

Cooking dried beans, once they are soaked, is simple. Store cooked beans in their cooking liquid, covered, in the refrigerator for up to a week.

Here are a few tips for soaking and cooking beans:

• To soak the beans, place them in a large pot and cover generously with cold water. Let stand overnight. Drain and rinse with fresh water before cooking.

• If you haven't time to soak the beans overnight, put them in a large saucepan, cover with water and bring to a boil. Reduce the heat and simmer the beans for about 5 minutes. Then remove from the heat and allow the beans to stand for about 1 hour. Drain and rinse and proceed with the recipe.

• The cooking times of different beans will vary according to type and freshness. Chick-peas, for instance, are often tougher and take longer to cook, while some black beans tend to cook quickly. Lentils do not need to be soaked and will cook in about 20 minutes. All beans should be cooked until tender.

• To cook beans after they have been soaked and drained, put them in a large pot, cover with cold water and bring to a boil; reduce the heat and simmer for 30 minutes to 1 hour, or until the beans are fork tender. Just keep checking every 10 minutes or so.

• Do not add salt to dried beans at the beginning of the cooking process because it will retard their tenderness. Add salt halfway through the cooking time.

• Do not add tomatoes, vinegar or any other acidic foods until about halfway through cooking; acid tends to toughen beans.

CHAPTER 3

THE LITTLE
DISHES
OF ITALY

ANTIPASTI

The word *antipasto* literally means "before the pasta," or first course. The *antipasto* can be the lightest, most creative component of the meal—perhaps a salad of white beans and fragrant sage or poached shellfish in a light vinaigrette. The Italians are also very fond of raw vegetables dipped in cold sauces such as garlic mayonnaise. All *antipasti* are meant to take the edge off hunger and set a relaxed pace to the courses that follow. In the U.S., we call such food snacks, starters and after-school treats; by any name, and in any language, the "little dishes" can play a big role in the healthy diet.

CANNELLINI BEAN DIP

*L*ow in fat and high in fiber, this dip is wonderful with strips of sweet red, green and yellow peppers, cherry tomatoes and celery sticks. It also makes a quick pasta sauce.

3	*cloves garlic*
¼	*cup chopped fresh basil*
2	*tablespoons chopped fresh marjoram*
1	*tablespoon lemon juice*
½	*teaspoon grated lemon rind*
1	*can (19 ounces) cannellini beans, rinsed and drained*
2–3	*drops of hot-pepper sauce*
	Fresh basil

In a food processor fitted with the steel blade, chop the garlic. Add the basil, marjoram, lemon juice and lemon rind; process until the herbs are finely chopped.

Add the beans and process for about 30 seconds, stopping the motor once and scraping down the sides of the bowl with a rubber spatula. The mixture should not be too smooth. Add the hot-pepper sauce. Serve garnished with fresh basil.

Preparation time: 5 minutes

Chef's note: This looks best when the mixture is rough, with large pieces of beans visible. You may want to reserve a tablespoon of the beans to add just before serving.

Per tablespoon: 13 calories, 0.1 g. fat (6% of calories), 1 g. dietary fiber, no cholesterol, 33 mg. sodium.

Garlicky Spinach Dip

Makes 2 cups

This emerald green dip of spinach and nonfat ricotta cheese goes beautifully with spears of fresh vegetables such as sweet red, yellow and orange peppers and yellow summer squash. It is also good with red and yellow cherry tomatoes.

½ *cup nonfat ricotta cheese*
¼ *cup nonfat sour cream*
2 *tablespoons orange juice*
1 *package (10 ounces) frozen chopped spinach, thawed and squeezed dry*
¼ *cup chopped scallions*
¼ *cup chopped fresh basil*
2 *tablespoons chopped fresh oregano*
2 *cloves garlic, minced*
⅛ *teaspoon ground nutmeg*
   Dash of hot-pepper sauce
   Salt and black pepper

In a food processor fitted with the steel blade, combine the ricotta, sour cream and orange juice. Add the spinach, scallions, basil, oregano, garlic, nutmeg and hot-pepper sauce. Process until smooth, stopping occasionally to scrape down the sides. Add salt and pepper to taste.

Pour into a medium bowl, cover and chill in the refrigerator for at least 30 minutes, or overnight.

Preparation time: 5 minutes
Chilling time: 30 minutes

Per tablespoon: 11 calories, trace of fat (3% of calories), 0.3 g. dietary fiber, 1 mg. cholesterol, 16 mg. sodium.

ROASTED GARLIC DIP

MAKES ½ CUP

*R*oasted garlic is tender and almost sweet. Here, the cloves are pureed with nonfat mayonnaise and nonfat yogurt into a lively dip for fresh raw vegetables such as broccoli, radishes, asparagus, carrots and bright sweet red peppers.

2 *whole heads garlic, ¼" sliced off the top to expose the cloves*

1 *teaspoon extra-virgin olive oil*

¼ *cup nonfat mayonnaise*

¼ *cup nonfat plain yogurt*

Cut off the bottom tips of the garlic heads so they will stand upright. Place the garlic in a small shallow baking dish and drizzle with the oil, allowing it to seep into each clove. Roast at 350° for 45 minutes, or until soft and golden brown.

Squeeze the soft cloves into a blender or food processor fitted with the steel blade; puree. Add the mayonnaise and yogurt. Mix well.

Preparation time: 5 minutes
Baking time: 45 minutes

Chef's note: The younger the garlic, the sweeter it will be and the less time it will need to roast.

Per teaspoon: 28 calories, 0.6 g. fat (19% of calories), no dietary fiber, trace of cholesterol, 102 mg. sodium.

ARTICHOKE-HERB SPREAD

MAKES ¾ CUP

rtichokes, a source of potassium and vitamin C, are very low in calories. This tangy spread is delicious on Crostini (page 31) or as a dip for sweet red pepper slices. Thinned with a little buttermilk, it makes a great pasta sauce.

1   *cup frozen artichoke hearts, cooked and drained*
1   *tablespoon nonfat plain yogurt*
1   *tablespoon minced garlic*
1   *tablespoon chopped fresh Italian parsley*
1   *teaspoon chopped fresh marjoram*
1   *teaspoon lemon juice*
    Salt and black pepper

In a food processor fitted with the steel blade, process the artichoke hearts, yogurt, garlic, parsley, marjoram and lemon juice until smooth. Add salt and pepper to taste.

Preparation time: 5 minutes

Chef's note: If you're not going to use the spread immediately, pack it into a jar, spoon a little olive oil over the surface, cover and refrigerate. It should keep one week.

Per tablespoon: 9 calories, 0.1 g. fat (5% of calories), trace of dietary fiber, trace of cholesterol, 15 mg. sodium.

ROASTED EGGPLANT SPREAD

MAKES 1¼ CUPS

A creamy but light spread for crackers and Crostini (page 31), this is also a wonderful dip for vegetables. This spread will keep, covered, several days in the refrigerator.

1   *pound eggplant (see note)*
1   *large clove garlic, thinly sliced*
1   *bay leaf*
2   *sprigs fresh oregano*
¼   *cup nonfat plain yogurt*
2   *teaspoons lemon juice*
1   *teaspoon chopped fresh marjoram*
1   *teaspoon chopped fresh parsley*
    Salt and black pepper

Cut slits in the eggplant and stick the garlic slices into the slits. Wrap the eggplant, bay leaf and oregano tightly in a large piece of foil and bake at 350° until the eggplant is completely soft all over, 1 to 1½ hours. Turn the eggplant over after 45 minutes.

Open the package and let it sit for 5 minutes. Discard the bay leaf, oregano and any liquid. When the eggplant is cool enough to handle, scrape the flesh and garlic into the bowl of a food processor fitted with the steel blade; discard the skin. Add the yogurt, lemon juice, marjoram and parsley. Process until smooth. Add salt and pepper to taste.

Preparation time: 5 minutes
Baking time: 1½ hours plus 5 minutes resting time

Chef's note: Try using the long, slender Japanese eggplants in this recipe. They are sweeter than the large round Western types.

Per tablespoon: 7 calories, 0.1 g. fat (6% of calories), trace of dietary fiber, 1 mg. cholesterol, 3 mg. sodium.

Lemon-Caper Tuna Spread

MAKES 1 CUP

*N*orthern Italy's *tonnato* sauce inspired this simple and easy spread. Serve with rounds of Italian bread, Crostini (page 31), crackers or fresh vegetables.

1   *can (3½ ounces) solid white tuna in water, drained*
2   *tablespoons nonfat cream cheese*
2   *tablespoons chopped fresh parsley*
1   *tablespoon nonfat mayonnaise*
1   *tablespoon lemon juice*
1   *teaspoon chopped fresh marjoram*
2   *dashes of hot-pepper sauce*
2   *tablespoons drained capers*

In a food processor fitted with the steel blade, process the tuna, cream cheese, parsley, mayonnaise, lemon juice, marjoram and hot-pepper sauce until smooth. Transfer to a small serving bowl and stir in the capers.

Preparation time: 10 minutes

Chef's note: Use this spread instead of tuna salad in sandwiches and add lots of fresh tomato and lettuce. It's also a delicious stuffing for cherry tomatoes.

Per tablespoon: 27 calories, 0.3 g. fat (11% of calories), 0.1 g. dietary fiber, 6 mg. cholesterol, 125 mg. sodium.

Yogurt Cheese

This ancient Mediterranean recipe produces a smooth spread from nonfat yogurt. It is delicious on its own spooned over fresh berries or scooped up with strips of sweet red peppers. It may be whisked with herbs and garlic into a dip or blended into low-oil vinaigrette. It's an excellent substitute for créme fraîche in a cool dessert sauce. Its advantage over plain nonfat yogurt is its thick, creamy body. Its advantage over nonfat sour cream is its clean and tangy flavor. It keeps two weeks, covered, in the refrigerator. Make a double or triple batch—it's delicious and healthful and nice to have on hand. The ingredient list is very simple: plain nonfat yogurt (without stabilizers, gelatin or sugar that will interfere with drainage or hamper flavor).

Dampen a cheesecloth in cold water and wring it out. Line a medium sieve with several layers of the cheesecloth. Spoon 1 quart of yogurt into the sieve and set over a large bowl to catch the dripping whey. Cover with plastic wrap and place the bowl in the refrigerator; allow to stand overnight, or longer. The longer the yogurt drains, the thicker the cheese will be. Turn the finished yogurt cheese into a bowl or container. (You may need to scrape away some of the cheese from the cloth with a knife.)

Here are several quick suggestions for enjoying the cheese:

• **Fruit Dip:** Blend 1 cup yogurt cheese with 1 teaspoon honey, ¼ teaspoon ground cinnamon, ⅛ teaspoon ground nutmeg and ⅛ teaspoon grated orange rind.

• **Rich Vinaigrette:** In your favorite vinaigrette recipe, replace 1 part oil with 2 parts yogurt cheese.

• **Potato Topper:** Top a baked potato with plenty of yogurt cheese and chopped fresh chives.

• **Grilled Veggie Topper:** Top grilled or oven-roasted vegetables (page 122) with yogurt cheese and chopped fresh basil.

• **Brown Sugar and Grapes:** Fill dessert glasses with a mix of red and green seedless grapes; top with yogurt cheese and sprinkle with brown sugar.

Herb-Garlic Yogurt Cheese

Makes 2 cups

*D*elicate and tangy yogurt cheese is marinated in olive oil and fresh herbs for a spectacular appetizer to serve with crusty bread, crostini or crackers. It's also good on baked potatoes.

1 *cup yogurt cheese (page 28)*
2 *teaspoons olive oil*
1 *teaspoon lemon juice*
1 *teaspoon chopped fresh thyme*
1 *teaspoon chopped fresh parsley*
1 *clove garlic, minced*
   Salt and black pepper

Divide the yogurt cheese into 4 rounds, flattening them lightly with your palms. Place in a wide, shallow bowl.

In a small bowl, whisk together the oil, lemon juice, oregano, parsley and garlic; add salt and pepper to taste. Pour over the rounds. Let marinate at room temperature for at least 30 minutes before serving (see note).

Preparation time: 5 minutes plus 30 minutes marinating time.

Chef's note: The longer the yogurt cheese marinates, the more flavorful it will be. It will keep, covered, in the refrigerator for 2 days. Allow it to come to room temperature before serving.

Per tablespoon: 13 calories, trace of fat (3% of calories), trace of dietary fiber, trace of cholesterol, 14 mg. sodium.

BRUSCHETTA

SERVES 4

*B*ruschetta, simple garlic toasts, are wonderful served unadorned or with fresh toppings. Try these variations—or experiment and create your own.

> 4 slices Italian-style or sourdough bread
> 2 large cloves garlic, cut in half lengthwise
> 1 tablespoon extra-virgin olive oil

Toast the bread under a broiler about 5″ from the heat or on a grill. While still hot, rub one side of each slice with the garlic, pressing the juice into the toast. Spread the olive oil over the garlic-rubbed side of the toast with a brush or your fingers.

Preparation time: 15 minutes
Cooking time: 5 minutes

Chef's note: Try these variations (each serves 4):

Tomato and Watercress: Layer the bruschetta with 1 cup watercress leaves and 1 large sliced tomato. Sprinkle with ¼ cup chopped red onions, 1 tablespoon drained capers and 1 teaspoon extra-virgin olive oil. Add salt and pepper to taste.

Cucumber, Sun-Dried Tomato and Olive: Layer the bruschetta with 1 small cucumber, peeled, seeded and thinly sliced lengthwise. Top with 4 sun-dried tomato halves, reconstituted and chopped (page 72). Sprinkle with 2 tablespoons imported and chopped black olives and 2 tablespoons chopped fresh basil. Add salt and pepper to taste.

Per Bruschetta: 117 calories, 3.4 g. fat (27% of calories), 0.8 g. dietary fiber, no cholesterol, 152 mg. sodium.

Per Tomato and Watercress variation: 143 calories, 4.6 g. fat (30% of calories), 1.6 g. dietary fiber, no cholesterol, 190 mg. sodium.

Per Cucumber, Sun-Dried Tomato and Olive variation: 142 calories, 4.2 g. fat (26% of calories), 1.9 g. dietary fiber, no cholesterol, 177 mg. sodium.

CROSTINI

SERVES 4

*C*rostini are the easy-to-make Italian croutons—use them in soups, as a base for spreads and on top of salads.

4 *large slices rustic Italian bread*
1 *tablespoon extra-virgin olive oil*
   Black pepper

Brush both sides of the bread with the oil and sprinkle with black pepper to taste.

Coat a baking sheet with no-stick spray. Put the bread on the baking sheet and bake at 350° for 15 minutes, turning once halfway through, until well toasted. Cut the bread into quarters.

Preparation time: 5 minutes
Baking time: 15 minutes

Chef's note: Crostini are at their best when made just before serving. They may also be prepared several hours ahead of time and kept at room temperature. Do not keep them overnight because they will taste stale the next day.

Per serving: 115 calories, 3.4 g. fat (28% of calories), 0.8 g. dietary fiber, no cholesterol, 152 mg. sodium.

TOP 8 TOPPERS

*T*op Crostini (page 31) or Bruschetta (page 30) with any of these quick and easy recipes, all ready in under 5 minutes. If you've no time to make the "bottoms," serve these toppers on whole-wheat crackers, lavosh or slices of crusty Italian bread. Each of these toppings is low-fat (with less than 30% of the calories from fat). Each serves four.

1. Red Pepper, Olive and Caper: Toss together ¼ cup chopped sweet red pepper, 2 tablespoons pitted and chopped imported black olives, 2 tablespoons pitted and chopped imported green olives and 1 tablespoon drained capers.

2. Fresh Tomato and Basil: Toss together ½ cup chopped fresh tomatoes, ¼ cup thinly sliced fresh basil and 2 teaspoons balsamic vinegar. Add salt and black pepper to taste.

3. White Bean and Sage: With the back of a fork, mash together ¼ cup well-drained canned white kidney beans with 2 teaspoons chopped fresh sage and 1 teaspoon lemon juice. Add salt and black pepper to taste.

4. Cucumber and Yogurt: Mix together ¼ cup peeled, seeded and sliced cucumbers, 2 tablespoons nonfat yogurt, 1 teaspoon chopped fresh oregano and 1 clove garlic, minced. Add salt and black pepper to taste.

5. Roasted Red Pepper and Caper: Chop half of a 7-ounce jar of drained roasted red peppers; mix together with 2 tablespoons drained capers.

6. Cream Cheese, Tomato and Onion: Spread each bruschetta with nonfat cream cheese and layer each with a thin slice of tomato and a thin slice of red onion. Sprinkle with balsamic vinegar and chopped fresh basil.

7. Cream Cheese and Olive: Mix ¼ cup nonfat cream cheese with 2 tablespoons sliced green olives stuffed with pimentos.

8. Sun-Dried Tomatoes and Olive: Mix ¼ cup chopped reconstituted sun-dried tomatoes (if using those packed in oil, rinse and drain well) with 2 tablespoons pitted and chopped imported black olives and 1 tablespoon chopped fresh basil.

CAPONATA

SERVES 4

*T*his southern Italian eggplant stew tastes best when the flavors have "married." Let it sit at least 2 hours before serving.

1	*teaspoon olive oil*
1	*eggplant, peeled and cut into 1" cubes*
1	*cup chopped fresh tomatoes or canned crushed tomatoes, drained*
1	*sweet red pepper, coarsely chopped*
1	*green pepper, coarsely chopped*
1	*onion, coarsely chopped*
3	*cloves garlic, minced*
15	*imported black olives, pitted and chopped*
¼	*cup drained capers*
¼	*cup chopped fresh Italian parsley*
2	*tablespoons chopped fresh marjoram*
1	*tablespoon red wine vinegar*

In a large no-stick frying pan over medium-high heat, warm the oil and sauté the eggplant for 2 minutes. Add the tomatoes, red peppers, green peppers, onions and garlic. Reduce the heat and simmer for 10 minutes, stirring occasionally. Add the olives, capers, parsley, marjoram and vinegar. Turn the caponata into a large bowl; cover and let sit for 2 hours before serving, or refrigerate overnight.

Preparation time: 15 minutes
Cooking time: 12 minutes plus 2 hours sitting time

Per serving: 115 calories, 4.2 g. fat (29% of calories), 2.3 g. dietary fiber, no cholesterol, 207 mg. sodium.

MINI-PITA PIZZAS

SERVES 4

*S*imple and quick, these pizzas are great with soup, for lunch or as an after- school snack. Use the basic recipe and add your own favorite toppings—or try any of these suggested variations.

> 2 *(4") whole-wheat mini-pita breads,*
> *split in half along the seam*
> ¼ *cup nonfat pizza sauce*
> 2 *tablespoons grated Parmesan cheese*

Put the pitas on a baking sheet and toast at 350° for 10 minutes, or until lightly browned and crisp. Spoon the pizza sauce over the 4 rounds and then top with the cheese. Return to the oven and bake for 7 to 9 minutes, or until the cheese is melted and the pizza is hot.

Preparation time: 2 minutes
Baking time: 19 minutes

Chef's note: Try these variations (each tops 4 pita halves):

Florentine: Mix ¼ cup chopped cooked spinach with 2 tablespoons nonfat ricotta, 2 tablespoons pitted and chopped imported black olives, an additional 1 tablespoon grated Parmesan cheese and a dash of nutmeg. Increase the baking time to 10 to 12 minutes, or until the filling is heated through.

Fresh Tomato: Mix together ¼ cup chopped tomatoes, 2 tablespoons shredded low-fat mozzarella and 1 tablespoon chopped red onions. Just before serving, sprinkle with 2 tablespoons chopped fresh basil.

Mixed Olive: Mix 2 tablespoons pitted and chopped imported black olives with 1 tablespoon pitted and chopped imported green olives and an additional 1 tablespoon grated Parmesan cheese.

Per Mini-Pita Pizza: 49 calories, 1.1 g. fat (21% of calories), 0.2 g. dietary fiber, 2 mg. cholesterol, 152 mg. sodium.

Per Florentine variation: 93 calories, 2.1 g. fat (20% of calories), 0.6 g. dietary fiber, 4 mg. cholesterol, 259 mg. sodium.

Per Fresh Tomato variation: 80 calories, 1.3 g. fat (14% of calories), 0.5 g. dietary fiber, 3 mg. cholesterol, 232 mg. sodium.

Per Mixed Olive variation: 85 calories, 2.2 g. fat (23% of calories), 0.4 g. dietary fiber, 4mg. cholesterol, 265 mg. sodium.

STUFFED CHERRY TOMATOES

SERVES 4

These bright tomatoes make a pretty addition to an antipasti platter or salad plate. The recipe makes good use of leftover cannellini or white kidney beans.

> 12 *large cherry tomatoes*
> ½ *cup cooked or canned white navy or cannellini beans, rinsed and drained*
> 2 *tablespoons lemon juice*
> 1 *tablespoon drained capers*
> 1 *tablespoon chopped fresh parsley*
> 1 *tablespoon fresh bread crumbs (page 14)*
> 2 *anchovy fillets, chopped (see note)*
> *Parsley*

Cut off the top of each tomato and hollow out about ½″ of the flesh.

In a medium bowl, combine the beans, lemon juice, capers, parsley, bread crumbs and anchovies. Spoon the bean mixture into the hollowed-out tomatoes and garnish with parsley.

Preparation time: 15 minutes

Chef's note: You may choose to omit the anchovies; they are salty and can have a strong taste. If you leave them out, substitute 1 teaspoon olive oil.

Per serving: 54 calories, 0.5 g. fat (7% of calories), 0.7 g. dietary fiber, 2 mg. cholesterol, 114 mg. sodium.

HERB-PICKLED MUSHROOMS

*B*ecause they're "pickled," these mushrooms will keep for up to 2 weeks in the refrigerator. They are nice to have on hand for a quick appetizer, to toss in salads or to serve as a condiment for grilled chicken or meat.

> 8 *ounces button mushrooms (see note)*
> 3 *cloves garlic*
> 3 *sprigs fresh rosemary*
> ¾ *cup water*
> ¼ *cup white wine vinegar*
> 10 *black peppercorns*
> ¼ *teaspoon sugar*
>   *Pinch of salt*

Pack the mushrooms into a wide-mouth pint-size jar. Add the garlic and rosemary, pressing them against the inside of the jar.

In a small saucepan over high heat, bring the water, vinegar, peppercorns, sugar and salt to a boil. Reduce the heat and simmer for 5 minutes. Pour the hot liquid over the mushrooms, making sure the mushrooms are completely covered. Cover the jar and refrigerate. Allow the mushrooms to marinate at least 8 hours or overnight.

Preparation time: 5 minutes
Cooking time: 5 minutes plus 8 hours marinating time

Chef's note: Look for the smallest, whitest mushrooms you can find.

Per ¼ cup: 18 calories, 0.3 g. fat (12% of calories), 1.3 g. dietary fiber, no cholesterol, 1 mg. sodium.

OFF THE SHELF
8 QUICK ANTIPASTI IDEAS

*P*ull these low-fat store-bought items from the pantry shelf and put together a sumptuous antipasti platter. Great for last-minute guests.

1. Tortellini Kabobs: Thread cooked packaged low-fat cheese tortellini on wooden skewers and serve with nonfat pasta sauce.

2. Herbed Roasted Peppers: Drain 1 jar (7 ounces) roasted red peppers and toss with 2 tablespoons chopped fresh basil. Serve with sliced bread or crackers.

3. Cream Cheese and Olives: Spread crackers with nonfat cream cheese and top with chopped, pitted and drained imported black olives and green olives.

4. Herbed Shrimp: Drain 1 can (3 ounces) shrimp and toss with 1 tablespoon chopped fresh parsley, 2 teaspoons olive oil and 1 teaspoon lemon juice. Serve with crusty bread or in endive.

5. White Bean Dip: Drain 1 can (19 ounces) cannellini or white kidney beans and mash lightly with the back of a fork. Add 2 tablespoons nonfat Italian dressing and 2 tablespoons chopped fresh parsley. Serve with crackers or crusty bread.

6. Veg Dip: Blend 1 cup nonfat yogurt (or better, Yogurt Cheese, page 28) with 2 tablespoons chopped fresh basil, 1 tablespoon lemon juice and 1 tablespoon drained capers. Serve as a dip for raw vegetables.

7. Artichoke Spread: Drain and chop 1 jar (3 ounces) marinated artichoke hearts and toss with 1 tablespoon lemon juice and 1 tablespoon chopped fresh parsley. Serve with crackers or crusty bread.

8. Melon with Pastrami: Wrap slices of honeydew or cantaloupe melon in slices of turkey pastrami. Secure with a toothpick.

Rosemary-Orange Carrots

SERVES 4

*B*athed in a fragrant marinade of rosemary and orange juice, these tender, tiny carrots make a pretty addition to an antipasti plate or a tossed green salad. They will keep several days in the refrigerator.

10	*ounces baby carrots*
2	*tablespoons white wine vinegar*
2	*tablespoons frozen orange juice concentrate, thawed*
1	*teaspoon Dijon mustard*
1	*teaspoon honey*
1	*teaspoon extra-virgin olive oil*
2	*tablespoons chopped fresh parsley*
1	*tablespoon chopped fresh rosemary (see note)*

Place the carrots on a microwave-safe plate and cover with plastic wrap. Microwave on high for 3 minutes, or until just tender.

While the carrots are cooking, whisk together the vinegar, juice concentrate, mustard and honey in a medium bowl. Whisk in the oil. Add the parsley and rosemary. Add the hot carrots and toss to coat. Refrigerate and serve chilled.

Preparation time: 5 minutes
Cooking time: 3 minutes

Chef's note: If fresh rosemary is difficult to find, you may substitute 1 teaspoon dried rosemary, crushed.

Per serving: 38 calories, 0.7 g. fat (15% of calories), 2.3 g. dietary fiber, no cholesterol, 28 mg. sodium.

(Not) Fried Zucchini

Serves 4

In Italy, tender zucchini blossoms are fried in a light batter for a popular antipasto served at outdoor *trattorias* (casual, family-style restaurants). This low-fat and low-calorie recipe replaces the batter with a tasty marinade and roasts the tender zucchini sticks into finger-licking-good snacks.

> 3   *small zucchini*
> ½   *cup balsamic vinegar*
> 1   *tablespoon chopped fresh rosemary*
> 4   *cloves garlic, minced*
>   *Salt and black pepper*

Cut the zucchini into thin wedges.

In a shallow bowl, whisk together the vinegar, rosemary and garlic; add salt and pepper to taste. Add the zucchini and toss so that all the sticks are thoroughly coated. Allow the zucchini to absorb the marinade for 2 to 3 minutes.

Coat a baking sheet with no-stick spray. Arrange the zucchini on the prepared baking sheet. Roast at 375° for 25 to 30 minutes, or until dark brown.

Preparation time: 5 minutes plus 2 minutes marinating time
Baking time: 25 minutes

Per serving: 49 calories, 0.2 g. fat (3% of calories), 1.5 g. dietary fiber, no cholesterol, 9 mg. sodium.

CHICKEN AND ARTICHOKE KABOBS

SERVES 4

*K*abobs are fun starters, especially in the summer when you're gathered with friends in the back yard for a barbecue. They also make a light supper served on pasta.

¼ *cup lemon juice*

2 *tablespoons virgin olive oil*

1 *tablespoon chopped fresh oregano*

1 *teaspoon Dijon mustard*

1 *teaspoon honey*

8 *ounces boneless, skinless chicken breast meat, cut into 2" cubes*

2 *cups artichoke hearts, frozen and thawed or canned and drained*

In a medium bowl, whisk together the lemon juice, oil, oregano mustard and honey. Add the chicken and toss to coat. Thread the meat alternately with the artichoke hearts onto 8 (6") wooden skewers (see note).

Grill the skewers over high heat or broil about 5" from the heat for 5 minutes, turning constantly, until the meat is springy to the touch and no longer pink.

Preparation time: 15 minutes
Cooking time: 5 minutes

Chef's note: Soak the wooden skewers in water for 10 minutes before threading the meat and artichokes. This will keep the wood from burning up on the grill. You may also use metal skewers that do not require soaking. These are generally 12" to 18" long, so you will need only 4 skewers.

Per serving: 132 calories, 4.8 g. fat (30% of calories), trace of dietary fiber, 23 mg. cholesterol, 372 mg. sodium.

Mussels Marinara

SERVES 4

*M*ussels are a wonderful source of iron and protein. Serve this hearty first course with crusty bread. It also makes a good main dish for two people served on a bed of pasta.

1 *pound mussels, scrubbed and debearded (see notes)*

1 *teaspoon olive oil*

¼ *cup chopped onions*

2 *cloves garlic, minced*

1 *can (14½ ounces) no-salt-added tomatoes, chopped (with juice)*

⅓ *cup white wine or clam juice*

1 *tablespoon lemon juice*

1 *tablespoon chopped fresh parsley*

2 *teaspoons chopped fresh oregano*

In a large saucepan over medium heat, heat the oil and sauté the onions and garlic for 1 minute, or until tender. Add the tomatoes (with juice), wine or clam juice, lemon juice, parsley and oregano. Add the mussels and cook until they have opened, about 10 minutes. Discard any mussels that have not opened.

Serve the mussels in their shells with the marinara sauce.

Preparation time: 5 minutes
Cooking time: 11 minutes

Chef's notes: Scrub the mussels under cold running water. Discard any that are already open or have broken shells.

Remove a mussel's "beard" (the clump of strong, dark material that clings to the shell) by tugging it off with your fingers. If that doesn't work, use pliers, but don't apply so much pressure you rip the mussel apart. Failing this, clip off what you can and leave the rest. Don't debeard mussels until right before cooking, or they will die and spoil.

Per serving: 96 calories, 1.6 g. fat (14% of calories), 1 g. dietary fiber, 32 mg. cholesterol, 177 mg. sodium.

ROASTED CLAMS WITH ZESTY FRESH TOMATOES

SERVES 4

*S*erve these clams in their shells topped with zesty fresh tomatoes. Leftovers may be tossed with pasta (but don't keep them more than a day). Clams are a good source of protein, iron and calcium.

1 *pound littleneck clams in the shell, scrubbed (see notes)*
1 *tablespoon extra-virgin olive oil*
1 *tablespoon lemon juice*
1 *plum tomato, chopped*
¼ *cup chopped scallions*
2 *tablespoons chopped fresh parsley*
   Salt and black pepper

Place the clams on a flat baking dish and roast at 450° for 10 minutes, or until they have opened. Discard any clams that have not opened.

While the clams are roasting, in a medium bowl whisk together the oil and lemon juice. Stir in the tomatoes, scallions and parsley; add salt and pepper to taste.

To serve, spoon the mixture onto the opened clams.

Preparation time: 5 minutes
Baking time: 10 minutes

Chef's notes: Littleneck clams are the smallest clams on the market. You may also use cherrystone clams, which are just a bit larger. Avoid chowder clams; they're too big and tough.

Scrub the clams under cold running water. Discard any that are already open or have broken shells.

Per serving: 207 calories, 5.7 g. fat (26% of calories), 0.6 g. dietary fiber, 76 mg. cholesterol, 131 mg. sodium.

Shrimp and White Beans with Sage

SERVES 4

*G*arlicky shrimp, mellow white beans and fragrant sage are tossed together in a zesty antipasto salad. This is pretty served on Belgian endive or crisp romaine lettuce with a few bright red and yellow cherry tomatoes.

> 2 *teaspoons olive oil*
> ¼ *pound small fresh shrimp, peeled and deveined*
> 2 *cloves garlic, minced*
> ½ *cup canned white kidney beans, rinsed and drained*
> 1 *tablespoon lemon juice*
> 1 *tablespoon drained capers*
> 2 *teaspoons chopped fresh sage*
> *Salt and black pepper*
> *Lettuce leaves or Belgian endive*
> 8 *red or yellow cherry tomatoes*

In a medium frying pan over medium heat, heat the oil and sauté the shrimp with the garlic for 2 minutes, or until the shrimp are pink. Add the beans, lemon juice, capers and sage, and continue cooking until the beans are heated through, about 1 minute. Add salt and pepper to taste.

Arrange the lettuce leaves or endive on 4 individual serving plates or a large platter. Spoon the mixture evenly over the leaves and garnish with the tomatoes.

Preparation time: 5 minutes
Cooking time: 5 minutes

Per serving: 91 calories, 2.8 g. fat (27% of calories), 0.8 g. dietary fiber, 44 mg. cholesterol, 87 mg. sodium.

Broccoli-Red Pepper Frittata

SERVES 8

*E*asy-to-make, this frittata may be served right from the oven or at room temperature. It will also make a light supper for four people.

6   *egg whites*
3   *cups cooked broccoli florets, drained*
1   *jar (7 ounces) roasted red peppers, drained*
1   *clove garlic, minced*
¼   *cup minced scallions*
    Salt and black pepper

In a large bowl, beat the egg whites with an electric mixer for 1 minute, or until light and foamy. Add the broccoli, red peppers, garlic and scallions; add salt and black pepper to taste.

Coat a 9″ pie pan with no-stick spray. Pour the egg mixture into the pan and bake at 350° for 25 minutes, or until the egg whites are set. Remove and allow to rest for 5 minutes. Loosen the edges with a spatula. Cut into wedges and serve.

Preparation time: 10 minutes
Baking time: 25 minutes plus 5 minutes resting time

Per serving: 37 calories, 0.3 g. fat (6% of calories), 2 g. dietary fiber, no cholesterol, 57 mg. sodium.

ROASTED CECI NUTS

MAKES 2 CUPS

*C*runchy after roasting, chick-pea "nuts" make a delicious low-fat, high-fiber alternative to peanuts. They are great for snacking, tossed in salads or on top of pasta. They will keep several days in an uncovered dish in a dry place. Do not refrigerate because they will become soggy.

> 2 *cups cooked or canned chick-peas, rinsed*
> *and drained (see note)*
> 1 *tablespoon olive oil*
> *Coarse salt*

In a medium bowl, toss the chick-peas with the oil to coat. Spread the chick-peas on a baking sheet and roast at 375° for 40 minutes, or until brown and crisp. Remove from the oven and sprinkle with salt to taste. Cool before turning into a bowl.

Preparation time: 2 minutes
Baking time: 40 minutes

Chef's notes: Dried chick-peas that have been soaked and cooked (page 20) seem better suited to roasting than canned chick-peas because they have absorbed less liquid and are firmer. They become drier and crisper during roasting.

Double or triple this recipe; these "nuts" make healthy snacks to have on hand. Recrisp at 375° for 5 minutes if they become soft.

Per ¼ cup: 29 calories, 0.8 g. fat (23% of calories), no dietary fiber,
no cholesterol, 2 mg. sodium.

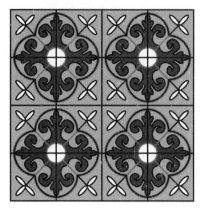

CHAPTER 4

THE
TRADITIONAL
TRIO

PASTA, POLENTA AND RISOTTO

Pasta, polenta and risotto are the cornerstones of Italian cooking. Served as a first course or entrée, they provide a luscious foundation for any number of creative vegetable, seafood and poultry dishes. Pasta, polenta and risotto are low in calories and fat. The sauce that accompanies them often is not. Here you'll find a medley of sauces and toppings; many are interchangeable. Vary the ingredients to suit the season, and create your own specialties *di casa*.

SPAGHETTI CARBONARA

SERVES 4

The story behind this old-time favorite dish is that several American soldiers who were serving in Italy in World War II convinced an Italian cook to create a pasta dish that celebrated their favorite foods—bacon and eggs. This version has all the richness but no eggs—a homey, comforting dish.

10 *ounces spaghetti*
4 *slices light turkey ham, chopped*
1 *shallot, minced*
1 *cup defatted chicken stock*
½ *cup fresh or frozen peas*
¼ *cup nonfat sour cream*
   Pinch of ground nutmeg
   Salt and black pepper
1 *tablespoon grated Parmesan cheese*

Cook the spaghetti in a large pot of boiling water for 10 to 12 minutes, or until just tender; drain well.

While the spaghetti is cooking, sauté the ham and shallots in a large no-stick frying pan over medium heat for 1 minute, or until the shallots begin to soften and the ham begins to brown. Add the stock and cook for 3 minutes, or until the liquid is reduced by half. Stir in the peas and heat through. Stir in the sour cream and continue cooking until the sauce is thick enough to coat the back of a spoon. Add the spaghetti and toss with the nutmeg; add salt and pepper to taste. Serve sprinkled with the Parmesan.

Preparation time: 5 minutes
Cooking time: 12 minutes

Per serving: 362 calories, 3.3 g. fat (8% of calories), 0.8 g. dietary fiber, 17 mg. cholesterol, 469 mg. sodium.

Scallops with Garlic and Parsley on Linguine

SERVES 4

*T*ender and sweet fresh scallops are lightly sautéed and tossed with garlic and parsley for a light entrée for four people or an elegant first course for eight.

10 *ounces linguine*

1 *pound bay scallops or large sea scallops, quartered*

1 *tablespoon extra-virgin olive oil*

1 *clove garlic, minced*

¼ *cup sliced scallions*

2 *tablespoons white wine or water*

1 *tablespoon chopped fresh parsley*

1 *tablespoon drained capers*

1 *tablespoon lemon juice*

Dash of hot-pepper sauce

Salt and black pepper

Cook the linguine in a large pot of boiling water for 10 to 12 minutes, or until just tender; drain well.

Wash the scallops in cold water. Drain and pat dry with a paper towel.

In a large frying pan over medium heat, heat the oil and sauté the garlic until it becomes a pale gold. Add the scallops and scallions and sauté for 1 minute, stirring constantly, until the scallops start to turn white. Add the wine or water, parsley, capers and lemon juice; cook for 3 minutes, or until the sauce is slightly reduced. Add the linguine; toss gently with the scallops and hot-pepper sauce; add salt and pepper to taste.

Preparation time: 5 minutes
Cooking time: 12 minutes

Per serving: 388 calories 6.6 g. fat (15% of calories), 0.2 g. dietary fiber, 0 mg. cholesterol, 283 mg. sodium.

PASTA SHELLS AND LITTLENECK CLAMS

SERVES 4

*S*erve this whimsical dish with the clams in their shells.

10 *ounces shell pasta*
2 *dozen littleneck clams, scrubbed (page 42)*
½ *cup chopped scallions*
⅔ *cup white wine or clam juice*
¼ *cup chopped fresh Italian parsley*
2 *tablespoons chopped fresh marjoram*
2 *cloves garlic, minced*
½ *cup diced sweet red peppers*
½ *cup diced green peppers*
Dash of hot-pepper sauce
Salt and black pepper
2 *tablespoons chopped fresh basil*

Cook the pasta in a large pot of boiling water for 7 to 10 minutes, or until just tender; drain well.

While the pasta is cooking, in a large saucepan combine the clams, scallions, wine or clam juice, parsley, marjoram and garlic. Bring to a boil over medium-high heat. Cover; reduce the heat and simmer until the clams open, about 8 minutes. Discard any clams that have not opened.

Add the pasta to the clams with the red peppers, green peppers and hot-pepper sauce; toss gently. Add salt and black pepper to taste. Cook over medium-high heat for 2 minutes, or until the pasta absorbs some of the juices. Sprinkle with the basil and serve immediately.

Preparation time: 5 minutes
Cooking time: 12 minutes

Per serving: 302 calories, 2.3 g. fat (7% of calories), 0.6 g. dietary fiber, 71 mg. cholesterol, 32 mg. sodium.

PASTA WITH SHRIMP, SUN-DRIED TOMATOES, BROCCOLI AND SHIITAKES

SERVES 4

In this recipe, the dark, woodsy shiitake mushrooms and sweet sun-dried tomatoes work beautifully with assertive broccoli and tender shrimp.

10	*ounces rotelle or penne*
1	*pound medium shrimp, peeled and deveined*
2	*cups broccoli florets*
8	*ounces shiitake mushrooms, stems removed and caps sliced ¼" thick (see note)*
4	*plum tomatoes, chopped*
2	*teaspoons lemon juice*
2	*cloves garlic, minced*
	Dash of hot-pepper sauce
¼	*cup reconstituted sun-dried tomatoes, cut in half (page 72)*
¼	*cup chopped fresh Italian parsley*
	Salt and black pepper
2	*tablespoons chopped fresh basil*

Cook the pasta in a large pot of boiling water for 10 to 12 minutes, or until tender; drain well.

While the pasta is cooking, set a large no-stick frying pan over medium-high heat. Sauté the shrimp, broccoli, mushrooms and plum tomatoes for 1 minute. Add the lemon juice, garlic and hot-pepper sauce. Reduce the heat, cover and cook for 3 minutes, or until the shrimp are pink and the broccoli is crisp-tender. Add the sun-dried tomatoes and parsley; add salt and black pepper to taste. Stir in the pasta. Top with the basil.

Preparation time: 10 minutes
Cooking time: 12 minutes

Chef's note: If fresh shiitake mushrooms are not available, use white button mushrooms. They have a milder flavor but will work just as well.

Per serving: 420 calories, 3.5 g. fat (7% of calories), 2.8 g. dietary fiber, 235 mg. cholesterol, 3 mg. sodium.

LEMON AND HERB RISO

SERVES 4

Riso, known in Greece as *orzo*, is a tiny, firm rice-shaped pasta that is difficult to overcook. It makes a toothsome side dish to poultry and lamb.

4	cups defatted chicken stock
1	teaspoon grated lemon rind
1	cup riso (orzo)
¼	cup chopped fresh basil
¼	cup chopped fresh Italian parsley
2	tablespoons chopped fresh marjoram
2	tablespoons lemon juice
	Salt and black pepper

In a large saucepan, bring the stock and lemon rind to a boil. Add the riso and cook for 10 to 15 minutes, or until just tender. Drain well.

Combine the riso, basil, parsley, marjoram and lemon juice. Add salt and pepper to taste. Serve hot, at room temperature or chilled.

Preparation time: 5 minutes
Cooking time: 15 minutes

Per serving: 215 calories, 1.6 g. fat (7% of calories). 0.2 g. dietary fiber, 49 mg. cholesterol, 480 mg. sodium.

PASTA PRIMAVERA

SERVES 4

Primavera is Italian for "springtime." This dish is a medley of fresh spring flavors. Vary your selection of vegetables with the season.

12   *ounces angel hair pasta*
3   *cloves garlic, minced*
1   *teaspoon extra-virgin olive oil*
1   *cup broccoli florets*
4   *stalks asparagus, cut into 1" pieces*
¼   *cup white wine or defatted chicken stock*
1   *sweet red pepper, cut into 1" pieces*
1   *green pepper, cut into 1" pieces*
5   *mushrooms, cut into 1" pieces*
¼   *cup sliced scallions*
1   *cup chopped fresh parsley*
¼   *cup chopped fresh basil*

Cook the pasta in a large pot of boiling water for 10 to 12 minutes, or until just tender; drain well.

While the pasta is cooking, in a large frying pan over medium heat, sauté the garlic in the oil for 1 minute. Add the broccoli and asparagus and toss. Add the white wine or stock; cover and cook for 1 minute. Add the red peppers, green peppers, mushrooms, scallions and parsley; cover and cook for 1 minute, or until the vegetables are tender-crisp. Uncover and cook for 1 minute, or until the liquid is reduced. Add the pasta and toss. Serve sprinkled with the basil.

Preparation time: 5 minutes
Cooking time: 12 minutes

Chef's note: Turn this dish into a sumptuous entrée by adding cooked chicken, turkey, fish or shrimp.

Per serving: 345 calories, 3.9 g. fat (10% of calories), 2.4 g. dietary fiber, 73 mg. cholesterol, 29 mg. sodium

Fettuccine Alfredo with Mushrooms

SERVES 4

*T*his is not quite the dish that the Roman restaurateur Alfredo di Lello first created in the 1920s, but he might be pleased with the rich, mushroomy sauce that enrobes the pasta, yet contains no cream or butter.

8   *ounces fettuccine*
8   *ounces mushrooms, sliced*
½   *cup sliced scallions*
1   *cup defatted chicken stock*
¼   *cup nonfat sour cream*
1   *tablespoon lemon juice*
    Pinch of ground nutmeg
    Salt and black pepper
2   *tablespoons grated Parmesan cheese*

Cook the fettuccine in a large pot of boiling water for 10 to 12 minutes, or until just tender; drain well.

While the fettuccine is cooking, in a large no-stick frying pan over medium heat, sauté the mushrooms and scallions for 1 minute. Add the chicken stock; cover and cook for 5 minutes, or until the mushrooms are tender. Uncover and cook for 2 to 3 minutes, or until the liquid is reduced by half. Stir in the sour cream and lemon juice and continue cooking until the sauce is thick enough to coat the back of a spoon.

Add the fettuccine and toss to coat. Stir in the nutmeg; add salt and pepper to taste. Serve sprinkled with the Parmesan.

Preparation time: 10 minutes
Cooking time: 12 minutes

Per serving: 245 calories, 2.8 g. fat (10% of calories), 1 g. dietary fiber, 51 mg. cholesterol, 207 mg. sodium.

LEMON, ASPARAGUS AND MUSHROOM FETTUCCINE

SERVES 4

*H*ere, fresh, almost sweet-tasting asparagus and earthy mushrooms are accented with lemon and sharp Asiago cheese. Serve this for a light supper or a hearty side dish. It reheats well in the microwave.

- 10 *ounces fettuccine*
- 1 *tablespoon extra-virgin olive oil*
- ¼ *cup chopped onions*
- 1 *clove garlic, minced*
- 6 *ounces portobello or white button mushrooms, sliced ¼" thick*
- 8 *ounces fresh asparagus, cut into 2" pieces*
- ¼ *cup defatted chicken stock*
- 2 *tablespoons lemon juice*
- 1 *teaspoon chopped fresh oregano*
- ¼ *cup grated Asiago or other sharp cheese*
- 1 *tablespoon chopped fresh parsley*

Cook the fettuccine in a large pot of boiling water for 8 to 10 minutes, or until just tender; drain well.

While the fettuccine is cooking, heat the oil in a large frying pan or wok over medium heat; sauté the onions and garlic for 1 minute, or until soft. Add the mushrooms and asparagus; toss together. Add the stock, lemon juice and oregano; cover and simmer for 3 minutes, or until the asparagus is tender. Add the fettuccine and toss along with the Asiago and parsley.

Preparation time: 5 minutes
Cooking time: 10 minutes

Chef's note: The mushroomy stock tinges the color of the pasta. To brighten this dish, garnish with more fresh parsley.

Per serving: 333 calories, 8 g. fat (21% of calories), 0.8 g. dietary fiber, 68 mg. cholesterol, 146 mg. sodium.

Tuscan Fettuccine

SERVES 4

A pasta that unites robust and earthy fava beans, sweet sun-dried tomatoes, lots of garlic and sage—all the flavors of the Italian countryside.

10	*ounces fettuccine*
2	*teaspoons virgin olive oil*
3	*cloves garlic, minced*
1	*cup broccoli florets*
¼	*cup defatted chicken stock*
1	*sweet red pepper, diced*
1	*cup canned fava beans, rinsed and drained*
¼	*cup chopped reconstituted sun-dried tomatoes (page 72)*
1	*tablespoon chopped fresh sage*
	Salt and black pepper
2	*tablespoons grated Asiago or other sharp cheese*

Cook the fettuccine in a large pot of boiling water for 10 to 12 minutes, or until just tender; drain well.

While the fettuccine is cooking, heat the oil in a large no-stick frying pan over medium heat; sauté the garlic and broccoli for 1 minute. Add the stock, reduce the heat, cover and cook for 2 minutes, or until the broccoli is bright green and just tender. Add the peppers, fava beans, tomatoes and sage; cook, uncovered, for 2 to 3 minutes, or until the peppers are tender and the liquid is reduced. Add salt and black pepper to taste. Add the fettuccine and cheese and gently toss.

Preparation time: 5 minutes
Cooking time: 12 minutes

Per serving: 357 calories, 5.8 g. fat (14% of calories), 3.1 g. dietary fiber, 64 mg. cholesterol, 221 mg. sodium.

SPAGHETTI WITH EGGPLANT AND TOMATOES

SERVES 4

This dish is from Sicily, where abundant eggplant is added to numerous tomato dishes. Often the eggplant is fried; here it is baked, then mixed with the tomatoes.

1	medium eggplant (about 1 pound), peeled and cut into ½" pieces
1	tablespoon plus 1 teaspoon olive oil
10	ounces spaghetti
½	cup minced onions
5	cloves garlic, minced
1½	pounds plum tomatoes, peeled, seeded and chopped
¼	cup grated Parmesan cheese
	Salt and black pepper
¼	cup chopped fresh basil

Coat a 13" × 9" baking dish with no-stick spray. Add the eggplant. Drizzle the eggplant with 1 tablespoon of the oil. Cover tightly and bake at 450° for 25 to 30 minutes, or until tender.

Near the end of the baking time, cook the spaghetti in a large pot of rapidly boiling water for 8 to 10 minutes, or until just tender; drain well.

Meanwhile, in a large no-stick frying pan over medium heat, sauté the onions and garlic in the remaining 1 teaspoon oil for 1 minute. Add the tomatoes; cover and cook for 2 minutes, or until soft. Uncover and cook for 2 minutes.

Add the eggplant, spaghetti and cheese; add salt and pepper to taste. Toss to mix; sprinkle with the basil.

Preparation time: 5 minutes
Cooking time: 30 minutes

Per serving: 425 calories, 8.5 g. fat (18% of calories), 2.5 g. dietary fiber, 5 mg. cholesterol, 138 mg. sodium

Herb-Garlic Yogurt Cheese (page 29)

Top to bottom: Caponata (page 33),
Bruschetta — Tomato and Watercress variation (page 30) and Bruschetta (page 30)

Mussels Marinara (page 41)

Spaghetti with Eggplant and Tomatoes (page 56)

Farfalle with Braised Bitter Greens (page 65)

Polenta with Mushroom-Tomato Sauce (page 74)

Polenta with Italian Sausage, Onions and White Beans (page 84)

Saffron Risotto with Vegetables (page 94)

FARFALLE WITH BRAISED BITTER GREENS

*U*se a combination of bitter greens such as beet greens, collards, kale, mustard greens, broccoli rabe and turnip greens in this quick pasta dish. Some are peppery, some pleasantly tart. They all are exceptionally healthful, with vitamins C and A, calcium, potassium, iron and fewer than 40 calories per cooked cup.

10	*ounces farfalle or other broad noodle*
1	*tablespoon virgin olive oil*
1	*small onion, chopped*
2	*cloves garlic, minced*
4	*cups mixed bitter greens*
¼	*cup defatted chicken stock*
¼	*cup chopped reconstituted sun-dried tomatoes (page 72)*
3	*dashes of hot-pepper sauce*
	Salt and black pepper
¼	*cup shredded Asiago or other sharp cheese*
¼	*cup pine nuts, toasted (page 71)*

Cook the pasta in a large pot of boiling water for 10 to 12 minutes, or until tender; drain well.

While the pasta is cooking, heat the oil in a large frying pan or wok over medium-high heat. Sauté the onions and garlic until soft. Add the greens and sauté for 1 minute. Add the stock and cook for 1 minute, or until the greens are soft. Add the tomatoes and hot-pepper sauce; add salt and pepper to taste.

Toss the bitter greens with the pasta and serve topped with the cheese and pine nuts.

Preparation time: 5 minutes
Cooking time: 12 minutes

Per serving: 380 calories, 12.4 g. fat (29% of calories) 2 g. dietary fiber, 68 mg. cholesterol, 186 mg. sodium.

Braised Peppers on Pasta

SERVES 4

*S*weet red peppers and a fiery chili pepper mingle in this bright dish.

10	ounces linguine
1	tablespoon olive oil
3	cloves garlic, minced
2	sweet red peppers, cut into 2" pieces
1	chili pepper, chopped (wear plastic gloves when handling)
¼	cup defatted chicken or vegetable stock
1	tablespoon chopped fresh oregano
½	cup chopped scallions
½	cup torn fresh basil
2	tablespoons lemon juice
2	tablespoons pine nuts, toasted (page 71)
	Grated Parmesan cheese

Cook the linguine in a large pot of boiling water for 10 to 12 minutes, or until just tender; drain well.

While the linguine is cooking, heat the oil in a large no-stick frying pan over medium heat. Sauté the garlic until it turns a light golden color, about 45 seconds. Add the red peppers and the chili peppers; stir in the stock. Bring the stock to a simmer; reduce the heat to low. Cover and cook for 2 minutes.

Stir in the oregano and cook, uncovered, for 2 minutes, or until the liquid in the pan is reduced by half. Stir in the scallions, basil and lemon juice. Serve the peppers over the linguine. Sprinkle with the pine nuts; top with the Parmesan.

Preparation time: 5 minutes
Cooking time: 12 minutes

Per serving: 319 calories, 7.8 g. fat (22% of calories), 1.1 g. dietary fiber, 62 mg. cholesterol, 45 mg. sodium.

BASIL BROCCOLI PESTO

SERVES 4

*P*esto is a wonderful, fresh-tasting, uncooked sauce from Genoa, traditionally made with basil, olive oil, pine nuts and Parmesan cheese. This recipe uses less oil and cheese and fewer pine nuts than the traditional recipe and calls for cooked broccoli to add body and flavor to the sauce.

   8   ounces angel hair pasta
   ½   cup defatted chicken stock
   2   cups chopped broccoli florets
   3   cloves garlic
   1   cup packed fresh basil leaves
   1   tablespoon pine nuts, toasted (page 71)
   1   tablespoon grated Parmesan cheese
       Salt and black pepper
  12   red cherry tomatoes, halved

Cook the pasta in a large pot of boiling water for 5 minutes, or until just tender; drain well.

While the pasta is cooking, bring the stock to a boil in a large saucepan over medium-high heat. Add the broccoli and cook for 5 minutes, or until tender. Set aside.

In a food processor fitted with the steel blade, chop the garlic, scraping down the sides. Add the basil and pine nuts and finely chop. Add 2 tablespoons of the stock and puree.

Remove the broccoli from the remaining stock and save the stock for another use. Add the broccoli and Parmesan to the food processor. Puree, scraping down the sides of the bowl frequently. Add salt and pepper to taste.

Toss the pesto and tomatoes with the hot pasta.

Preparation time: 10 minutes
Cooking time: 5 minutes

Per serving: 246 calories, 3.6 g. fat (13% of calories), 2.2 g. dietary fiber, 50 mg. cholesterol, 116 mg. sodium.

PASTA PUTTANESCA

SERVES 4

*M*ade with no anchovies and fewer olives than its rich namesake, this lighter version of a classic sauce is every bit as zesty.

12	ounces penne or rigatoni
1	tablespoon olive oil
3	cloves garlic, minced
2½	cups chopped fresh or canned plum tomatoes, drained
½	cup pitted and chopped imported black olives
1	tablespoon drained capers
2	teaspoons chopped fresh Italian parsley
2	teaspoons chopped fresh marjoram
¼	teaspoon red-pepper flakes
	Salt and black pepper
	Basil leaves

Cook the pasta in a large pot of boiling water for 10 minutes, or until tender; drain well.

While the pasta is cooking, in a large no-stick frying pan over medium-high heat, heat the oil and sauté the garlic for 1 to 2 minutes, or until it becomes soft.

Add the tomatoes, olives, capers, parsley, marjoram and red-pepper flakes; cook over low heat for 10 minutes, or until the sauce begins to thicken. Add salt and black pepper to taste.

Add the cooked pasta to the sauce and toss to coat. Serve garnished with basil.

Preparation time: 10 minutes
Cooking time: 15 minutes

Per serving: 363 calories, 7.4 g. fat (18% of calories), 1.6 g. dietary fiber, 73 mg. cholesterol, 93 mg. sodium.

FUSILLI WITH FRESH TOMATOES

SERVES 4

You will need fresh, ripe plum tomatoes and fresh basil (lots of it). This luscious dish may be served warm or at room temperature.

8 *ounces fusilli*
1 *tablespoon extra-virgin olive oil*
1 *tablespoon balsamic vinegar*
6 *plum tomatoes, peeled, seeded and chopped*
1 *cup torn fresh basil*
½ *cup chopped red onions*
   Salt and black pepper
   Grated Parmesan cheese

Cook the fusilli in a large pot of boiling water for 10 to 12 minutes, or until just tender; drain well.

While the fusilli is cooking, in a medium bowl whisk together the oil and vinegar. Add the tomatoes, basil and onions; add salt and pepper to taste. Serve the tomatoes over the fusilli; sprinkle with the Parmesan.

Preparation time: 5 minutes
Cooking time: 12 minutes

Chef's note: This fresh tomato sauce is delicious on polenta and risotto, too.

Per serving: 276 calories, 5.6 g. fat (18% of calories), 2.7 g. dietary fiber, 49 mg. cholesterol, 27 mg. sodium.

PASTA WITH SPINACH, SUN-DRIED TOMATOES AND WHITE BEANS

SERVES 4

*I*n this wonderfully satisfying but light dish, the white beans are a mellow contrast to the sweet sun-dried tomatoes.

8	ounces penne
1	teaspoon olive oil
1	green pepper, diced
2	cloves garlic, minced
1	can (15 ounces) white navy or cannellini beans, rinsed and drained
1	can (14 ounces) plum tomatoes (with juice)
1	package (10 ounces) chopped frozen spinach, thawed and squeezed dry
¼	cup chopped reconstituted sun-dried tomatoes (page 72)
2	teaspoons chopped fresh oregano
2	tablespoons chopped fresh basil
	Dash of hot-pepper sauce
	Salt and black pepper

Cook the penne in a large pot of boiling water for 10 to 12 minutes, or until tender; drain well.

While the penne is cooking, heat the oil in a large no-stick frying pan over medium heat; sauté the peppers and garlic for 3 minutes, or until the peppers are slightly wilted. Add the beans, plum tomatoes (with juice), spinach, sun-dried tomatoes and oregano; simmer for 10 minutes.

Add the penne, basil and hot-pepper sauce; add salt and black pepper to taste. Toss to mix.

Preparation time: 10 minutes
Cooking time: 12 minutes

Per serving: 338 calories, 3.9 g. fat (9% of calories), 9.1 g. dietary fiber, 49 mg. cholesterol, 445 mg. sodium.

WILD MUSHROOM PESTO

SERVES 4

*P*orcini mushrooms, also known as *cèpes*, star in this earthy pasta sauce. In the U.S., these dark, woodsy treasures are generally only available dried. This rich, almost meaty-tasting pesto is great on pasta, grilled chicken and pizza.

½ cup defatted chicken stock
2 ounces dried porcini mushrooms, rinsed
3 plum tomatoes, finely chopped
½ cup chopped scallions
1 tablespoon chopped fresh parsley
2 teaspoons chopped fresh rosemary
2 dashes of hot-pepper sauce
1 tablespoon pine nuts, toasted (see note)

In a medium saucepan, bring the stock to a boil. Add the mushrooms, tomatoes, scallions, parsley, rosemary and hot-pepper sauce. Set the pesto aside for 15 to 20 minutes, or until the mushrooms are plump and soft.

In a food processor fitted with the steel blade, chop the pesto mixture with on/off pulses until chunky. To serve, toss with hot pasta or spoon over grilled chicken or pizza; sprinkle with the pine nuts.

Preparation time: 5 minutes
Cooking time: 5 minutes with 15 minutes standing time

Chef's note: Toasting heightens the flavor of pine nuts. Toast them on a baking sheet at 350° for 5 minutes, or until they turn golden brown.

Per serving: 323 calories, 3.6 g. fat (10% of calories), 1.6 g. dietary fiber, 61 mg. cholesterol, 80 mg. sodium.

SUN-DRIED TOMATOES

Sun-dried tomatoes are plum tomatoes that have been split and dried to look something like flat ruby prunes. They are sweet and pungent, adding a distinct flavor to pastas, salads and sauces.

Less expensive when purchased in bulk, dried tomatoes are sold in their dry form or packed in oil. The dry ones must be reconstituted before using; reconstitute only the amount you need for any given recipe. Here's how: Put the tomatoes in a pot and add enough water to cover. Bring to a boil; reduce the heat and simmer for 10 minutes, or until the tomatoes are soft. Drain the liquid (and save it to add to soups or sauces). Spread the tomatoes on a paper towel and cover them with another paper towel to blot out extra moisture.

SUN-DRIED TOMATO PESTO

SERVES 4

*F*lavorful and rich-tasting though it is, this sauce is almost oil-free —and a little bit goes a long long way. Stir it into hot pasta, tossing to coat evenly. Spread it on Bruschetta (page 30) or simple crackers or stir it into cooked white or brown rice. It will keep up to a week, covered and refrigerated.

> 2 *cups defatted chicken stock*
> 1 *cup sun-dried tomatoes*
> ¼ *cup fresh basil*
> 2 *tablespoons chopped fresh parsley*
> 1 *clove garlic*
> *Pinch of sugar*

In a small saucepan over medium heat, bring the stock to a simmer and add the tomatoes. Cook for 10 minutes, or until the tomatoes are reconstituted and soft.

In a food processor fitted with the steel blade, process the basil, parsley, garlic and sugar until finely minced. Add the tomatoes and stock; puree.

Preparation time: 5 minutes
Cooking time: 10 minutes

Per serving: 49 calories, 0.1 g. fat (1% of calories), 0.9 g. dietary fiber, no cholesterol, 253 mg. sodium.

POLENTA WITH MUSHROOM-TOMATO SAUCE

SERVES 4

*T*hree types of polenta are available: *Traditional polenta*, trickiest to work with, takes the longest to cook. *Instant polenta*, more finely ground, is ready in half the time. *Precooked packaged polenta* is sold in the produce section of the supermarket. This recipe, and those that follow, call for instant polenta, but they all would be equally successful made with the traditional or precooked polenta.

3½ *cups defatted chicken stock*
1 *cup instant polenta*
1 *tablespoon olive oil*
2 *shallots, minced*
2 *teaspoons chopped fresh rosemary*
4 *cups thinly sliced mushrooms (a mix of shiitake, portobello and button)*
1 *cup canned crushed tomatoes*
¼ *cup white wine or no-salt-added tomato juice*
1 *tablespoon balsamic vinegar*
2 *tablespoons grated Parmesan cheese*
2 *tablespoons chopped fresh Italian parsley*
   Salt and black pepper

In a medium saucepan, bring the stock to a boil; reduce the heat to low. While the stock is simmering, add the polenta in a slow, steady stream, stirring constantly. Cook the polenta over low heat for 10 minutes, or until very thick, stirring occasionally.

While the polenta is cooking, heat the oil in a large no-stick frying pan over medium heat. Add the shallots and rosemary; cook for 2 minutes, or until the shallots are golden. Stir in the mushrooms, tomatoes, wine or tomato juice and vinegar; bring to a boil. Cover, reduce the heat, and simmer for 5 minutes.

Uncover and cook for 15 to 20 minutes, or until the sauce thickens. Toss in the Parmesan and parsley; add salt and pepper to taste. To serve, spoon the polenta onto a large platter or 4 individual plates; top with the sauce.

Preparation time: 10 minutes
Cooking time: 30 minutes

Chef's notes: To make this recipe a day ahead, coat an 8″ × 5″ loaf pan with no-stick spray. Turn the cooked polenta into the prepared loaf pan, cover with plastic wrap and refrigerate overnight. Cover and refrigerate the sauce overnight.

To serve, turn the polenta out onto a cutting board and cut into 2″ slices. Coat a baking sheet with no-stick spray. Place the polenta slices on the baking sheet and bake at 400° for 10 minutes, or until golden brown. Reheat the sauce and serve over the polenta slices.

Per serving: 214 calories, 5.9 g. fat (24% of calories), 6.2 g. dietary fiber, 2 mg. cholesterol, 583 mg. sodium.

EGGPLANT SAUCE

MAKES 1 CUP

*D*ense and savory, this sauce is best on any sturdy pasta such as bow ties or penne. It will keep several days in the refrigerator.

1   *small eggplant, peeled and cut into 2″ cubes*
1   *clove garlic, minced*
1   *teaspoon olive oil*
¼   *cup defatted chicken stock*
1   *tablespoon chopped fresh parsley*
1   *teaspoon tomato paste*
1   *teaspoon chopped fresh oregano*
1   *teaspoon balsamic vinegar*

In a large no-stick frying pan over medium heat, sauté the eggplant and garlic in the oil for 1 minute. Add the stock, reduce the heat, cover and cook for 7 to 10 minutes, or until the eggplant is very soft. Stir in the parsley, tomato paste, oregano and vinegar; cook for 1 to 2 minutes, or until the mixture resembles a chunky sauce. (For a smooth sauce, transfer the eggplant mixture to a food processor fitted with the steel blade and puree.)

Preparation time: 5 minutes
Cooking time: 13 minutes

Per ¼ cup: 43 calories, 1.4 g. fat (26% of calories), 0.2 g. dietary fiber, no cholesterol, 65 mg. sodium.

10 Fresh Ways to Sauce
Pasta, Polenta and Risotto

These fast and easy mini-recipes are a snap. Many are interchangeable and may be tossed with pasta, spooned onto polenta or stirred into risotto. All of them make enough sauce for a pasta, polenta or risotto to serve four people.

1. Fresh Tomato: Chop 4 fresh plum tomatoes and toss with ½ cup chopped fresh basil, 2 teaspoons balsamic vinegar and 1 clove garlic, minced. Add salt and black pepper to taste. Toss with drained hot pasta or serve on soft, grilled or baked polenta.

2. Oven-Roasted Vegetable: Sprinkle 2 cups oven-roasted vegetables (page 122) with 2 teaspoons balsamic vinegar and 1 teaspoon chopped fresh oregano. Add salt and black pepper to taste. Toss with drained hot pasta or serve on soft, grilled or baked polenta or over simple risotto.

3. Lemon Caper Cream: Stir together ½ cup nonfat sour cream with 2 tablespoons chopped fresh parsley, 2 teaspoons drained capers, 1 teaspoon fresh juice and ⅛ teaspoon grated lemon rind. Toss with drained hot pasta.

4. Red Pepper and Olive: In a blender or food processor fitted with the steel blade, puree ½ cup roasted red peppers with 1 teaspoon lemon juice and ¼ teaspoon extra-virgin olive oil. Add 1 tablespoon pitted and chopped green olives and blend with on/off pulses. Toss with drained hot pasta or spoon over soft polenta.

5. Herb and Pine Nut: Lightly toss drained hot pasta with 2 teaspoons extra-virgin olive oil, 2 teaspoons chopped fresh basil, 2 teaspoons chopped fresh parsley and 1 teaspoon chopped fresh oregano, Sprinkle with 3 tablespoons pine nuts, toasted (page 71).

6. Creamy Tomato: Stir together ¼ cup no-salt tomato paste with ¼ cup nonfat sour cream. Toss with drained hot pasta.

7. Creamy Bean: In a food processor fitted with the steel blade, puree ½ cup drained canned white navy or cannellini beans with 2 tablespoons chopped fresh basil, 1 teaspoon lemon juice and 1 teaspoon extra-virgin olive oil. Add salt and black pepper to taste. (Do not overprocess; the puree should be rough.) Toss with drained hot pasta or spoon over soft polenta.

8. Zesty Tomato: Warm 1 cup mild fresh tomato salsa. Toss with drained hot pasta, spoon over soft or grilled polenta or stir into risotto the last minute of cooking. Garnish with 2 tablespoons chopped fresh basil.

9. Quick Florentine: In a food processor fitted with the steel blade, puree ½ cup thawed frozen chopped spinach with ¼ cup nonfat sour cream, a dash of ground nutmeg and a dash of hot-pepper sauce. Add salt and black pepper to taste. Warm the sauce and toss with drained hot pasta.

10. Simple Shrimp: Toss 1 cup cooked shrimp with 1 tablespoon lemon juice, 1 teaspoon extra-virgin olive oil and 1 teaspoon drained capers. Add salt and black pepper to taste. Toss with drained hot pasta or spoon over hot polenta; serve with 2 tablespoons chopped fresh parsley.

TOASTED MUSHROOM POLENTA

SERVES 4

*M*ake this savory replacement for bread to serve with a hearty stew, salad or soup. It will keep for several days, covered, in the refrigerator.

3½	*cups defatted chicken stock*
1	*cup instant polenta*
1	*teaspoon chopped fresh rosemary*
1	*teaspoon chopped fresh oregano*
	Salt and black pepper
1	*cup sliced dark mushrooms (portobello, shiitake or cremini)*
¼	*cup chopped onions*
¼	*cup tomato juice*
1	*tablespoon balsamic vinegar*

In a medium saucepan, bring the stock to a boil; reduce the heat to low. While the stock is simmering, add the polenta in a slow, steady stream, stirring constantly. Add the rosemary and oregano. Cook the polenta over low heat for 10 minutes, or until very thick, stirring occasionally. Add salt and pepper to taste.

While the polenta is cooking, in a large no-stick frying pan over medium-high heat, sauté the mushrooms and onions for 3 minutes. Add the tomato juice and vinegar; cover and cook for 5 minutes, or until the mushrooms are tender. Uncover and continue cooking for 1 to 2 minutes, or until the liquid has evaporated. Stir into the polenta.

Coat an 8″ pie plate or an 8″ × 8″ baking dish with no-stick spray. Spread the polenta into the prepared pie plate or baking dish. Allow to cool for 15 minutes, or chill overnight.

Coat a baking sheet with no-stick spray. Cut the polenta into wedges or squares and place on the prepared baking sheet. Toast at 450° for 5 to 7 minutes per side, or until lightly browned.

Preparation time: 10 minutes
Cooking time: 10 minutes
Cooling time: 15 minutes
Baking time: 14 minutes

Per serving: 155 calories, 1.2 g fat (7% of calories), 5 g. dietary fiber, no cholesterol, 479 mg. sodium.

GRILLED POLENTA
WITH ROASTED ONIONS AND RAISINS

SERVES 4

Onions become meltingly sweet when roasted; here they are nicely complemented by golden raisins. The grilled polenta adds its toasty, mellow flavors to this complex dish. Serve as a side to simple grilled poultry or fish.

3½ *cups defatted chicken stock*
1 *cup instant polenta*
½ *cup golden raisins*
¼ *cup orange juice*
2 *tablespoons sherry or 1 tablespoon balsamic vinegar*
4 *medium onions, cut crosswise into 1″ slices*
1 *teaspoon extra-virgin olive oil*
    Toasted pine nuts (page 71)

In a medium saucepan, bring the stock to a boil; reduce the heat to low. While the stock is simmering, add the polenta in a slow, steady stream, stirring constantly. Cook the polenta over low heat for 10 minutes, or until very thick, stirring occasionally. Coat an 8″ pie plate with no-stick spray. Spread the cooked polenta evenly in the prepared pie plate; chill in the refrigerator for 15 minutes.

Meanwhile, in a small cup combine the raisins, orange juice and sherry or vinegar. Set aside to allow the raisins to plump.

Coat a 13″ × 9″ baking dish with no-stick spray. Brush the onions with the oil and place, cut side down, in the prepared dish. Bake at 375° for 20 minutes. Turn the onions over and bake for 10 minutes, or until slightly charred. Spoon the raisins and liquid over the onions and bake for 2 minutes.

Cut the polenta into wedges and grill over high heat or broil about 5″ from the heat for 1 minute per side, or until lightly browned. Place the wedges on a serving plate and spoon the onion mixture over them. Sprinkle with the pine nuts.

Preparation time: 5 minutes
Cooking time: 10 minutes
Chilling time: 15 minutes
Baking time: 32 minutes
Grilling time: 2 minutes

Per serving: 272 calories, 3.7 g. fat (12% of calories), 6.8 g. dietary fiber, no cholesterol, 430 mg. sodium.

POLENTA WITH SPRING VEGETABLE STEW

*P*olenta provides a creamy background for this rich stew of asparagus, leeks, mushrooms and peas.

3½ *cups defatted chicken stock*
1 *cup instant polenta*
1 *cup vegetable stock*
1 *cup diced onions*
1 *cup diced leeks (see note)*
1 *cup quartered mushrooms*
2 *tablespoons orange juice*
1 *tablespoon chopped fresh Italian parsley*
2 *cloves garlic, diced*
1 *teaspoon chopped fresh rosemary*
1 *teaspoon grated orange rind*
1 *cup asparagus cut into 1" pieces*
1 *cup fresh or frozen peas*
   Salt and black pepper
2 *tablespoons chopped fresh basil*

In a medium saucepan, bring the chicken stock to a boil; reduce the heat to low. While the stock is simmering, add the polenta in a slow, steady stream, stirring constantly. Cook the polenta over low heat for 10 minutes, or until very thick, stirring occasionally.

While the polenta is cooking, in a large no-stick frying pan over medium-high heat, bring the vegetable stock to a simmer. Add the onions, leeks, mushrooms, orange juice, parsley, garlic, rosemary and grated orange rind. Cover and cook for 15 minutes, or until the vegetables are soft.

Add the asparagus; cover and cook for 5 minutes, or until the asparagus is bright green and crisp-tender. Add the peas and cook, uncovered, for 1 minute, or until heated through. Add salt and pepper to taste. To serve, spoon the polenta onto a large platter or 4 individual plates; top with the stew and sprinkle with basil.

Preparation time: 15 minutes
Cooking time: 21 minutes

Chef's note: To clean leeks, trim the rootlets and leaf ends. Slit the leeks from top to bottom and wash thoroughly to remove all the dirt trapped between the leaf layers.

Per serving: 225 calories, 1.6 g. fat (6% of calories), 7.1 g. dietary fiber, no cholesterol, 533 mg. sodium.

Polenta with Italian Sausage, Onions and White Beans

SERVES 4

A hearty, homey dish for a cold winter night. Who says comfort food can't be healthful?

3½	*cups defatted chicken stock*
1	*cup instant polenta*
½	*Italian sausage (2 ounces), hot or sweet*
1	*small onion, thinly sliced*
2	*tablespoons orange juice*
1	*can (19 ounces) cannellini beans*
1	*tablespoon chopped fresh oregano*
1	*teaspoon fennel seeds*
1	*teaspoon grated orange rind*
2	*tablespoons chopped fresh parsley*

In a medium pot, bring the stock to a boil; reduce the heat to low. While the stock is simmering, add the polenta in a slow, steady stream, stirring constantly. Cook the polenta over low heat for 10 minutes, or until very thick, stirring occasionally.

While the polenta is cooking, in a large no-stick frying pan over medium-high heat, cook the sausage for 3 minutes, turning often to brown evenly. Cover and cook for 2 to 3 minutes, or until the sausage is no longer pink in the center. Remove the sausage, slice ½" thick and set aside; drain off the fat and wipe the pan clean.

Return the pan to the heat and sauté the onions for 2 minutes, or until they begin to soften. Add the orange juice; cover and cook for 3 to 4 minutes, or until the onions are very soft. Add the beans (with liquid), oregano, fennel seeds, orange rind, parsley and sausage; mix well.

To serve, spoon the polenta onto a large platter or 4 individual plates; top with the bean mixture and sprinkle with the parsley.

Preparation time: 10 minutes
Cooking time: 12 minutes

Per serving: 268 calories, 4.7 g. fat (14% of calories), 13 g. dietary fiber, no cholesterol, 688 mg. sodium.

LEMON-PEPPER POLENTA
WITH BAKED FISH AND PEPPERS

SERVES 4

Peppery polenta makes a zesty base for a light fish such as sole. The polenta is also delicious as a simple side dish for grilled lamb or chicken.

3 cups water

¼ cup plus 2 tablespoons lemon juice

1 teaspoon grated lemon rind

1 teaspoon ground black pepper

1 cup instant polenta

1 pound sole fillets (see note)

1 sweet red pepper, cut into 1" pieces

¼ cup chopped scallions

2 tablespoons pitted and chopped imported black olives

2 tablespoons drained capers

2 tablespoons chopped fresh oregano
Lemon wedges

In a medium saucepan, bring the water, ¼ cup of the lemon juice, lemon rind and black pepper to a boil; reduce the heat to low. While the water is simmering, add the polenta in a slow, steady stream, stirring constantly. Cook the polenta over low heat for 10 minutes, or until very thick, stirring occasionally.

While the polenta is cooking, coat a 13" × 9" baking dish with no-stick spray. Place the fillets in the prepared baking dish; top with the red peppers, scallions, olives, capers, oregano and the remaining 2 tablespoons lemon juice. Bake at 425° for 8 to 15 minutes, depending on the thickness of the fillets, or until the fish turns opaque and just begins to flake when gently pressed.

To serve, spoon the polenta onto a large platter or individual plates; top with the fish-and-pepper mixture. Garnish with lemon wedges.

Preparation time: 10 minutes
Cooking time: 10 minutes
Baking time: 15 minutes

Chef's note: You may substitute other fish; just be sure to adjust the baking time accordingly. Red snapper, halibut and thick pieces of cod may take around 20 minutes.

Per serving: 230 calories, 2.8 fat (11% of calories), 5.4 g. dietary fiber, 53 mg. cholesterol, 166 mg. sodium.

TRUE FISH TALES

Fish is a hero when it comes to healthy food. Low-calorie, low-saturated fat and high-protein, fish can help lower cholesterol levels, reduce risk of heart disease and protect against some cancers. Omega-3 fatty acids found in fish oil take much of the credit for these benefits.

In a study of two low-fat diets, half the Australian participants ate a variety of lean protein foods; the other half ate one serving of fish per day. Both kept their fat level to 30 percent of calories. Total cholesterol and bad LDL cholesterol fell for everyone, but the fish eaters got a bonus: They raised their levels of beneficial HDL cholesterol.

Sardines, tuna, mackerel and salmon are especially high in omega-3 fatty acids, but all types of seafood contain this healthful substance. Eating fish two or three times a week will help you reap its benefits.

When buying fish, look for:

• Whole fish that have clear eyes and gills that are bright red or pink, not brownish. The skin should be shiny, and it should feel firm and spring back when pressed with the finger. If the head has been removed, make sure there's no discoloration at the neck.

• Steaks or fillets with flesh that's transparent, not opaque, dull or spongy.

• Flesh that's plump and moist with a tight, firm grain. It should be firm and elastic when touched.

• The absence of an unpleasant fishy smell.

• White-fleshed fish that have no areas of deep color (which would indicate bruising).

Traditional Risotto with Sweet Onions

SERVES 4

*H*ere, the risotto is cooked on the stovetop, using the traditional method of adding boiling stock to the rice only as quickly as it is absorbed. Patience and a strong, steady arm are the key. A smooth, velvety risotto makes it well worth the work.

1	tablespoon extra-virgin olive oil
1	cup chopped sweet onions (Walla Walla or Vidalia)
1	cup Arborio rice
1	teaspoon grated orange rind
4–5	cups simmering defatted chicken stock
1	tablespoon orange juice
½	cup chopped scallions
	Salt and black pepper
2	tablespoons grated Parmesan cheese
2	tablespoons fresh chopped chives

In a large heavy-bottomed saucepan over medium-high heat, heat the oil and sauté the onions for 10 minutes, or until soft and starting to brown. Stir in the rice and orange rind and toss to coat. Cook for 1 minute, stirring constantly.

While the onions are cooking, bring the stock to a simmer in a medium saucepan over medium heat. Maintain the simmer.

Slowly add ½ cup of the stock and the orange juice to the onion mixture, stirring constantly. Continue stirring until the stock is absorbed by the rice. Slowly add ½ cup of the stock at a time, stirring constantly as the rice absorbs the stock. Keep adding and stirring until all of the stock has been absorbed and the risotto is creamy but still firm to the bite.

Stir in the scallions; add salt and pepper to taste. Sprinkle with the Parmesan and chives.

Preparation time: 5 minutes
Cooking time: 30 minutes

Per serving: 255 calories, 4.7 g. fat (17% of calories), 1 g. dietary fiber, 2 mg. cholesterol, 530 mg. sodium.

SPINACH RISOTTO

SERVES 4

*M*icrowaving risotto saves the cook time and effort over the usual stovetop method. Just add the liquid in two parts and stir twice. No need to stand at the stove, stirring constantly. But each cooking method will yield a differently textured risotto. Stovetop risotto is very creamy; microwave risotto tends to be a bit drier and the rice firmer.

1	tablespoon virgin olive oil
1	cup Arborio rice
½	cup finely chopped onions
1	clove garlic, minced
1	teaspoon grated lemon rind
⅛	teaspoon ground nutmeg
2½	cups vegetable stock
1	tablespoon lemon juice
1	pound fresh spinach, washed, dried and torn
	Salt and black pepper
2	tablespoons grated Parmesan cheese

In a large microwave-safe bowl, microwave the oil for 1 minute on high. Stir in the rice, onions, garlic, lemon rind and nutmeg. Microwave, uncovered, for 1 minute. Stir in 1½ cups of the stock and the lemon juice. Microwave for 10 minutes, stirring once halfway through cooking.

Stir in the remaining 1 cup stock. Microwave for 15 minutes, stirring once halfway through cooking.

Stir in the spinach. Add salt and pepper to taste. Sprinkle with the Parmesan.

Preparation time: 5 minutes
Microwaving time: 27 minutes

Per serving: 265 calories, 5.1 g. fat (17% of calories), 3.3 g. dietary fiber, 3 mg. cholesterol, 442 mg. sodium.

HERBED SWEET POTATO RISOTTO

SERVES 4

*S*weet potatoes and sage, the mellow and musky flavors of autumn, blend here in a low-fat take on traditional *risotto alla zucca* ("risotto with sweet pumpkin"). The Italian version is made with locally grown, very sweet pumpkins that have a flavor similar to our sweet potatoes.

> 1   *tablespoon virgin olive oil*
> 2   *cups cubed (1") sweet potatoes*
> 1   *cup Arborio rice*
> ½   *cup chopped onions*
> 1   *tablespoon chopped fresh sage*
> 1   *teaspoon grated orange rind*
> ⅛   *teaspoon ground nutmeg*
> 2   *cups defatted chicken stock*
> ¼   *cup orange juice*
>   *Salt and black pepper*
> 2   *tablespoons grated Parmesan cheese*
> 2   *tablespoons chopped fresh Italian parsley*

In a large microwave-safe bowl, microwave the oil for 1 minute on high. Stir in the sweet potatoes, rice, onions, sage, orange rind and nutmeg. Microwave, uncovered, for 1 minute. Stir in 1½ cups of the stock. Microwave for 10 minutes, stirring once halfway through cooking.

Stir in the remaining ½ cup stock and orange juice. Microwave for 15 minutes, stirring once halfway through cooking.

Add salt and pepper to taste. Sprinkle with the Parmesan and parsley.

Preparation time: 5 minutes
Microwaving time: 27 minutes

Per serving: 316 calories, 4.8 g. fat (14% of calories), 0.5 g. dietary fiber, 2 mg. cholesterol, 299 mg. sodium.

ASPARAGUS RISOTTO

SERVES 4

*I*n this elegant dish, the risotto cooks in the asparagus stock for extra flavor. Sun-dried tomatoes add a sweet, colorful touch. Serve for a simple supper or side dish.

> 1   *pound asparagus, cut into 2" pieces,*
>   *tips reserved*
> 1   *tablespoon olive oil*
> 1   *cup Arborio rice*
> ½   *cup finely chopped onions*
> 2   *cups defatted chicken stock*
> 4   *sun-dried tomato halves, reconstituted*
>   *and chopped (page 72)*
> 2   *tablespoons chopped fresh parsley*
> 2   *tablespoons grated Parmesan cheese*

In a large frying pan of rapidly boiling water, blanch the asparagus tips for 2 to 3 minutes, or until vivid green. Remove the asparagus from the pan and set aside; reserve the cooking water.

In a large microwave-safe bowl, microwave the oil for 1 minute on high. Stir in the rice and onions. Microwave, uncovered, for 1 minute. Stir in 1½ cups of the reserved cooking water. Microwave for 10 minutes, stirring once halfway through cooking.

Stir in the stock. Microwave for 15 minutes, stirring once halfway through cooking. Stir in the asparagus (except for the tips), tomatoes and parsley. Microwave for 1 minute, or until heated through.

To serve, arrange the asparagus tips on top of the risotto; sprinkle with the Parmesan.

Preparation time: 5 minutes
Cooking time: 3 minutes
Microwaving time: 28 minutes

Per serving: 281 calories, 5 g. fat (16% of calories), 0.8 g. dietary fiber, no cholesterol, 308 mg. sodium.

ARTICHOKE, TOMATO AND MUSHROOM RISOTTO

SERVES 4

*A*rtichokes and earthy mushrooms blend well in this dish. Serve as an entrée for four or a side dish for six or eight people.

1	*tablespoon virgin olive oil*
1	*cup Arborio rice*
1	*cup chopped mushrooms (see note)*
3⅓	*cups defatted chicken stock*
1	*can (14 ounces) artichoke hearts, drained and quartered*
1	*tablespoon lemon juice*
1	*tablespoon chopped fresh oregano*
½	*cup chopped fresh tomatoes*
½	*cup chopped scallions*
2	*tablespoons grated Parmesan cheese*
	Salt and black pepper
¼	*cup chopped fresh basil*

In a large microwave-safe bowl, microwave the oil for 1 minute on high. Stir in the rice and mushrooms. Microwave, uncovered, for 1 minute. Stir in 2 cups of the stock. Microwave for 15 minutes, stirring once halfway through the cooking. Stir in the remaining 1⅓ cups stock, artichokes, lemon juice and oregano. Microwave for 10 minutes, stirring once halfway through cooking.

Stir in the tomatoes, scallions and Parmesan; add salt and pepper to taste. Sprinkle with the basil just before serving.

Preparation time: 5 minutes
Microwaving time: 27 minutes

Chef's note: Fresh shiitake mushrooms, if you can find them, will give this dish a rich mushroom flavor. Otherwise, fresh white button mushrooms will work well, too.

Per serving: 273 calories, 5 g. fat (16% of calories), 0.8 g. dietary fiber, 2 mg. cholesterol, 489 mg. sodium.

SAFFRON RISOTTO WITH VEGETABLES

*S*affron, from the yellow-orange stigmas of a small purple crocus, is the world's dearest spice. Each flower provides only three stigmas, which must be carefully hand picked and then dried, an extremely labor-intensive process. Fortunately, a little of this expensive spice goes a long way. It is sold in threads and powdered form. The threads tend to have more flavor and keep longer. They must be crushed before using. Saffron is pungent and aromatic and, in this dish, turns the risotto into a lovely golden backdrop for the bright peas and tomatoes.

1 tablespoon virgin olive oil
1 cup Arborio rice
½ cup finely chopped onions
½ cup finely chopped shiitake mushrooms
2 cloves garlic, minced
1 teaspoon Dijon mustard
½ teaspoon crushed saffron threads (see note)
⅛ teaspoon ground nutmeg
　Pinch of ground cloves
3 cups vegetable stock or defatted chicken stock
¼ cup orange juice
1 teaspoon grated orange rind
¼ cup fresh or frozen peas
1 plum tomato, diced
1 teaspoon chopped fresh thyme
2 tablespoons chopped fresh basil
　Salt and black pepper

In a large microwave-safe bowl, microwave the oil for 1 minute on high. Stir in the rice, onions, mushrooms, garlic, mustard, saffron, nutmeg and cloves. Microwave, uncovered, for 1 minute.

Stir in 2 cups of the stock, the orange juice and orange rind. Microwave for 10 minutes, stirring once halfway through cooking. Stir in the remaining 1 cup stock. Microwave for 15 minutes, stirring once halfway through cooking.

Gently stir in the peas, tomatoes and thyme. Microwave for 1 minute, or until heated through. Stir in the basil; add salt and pepper to taste.

Preparation time: 10 minutes
Microwaving time: 27 minutes

Chef's note: You may use powdered saffron, but the flavor will not be quite as pronounced. Increase the quantity to ¾ or 1 teaspoon, depending on taste.

Per serving: 261 calories, 4 g. fat (14% of calories), 0.8 g. dietary fiber, no cholesterol, 375 mg. sodium.

CHAPTER 5

VEGETABLES AND LEGUMES

In Italy, none of the good earth is left idle. Tomatoes grow in the center of a parking lot, lettuces flourish along a railroad line. Fresh produce is an everyday fact of life. Fresh vegetables and legumes are the most nutritious foods we can eat, the platform of a healthful diet. Crisp, bright and beautiful, vegetables add variety and flavor, color and texture to a meal. Legumes such as lentils, dried beans and nuts, all no-cholesterol sources of protein, are replacing meat on the training table. With these easy, fresh recipes for side dishes and entrées, no one will have to say, "eat your vegetables."

GARDEN ASPARAGUS WITH LEMON AND GARLIC

SERVES 4

*H*ere's one of those spring dishes that reminds us of how good things taste when truly fresh. Use garden fresh or farmer's market asparagus.

> 2   *pounds asparagus, trimmed (see note)*
> 2   *teaspoons olive oil*
> 1   *teaspoon minced garlic*
> ¼   *cup lemon juice*
>   *Coarse salt*
>   *Ground black pepper*
> 3   *tablespoons chopped fresh Italian parsley*

Bring a large pot of water to a boil. Blanch the asparagus for 2 to 3 minutes, or until bright green and crisp-tender. (Watch the pot; this happens quickly.) Drain the asparagus and refresh in ice water to stop the cooking. Drain well; set in a serving dish.

In a small frying pan over medium-high heat, heat the oil and sauté the garlic for 1 minute, or until just tender—do not allow it to brown. Stir in the lemon juice; add salt to taste. Drizzle over the asparagus. Sprinkle with the pepper; garnish with the parsley.

Preparation time: 5 minutes
Cooking time: 5 minutes

Chef's note: To trim the asparagus: cut off ¼″ from the stems. Using a vegetable peeler or a small paring knife, starting at the stem, peel off the thin, woody layer, running the knife or peeler up the asparagus until the shoot becomes tender. This method yields more asparagus than the conventional practice of breaking off the woody stems.

Per serving: 78 calories, 2.9 fat (28% of calories), 0.2 g. dietary fiber, no cholesterol, 10 mg. sodium.

Peperonata

*S*erve this bright pepper stew warm or at room temperature. It is also delicious on Bruschetta (page 30) for an antipasto.

> 1 teaspoon olive oil
> ¼ cup chopped red onions
> 2 cloves garlic, minced
> 1 sweet red pepper, cut into ⅛" strips
> 1 yellow pepper, cut into ⅛" strips
> 1 green pepper, cut into ⅛" strips
> 2 plum tomatoes, chopped
>   Salt and black pepper
> 2 tablespoons chopped fresh basil

In a large no-stick frying pan over low heat, warm the oil. Add the onions and garlic and sauté for 1 to 2 minutes, or until tender. Add the red peppers, yellow peppers, green peppers and tomatoes; cover and simmer for 10 minutes. Uncover and cook for 5 minutes, or until the juices are reduced by half. Add salt and pepper to taste. Sprinkle with the basil.

Preparation time: 5 minutes
Cooking time: 17 minutes

Chef's note: The less basil cooks, the better it tastes. Add it to cooked food just before serving.

Per serving: 44 calories, 1.5 g. fat (26% of calories), 1.8 g. dietary fiber, no cholesterol, 7 mg. sodium.

White Beans, Peppers and Tomatoes

SERVES 4

*F*ragrant with rosemary and orange, this dish makes a light entrée for four people or a satisfying side dish or first course for four to six.

½ *cup chopped peppers*

½ *cup chopped tomatoes*

¼ *cup chopped red onions*

¼ *cup defatted chicken stock*

1 *clove garlic, minced*

1 *can (15 ounces) white kidney or navy beans, rinsed and drained*

1 *tablespoon orange juice*

1 *teaspoon chopped fresh rosemary*

1 *teaspoon grated orange rind*

Salt and black pepper

In a large frying pan, combine the peppers, tomatoes, onions, stock and garlic; cover and cook over medium heat for 3 minutes, or until the peppers are soft. Add the beans, orange juice, rosemary and orange rind; cook and stir for 2 minutes, or until hot. Add salt and pepper to taste.

Preparation time: 5 minutes
Cooking time: 5 minutes

Chef's note: This is one dish that tastes especially good the next day when the flavors have had some time to "marry." Serve cool or at room temperature as a main course salad on a bed of lettuce.

Per serving: 111 calories, 0.5 g. fat (4% of calories), 5.8 g. dietary fiber, no cholesterol, 379 mg. sodium.

BAKED FENNEL

SERVES 4

*I*n this dish, the fennel becomes golden and fragrant. It makes a simple side dish for roast chicken. Garnish with chopped fennel fronds.

1	*pound fennel bulbs, cored and sliced ½" thick (see note)*
2	*cups finely chopped onions*
½	*cup defatted chicken stock*
1	*teaspoon extra-virgin olive oil*
¼	*teaspoon lemon juice*
	Salt and black pepper

In a small baking dish, mix together the fennel, onions, stock, oil and lemon juice.

Cover tightly and bake at 450° for 35 minutes, or until the fennel is soft. Uncover and bake for 5 to 10 minutes, or until the fennel becomes golden. Add salt and pepper to taste.

Preparation time: 5 minutes
Baking time: 45 minutes

Chef's notes: To prepare a fennel bulb, trim the outer leaves. Cut off the stalks and set aside. Cut the bulb in half, remove and discard the core and then cut the bulbs and stalks (up to the feathery fronds). Reserve the fronds for garnish, if desired.

Fennel is also delicious baked in the same pan as a roasting chicken.

Per serving: 58 calories, 1.6 g. fat (22% of calories), 1.3 g. dietary fiber, no cholesterol, 166 mg. sodium.

BRAISED FENNEL AND TOMATOES

SERVES 4

*T*he anise flavors of this celery-like vegetable are played up with toasted anise seeds in a slow braise that makes the fennel fragrant and tender. The tomatoes add a touch of sweetness.

> 1 *teaspoon anise seeds (see note)*
> 1 *fennel bulb, cored and cut into ¼" pieces (page 100)*
> 1 *teaspoon olive oil*
> ½ *cup sliced onions*
> 1 *clove garlic, sliced*
> ¼ *cup defatted chicken stock*
> 3 *plum tomatoes*
> 1 *teaspoon red wine vinegar*
>   *Salt and black pepper*

Put the anise seeds in a small no-stick frying pan and toast over high heat, shaking the pan occasionally, for 1 minute, or until they smell fragrant. Set the seeds aside.

In a large frying pan over medium heat, heat the oil and sauté the onions and garlic for 1 minute, or until soft. Add the fennel and toss.

Add the stock. Reduce the heat, cover and cook for 5 minutes, or until the fennel is tender. Add the tomatoes and vinegar and cook, uncovered, for 2 minutes, or until the liquid is reduced by half and the tomatoes are tender. Add salt and pepper to taste.

Sprinkle with the anise seeds before serving.

Preparation time: 5 minutes
Cooking time: 9 minutes

Chef's note: Anise seeds have a distinct licorice flavor. Taste one before using them in this recipe. You may choose to leave them out.

Per serving: 44 calories, 1.6 g. fat (29% of calories), 1.5 g. dietary fiber, no cholesterol, 58 mg. sodium.

STUFFED ZUCCHINI

SERVES 4

*Z*ucchini threatening to overtake your garden? Try doubling this recipe and freezing a batch to microwave for a quick and easy supper.

> 4 *zucchini*
> ¼ *cup finely chopped onions*
> 1 *clove garlic, minced*
> 2 *plum tomatoes, finely chopped*
> 2 *tablespoons chopped fresh Italian parsley*
> 1 *teaspoon chopped fresh marjoram*
> *Salt and black pepper*
> ¼ *cup toasted bread crumbs*
> 2 *tablespoons grated Parmesan cheese*

Cut each zucchini lengthwise in half. Scoop out the pulp, leaving a shell. Reserve the pulp.

In a medium no-stick frying pan over low heat, sauté the onions and garlic for 1 minute. Add the zucchini pulp, tomatoes, parsley and marjoram; add salt and pepper to taste. Cook, stirring frequently, for 5 minutes, or until the zucchini is tender.

Spoon the filling into the zucchini shells. Sprinkle the top of each zucchini evenly with the bread crumbs and Parmesan.

Spray a baking sheet with no-stick spray. Place the zucchini on the baking sheet and roast at 350° for 15 minutes, or until the zucchini are hot and the top is brown and bubbly.

Preparation time: 10 minutes
Cooking time: 6 minutes
Baking time: 15 minutes

Chef's note: This makes a nice side dish for four. To make it into an entrée, add ¼ cup shredded mozzarella cheese to the cooked tomato and zucchini mixture.

Per serving: 59 calories, 1.5 g. fat (20% of calories), 3.1 g. dietary fiber, 2 mg. cholesterol, 83 mg. sodium.

BAKED STUFFED TOMATOES

SERVES 4

*P*lump with herb stuffing, these tomatoes seem to "ripen" in the oven, their natural sweetness combining deliciously with the garlic, parsley and basil.

> 4 *plum tomatoes (see note)*
> 1 *cup fresh bread crumbs*
> ¼ *cup chopped fresh Italian parsley*
> 2 *tablespoons nonfat mayonnaise*
> 2 *teaspoons balsamic vinegar*
> 1 *clove garlic, minced*
> *Salt and black pepper*
> 2 *tablespoons chopped fresh basil*

Coat a small baking sheet with no-stick spray. Slice the tomatoes in half lengthwise and remove and discard the seeds and pulp, leaving the shells intact. Set on the prepared baking sheet.

In a small bowl, combine the bread crumbs, parsley, mayonnaise, vinegar and garlic; add salt and pepper to taste. Fill the tomato shells with the bread crumb mixture.

Bake at 350° for 15 to 20 minutes, or until the tomatoes are soft and the stuffing is heated through. Sprinkle with the basil just before serving.

Preparation time: 5 minutes
Baking time: 20 minutes

Chef's note: Instead of plum tomatoes, you may use 2 large garden tomatoes; halve crosswise. Increase the baking time to 25 to 30 minutes, then check for doneness. Allow one half per person.

Per serving: 67 calories, 0.9 g. fat (11% of calories), 2.1 g. dietary fiber, no cholesterol, 166 mg. sodium.

SICILIAN STUFFED EGGPLANT

*I*n this recipe, a rich, savory filling of eggplant is served on the eggplant peel and topped with tomato sauce. Serve this satisfying dish as an entrée for four people or a side dish for eight.

1   *medium eggplant (about 1 pound)*
2   *teaspoons olive oil*
1   *cup chopped onions*
1   *clove garlic, minced*
1   *cup fresh bread crumbs*
4   *tablespoons grated Parmesan cheese*
¼   *cup chopped fresh Italian parsley*
   Salt and black pepper
1   *cup no-salt-added tomato sauce*
¼   *cup chopped fresh basil*

Cut the eggplant lengthwise into quarters, and again in half crosswise, yielding 8 pieces. Put the eggplant in a large saucepan, cover with water and bring to a boil. Cover, reduce the heat and simmer for 8 minutes, or until the pulp can be removed easily from the peel. Spoon the pulp from the peel; save the peel. Mash the pulp and set aside.

Heat the oil in a large no-stick frying pan over medium heat. Add the eggplant pulp, onions and garlic and sauté for 7 minutes, or until tender. Stir in the bread crumbs, 2 tablespoons of the Parmesan and parsley; add salt and pepper to taste. Place the peels in a large baking dish or on a baking sheet and spoon the eggplant mixture onto the peels. Bake at 350° for 20 minutes, or until hot and bubbly.

In a small saucepan, heat the tomato sauce. Spoon the sauce over the eggplant; top with the remaining 2 tablespoons Parmesan and the basil.

Preparation time: 10 minutes
Cooking time: 15 minutes
Baking time: 20 minutes

Per serving: 145 calories, 4.8 g. fat (29% of calories), 2 g. dietary fiber, 5 mg. cholesterol, 196 mg. sodium.

SUGAR SNAP PEAS WITH MINT

SERVES 4

*S*ugar snap peas, also called sugar peas, are entirely edible—pod and all. A cross between the English pea and the snow pea, the sweet and crunchy sugar snaps are well-named. They are best raw or very lightly cooked, as in this recipe.

1¼ *pounds sugar snap peas*
3 *tablespoons orange juice*
2 *teaspoons extra-virgin olive oil*
½ *cup orange segments*
8 *mint leaves*
2 *teaspoons slivered almonds, toasted (see note)*
  Salt and black pepper

In a medium saucepan, blanch the peas in rapidly boiling water for 2 minutes, or until bright green and crisp-tender. Plunge immediately into ice water. Drain. Turn into a large bowl.

In a small cup, whisk together the orange juice and oil. Pour over the peas and toss to coat. Gently toss in the orange segments, mint and almonds. Add salt and pepper to taste.

Preparation time: 5 minutes
Cooking time: 2 minutes

Chef's note: Toasting almonds intensifies their flavor. Spread the almonds on a baking sheet and toast at 350° for 5 to 8 minutes, or until they begin to turn brown and smell nutty.

Per serving: 90 calories, 2.2 g. fat (21% of calories), 0.7 g. dietary fiber, no cholesterol, 6 mg. sodium.

MEDITERRANEAN CAULIFLOWER

SERVES 4

*A*n interesting cauliflower dish that's a good example of the Arabic flavors that influence Mediterranean cuisine. Sweet with raisins and honey, sour with red wine vinegar, this side dish is delicious served hot or at room temperature.

> 2 *cups cauliflower florets*
> 1 *clove garlic, minced*
> ¼ *cup raisins*
> 2 *tablespoons red wine vinegar*
> 1 *tablespoon water*
> 1 *tablespoon pine nuts, toasted (page 71)*

In a large no-stick frying pan over medium heat, sauté the cauliflower and garlic for 1 minute, or until the garlic begins to soften. Add the raisins, vinegar and water. Cover and cook for 5 to 7 minutes, or until the cauliflower is crisp-tender. Serve sprinkled with the pine nuts.

Preparation time: 5 minutes
Cooking time: 8 minutes

Chef's note: This cauliflower dish is very good served on soft polenta or over pasta. Add cooked chicken for a simple one-dish supper.

Per serving: 65 calories, 2.4 g. fat (30% of calories), 1.9 g. dietary fiber, no cholesterol, 12 mg. sodium.

BAKED RADICCHIO

SERVES 4

*R*adicchio's distinctive bite is as bright as its beautiful magenta leaf. Here, the flavor is tempered by baking with vegetables and a little oil. This makes a marvelous companion to roast chicken or sautéed chicken breasts.

1	*pound radicchio*
¾	*cup diced carrots*
¾	*cup diced celery*
½	*cup chopped onions*
¼	*cup minced shallots*
¼	*cup water*
	Salt and black pepper
1	*teaspoon extra-virgin olive oil*

Trim and clean the radicchio. Cut into quarters and remove the core.

In a medium baking dish, combine the carrots, celery, onions, shallots and water. Lay the radicchio on top of the vegetables. Add salt and pepper to taste. Cover tightly with foil.

Bake at 400° for 15 minutes. Lower the heat to 350° and continue baking for 25 minutes, or until the radicchio is tender. Sprinkle with the oil before serving.

Preparation time: 10 minutes
Baking time: 40 minutes

Per serving: 44 calories, 1.2 g. fat (24% of calories), 2.1 g. dietary fiber, no cholesterol, 37 mg. sodium.

MARINATED VEGETABLES

SERVES 8

*M*ake this dish a day or two ahead so the vegetables absorb the marinade and the flavors have time to blend.

Marinade

½ *cup white wine vinegar*

1 *teaspoon lemon juice*

1 *teaspoon Dijon mustard*

1 *clove garlic, minced*

1 *teaspoon sugar*

1 *tablespoon extra-virgin olive oil*

2 *tablespoons chopped fresh marjoram*

2 *tablespoons chopped fresh Italian parsley*

Vegetables

8 *ounces new potatoes, scrubbed and cut into 2" pieces*

1 *cup broccoli florets*

1 *sweet red pepper, cut into 2" pieces*

1 *cup quartered fresh mushrooms*

½ *cup sliced scallions*

2 *tablespoons pitted and sliced imported black olives*

Salt and black pepper

To make the marinade: In a large bowl, whisk together the vinegar, lemon juice, mustard, garlic and sugar. Whisk in the oil. Stir in the marjoram and parsley.

To make the vegetables: In a large microwave-safe dish, microwave the potatoes on high for 8 minutes, or until fork-tender. Add to the marinade while still hot. Microwave the broccoli florets for 3 minutes, or until bright green and fork-tender; add to the marinade. Add the peppers, mushrooms, scallions and olives; toss to coat with the marinade. Add salt and black pepper to taste. Cover with plastic wrap and chill in the refrigerator for at least 20 minutes or overnight.

Preparation time: 15 minutes
Microwaving time: 11 minutes
Chilling time: 20 minutes

Per serving: 44 calories, 0.9 g. fat (17% of calories), 0.9 g. dietary fiber, no cholesterol, 15 mg. sodium.

PARSLEYED CARROTS WITH GARLIC AND CAPERS

SERVES 4

Sweet, tangy and colorfully flecked with parsley, these carrots will ensure everyone eats all his or her vegetables.

2	*teaspoons minced garlic*
2	*teaspoons olive oil*
8	*medium carrots, thinly sliced*
¼–1	*cup water*
2	*tablespoons chopped fresh Italian parsley*
1	*tablespoon drained capers*

In a no-stick frying pan, gently cook the garlic in the oil for 3 minutes, or until the garlic becomes tender.

Add the carrots and ¼ cup of the water. Cook gently, uncovered, until the water has evaporated. Continue cooking for 5 to 10 minutes, or until the carrots are just barely tender, adding water ¼-cup at a time as it evaporates. Stir in the parsley and capers.

Preparation time: 5 minutes
Cooking time: 15 minutes

Chef's note: The cooking time will depend on the age and size of the carrots.

Per serving: 90 calories, 2.5 g. fat (24% of calories), 4.7 g. dietary fiber, no cholesterol, 82 mg. sodium.

CARROTS COOKED IN MILK

SERVES 4

*I*n this old-fashioned Italian recipe, milk adds sweetness and body to the carrots. Herbs add a finishing touch.

1   *pound mini-carrots*
½   *cup skim milk*
2   *sprigs fresh tarragon, mint or parsley (see note)*
    Pinch of ground nutmeg
1   *teaspoon red wine vinegar*
    Salt and black pepper

Cut the carrots into thin strips 2″ by ¼″. Put the carrots and milk into a medium saucepan over high heat. Bring the milk to a boil, but be careful it does not boil over. Reduce the heat; add the tarragon, mint or parsley and nutmeg. Cover and simmer for 2 minutes; uncover and continue cooking for 8 to 10 minutes, or until the carrots are tender and the milk is absorbed. Remove and discard the tarragon, mint or parsley.

Sprinkle with the vinegar. Add salt and pepper to taste.

Preparation time: 5 minutes
Cooking time: 15 minutes

Chef's note: Use fresh, not dried herbs in this recipe. The dried tend to give the dish a bitter taste.

Per serving: 62 calories, 0.3 g. fat (4% of calories), 3.6 g. dietary fiber, 1 mg. cholesterol, 56 mg. sodium.

Baby Artichokes with Basil and Tomatoes

SERVES 4

*T*his dish is best made with the two-ounce bite-sized artichoke buds prized in Rome—so young that their hearts are not yet covered with thistle. Look for them February through May.

> 2   *teaspoons olive oil*
> 1   *cup chopped onions*
> 4   *baby artichokes, chokes removed (see note)*
> 2   *tablespoons defatted chicken stock*
> 1   *cup chopped fresh tomatoes*
> 2   *tablespoons chopped fresh basil*
> 2   *teaspoons lemon juice*
>   *Salt and black pepper*
> 1   *teaspoon minced fresh Italian parsley*

Heat the oil in a medium no-stick frying pan over medium-high heat. Add the onions and sauté for 1 to 2 minutes, or until soft. Add the artichokes and cook for 3 to 5 minutes, or until the edges of the artichokes begin to brown.

Add the stock and simmer for 2 to 3 minutes. Add the tomatoes, basil and lemon juice; cover and cook for 20 minutes, or until the artichokes can be pierced with a knife. Add salt and pepper to taste. Sprinkle with the parsley.

Preparation time: 10 minutes
Cooking time: 30 minutes

Chef's note: To remove the choke, cut the artichoke in half lengthwise. Then use a small, sharp paring knife to cut along the perimeter of the pale green "choke" nestled in the center of the artichoke. If baby artichokes are not available, substitute frozen artichokes that have been thawed, and reduce the cooking time from 20 to 10 minutes.

Per serving: 105 calories, 2.6 g. fat (20% of calories), 5.2 g. dietary fiber, no cholesterol, 134 mg. sodium.

LEMONY GREEN BEANS WITH SUNCHOKES

SERVES 4

*S*unchokes are also known as Jerusalem artichokes, although they are not artichokes but the roots of a sunflower. In Italy, "sunflower" is *girasole*, which sounds something like Jerusalem; hence, the name. This confusion may explain why sunchokes are not more popular. They have a deliciously nutty flavor and crunchy texture and are great with braised vegetables.

> 1 *pound green beans, trimmed*
> ½ *cup sliced sunchokes (see note)*
> ¼ *cup defatted chicken stock*
> ¼ *cup lemon juice*
> 1 *tablespoon fresh chopped oregano*
> 1 *teaspoon Dijon mustard*
> 1 *teaspoon honey*
>   *Coarsely ground black pepper*

In a large no-stick frying pan over medium heat, combine the green beans, sunchokes, stock and lemon juice; cover and cook for 3 minutes, or until the beans are tender. Add the oregano, mustard and honey; cook and stir for 1 minute, or until the liquid is reduced to a glaze. Add pepper to taste.

Preparation time: 5 minutes
Cooking time: 4 minutes

Chef's note: Sunchokes, available in most supermarkets, are in season from fall through early spring. They are best when very firm. To prepare, remove the tough outer layer with a sharp knife or vegetable peeler.

Per serving: 66 calories, 0.4 g. fat (5% of calories), 0.3 g. dietary fiber, no cholesterol, 51 mg. sodium.

Marinated Vegetables (page 108)

Asparagus with Roasted Peppers and Olives (page 121)

114

Lemon Sole with Asparagus (page 131)

Salmon with Lemon and Herbs (page 134)

Grilled Shrimp with Potatoes, Peas and Basil (page 148)

117

Roasted Chicken with Lemon and Garlic (page 154)

Roasted Eggplant, Pepper and Onion Salad (page 231),
Lemon-Herb Chicken Breasts (page 158)

Mediterranean Turkey in Apricot Sauce (page 167)

Asparagus with Roasted Peppers and Olives

SERVES 4

A lively dish that's wonderful alongside grilled or broiled pork or chicken. Tossed with pasta, it becomes a light meal. It is equally good hot or at room temperature.

1 sweet red pepper

1 pound asparagus, cut into 1" pieces

2 cloves garlic, minced

2 tablespoons lemon juice

2 tablespoons pitted and chopped imported black olives

1 tablespoon chopped fresh Italian parsley

Dash of hot-pepper sauce

Salt and black pepper

2 tablespoons shredded fontina or provolone cheese

Roast the red pepper by placing on a high gas flame, on a hot grill or under the broiler for 10 minutes, turning until all sides are black. Wrap the pepper in a damp towel and allow to rest for 5 minutes, or until cool enough to handle. Using your finger or a sharp knife, peel off the skin; rub off any black charred spots with the damp towel. Cut the peppers into ½" pieces.

In a large no-stick frying pan over medium-high heat, cook the asparagus and garlic for 1 minute, stirring constantly. Add the lemon juice; cover and cook for 2 minutes, or until the asparagus is bright green and crisp-tender.

Remove from the heat. Stir in the red peppers, olives, parsley and hot-pepper sauce; add salt and black pepper to taste. Serve topped with the fontina or provolone.

Preparation time: 5 minutes
Cooking time: 13 minutes plus 5 minutes resting time

Per serving: 52 calories, 1.8 g. fat (27% of calories), 0.4 g. dietary fiber, 4 mg. cholesterol, 43 mg. sodium.

Oven roasting brings an ancient cooking method to the contemporary kitchen. The intense heat and long cookingtime produces vegetables of intense flavor with crisp skin and tender flesh. This is the only kind of vegetable cookery where overcooking is not an issue; the browner and crisper, the better. The vegetables need only to be stirred a few times and watched so they don't burn.

Roasted vegetables are as versatile as they are delicious. Here are a few suggestions.

- **First-Course Salad:** Sprinkle roasted vegetables with a little balsamic vinegar and serve on lettuce.

- **Pasta or Polenta:** Toss roasted vegetables with pasta or spoon onto soft polenta and sprinkle with a little grated Parmesan cheese.

- **Pizza:** Serve roasted vegetables on ready-made pizza crusts and sprinkle with shredded low-fat mozzarella and grated Parmesan cheese.

OVEN-ROASTED VEGETABLES

SERVES 4

4 cups vegetables cut into 1" pieces
1 teaspoon extra-virgin olive oil
2 teaspoons salt

In a large bowl, toss the vegetables with the oil. Spread on a baking sheet. Sprinkle with the salt. Roast at 400° for 15 to 30 minutes, or until the vegetables are brown and crisp, shaking the pan once or twice.

GENERAL ROASTING GUIDE

Here is a list of vegetables and their approximate roasting times.

Some vegetables such as corn, peas and asparagus are more delicate and should not roast as long as potatoes, carrots, onions and other root vegetables. If using a mix of vegetables, add the more delicate varieties halfway through cooking.

Roast these vegetables for 20 to 30 minutes (all should be cut into 1″ pieces):

- carrots
- eggplant
- garlic cloves
- mushrooms
- onions
- pattypan squash
- peppers
- potatoes
- sweet potatoes
- winter squash
- zucchini

Roast these vegetables for 10 to 20 minutes:

- asparagus
- corn kernels
- green beans
- okra
- peas
- sugar snap peas
- tomatoes

ROASTED PEPPERS IN MARINADE

SERVES 4

*R*oasting sweetens the peppers and gives them a hint of smokiness. Roasted peppers are versatile and delicious. Serve them with grilled or sautéed chicken, pork or fish. Toss them with pasta or into a green salad. Stir them into risotto or spoon onto polenta. Scoop up roasted peppers with Bruschetta (page 30) or Crostini (page 31) or crusty Italian bread. They're great in a sliced turkey sandwich or on a hamburger.

1   *large sweet red pepper, roasted (see note)*
1   *large yellow pepper, roasted*
1   *large orange pepper, roasted*
2   *tablespoons chopped fresh basil*
1   *tablespoon balsamic vinegar*
1   *clove garlic, minced*

Slice the peppers into ½″ strips.

In a medium bowl, combine the peppers, basil, vinegar and garlic; toss to mix. Allow to marinate for at least 5 minutes before serving.

Preparation time: 5 minutes
Cooking time: 10 minutes plus 5 minutes resting time and 5 minutes marinating time.

Chef's notes: To roast peppers, place them over a high gas flame, on a hot grill or under the broiler about 5″ from the heat. Roast for 10 minutes, turning the peppers often until all sides are black. Wrap the peppers in damp towels and allow to rest for 5 minutes, or until cool enough to handle. Using your fingers or a sharp knife, peel off the skin; rub off any black charred spots with the damp towel. Remove the seeds and veins.

Roasted peppers are a staple in the well-stocked Italian kitchen. They will keep, covered, in the refrigerator for several days.

Per serving: 20 calories, 0.1 g. fat (4% of calories), 0.9 g. dietary fiber, no cholesterol, 2 mg. sodium.

ROASTED ROSEMARY POTATOES

SERVES 4

*C*risp outside, tender inside, these potatoes are finger-lickin' good.

2 *cups quartered new potatoes*
2 *tablespoons chopped fresh rosemary*
Coarse salt

Coat a baking sheet with no-stick spray. Spread the potatoes on the baking sheet and coat lightly with no-stick spray. Sprinkle the rosemary and salt over the potatoes.

Roast the potatoes at 425° for 30 to 40 minutes, shaking the baking sheet twice during the roasting time to keep the potatoes from sticking.

Preparation time: 5 minutes
Cooking time: 40 minutes

Chef's note: These are also delicious tossed with Basic Balsamic Vinaigrette (page 210) or nonfat mayonnaise; serve at room temperature or chill.

Per serving: 75 calories, 0.2 g. fat (2% of calories), 1.9 g. dietary fiber, no cholesterol, 4 mg. sodium.

BRUSSELS SPROUTS AND POTATOES

SERVES 4

*B*russels sprouts, mini-cabbages packed with vitamin C, are also members of the cancer-preventing crucifer family. Their distinctive flavor partners nicely with gentle baby potatoes in a delicious side dish.

8   *ounces new potatoes, halved*
8   *brussels sprouts (see note)*
2   *teaspoons extra-virgin olive oil*
2   *cloves garlic, minced*
1   *teaspoon chopped fresh oregano*
     Salt and black pepper

In a large saucepan, cover the potatoes with water; bring to a boil over high heat and cook for 5 to 8 minutes, or until fork-tender. Add the brussels sprouts and cook for 5 minutes, or until fork-tender. Drain, reserving ½ cup of the cooking liquid.

In a large no-stick frying pan over medium-high heat, heat the oil and sauté the garlic for 3 minutes, or until it is just beginning to color. Add the potatoes, brussels sprouts, ¼ cup of the reserved cooking liquid, and oregano; add salt and pepper to taste. Cover and heat through, adding more liquid as needed.

Preparation time: 10 minutes
Cooking time: 16 minutes

Cook's note: To prepare fresh brussels sprouts, trim ¼″ from the bottom and score the trimmed sprouts with a deep ✕.

Per serving: 93 calories, 2.6 g. fat (23% of calories), 2.4 g. dietary fiber, no cholesterol, 15 mg. sodium.

WHIPPED POTATOES

SERVES 4

*M*ashed potatoes are an international comfort food. In this recipe they are seasoned with a hint of nutmeg and Parmesan cheese.

> 1¼ *pounds russet potatoes, peeled and cut into ½" cubes*
> ¼ *cup nonfat buttermilk*
> *Pinch of ground nutmeg*
> *Salt and black pepper*
> *Grated Parmesan cheese*

Rinse the potatoes with cold water and put into a large saucepan. Add enough cold water to cover.

Cover the pan and bring the water to a boil. Lower the heat to medium-low and simmer the potatoes for 20 minutes, or until very tender.

Remove the pan from the heat. Drain the potatoes and whip with a hand masher or electric mixer until the potatoes are smooth. Add the buttermilk and nutmeg; add salt and pepper to taste.

Serve the potatoes sprinkled with the Parmesan.

Preparation time: 10 minutes
Cooking time: 20 minutes

Chef's note: This recipe is also delicious (and very nutritious) made with sweet potatoes or yams.

Per serving: 126 calories, 0.2 g. fat (1% of calories), no dietary fiber, no cholesterol, 23 mg. sodium.

CHAPTER 6

FAST-FIXING
FISH AND
SHELLFISH

FRUIT OF THE SEA

he necklaces of little fishing villages that string the
Mediterranean and Adriatic shores of Italy are famous
for their seafood. Every day brings a bountiful harvest of fish
and shellfish too numerous to name. Fish and shellfish are
extremely low in calories and excellent sources of protein. The
small amount of fat that fish contains may be beneficial to
the heart, but the true reason Italians love *frutti di mare* is
because it's delicious.

Swordfish with Tomatoes, Onions and Olives

SERVES 4

*S*wordfish's firm texture and assured flavor stand up to an assertive sauce of tomatoes, onions and olives.

> 1 *swordfish steak (about 1 pound)*
> ½ *cup chopped tomatoes*
> ½ *cup chopped onions*
> ¼ *cup defatted chicken stock*
> 4 *imported green olives, pitted and chopped*
> 2 *tablespoons lemon juice*
> 2 *teaspoons chopped fresh oregano*
> 2 *cloves garlic, minced*

In a large no-stick frying pan over medium heat, sear the swordfish for 1 minute per side, or until brown. Transfer to a shallow baking dish and tent with foil. Set aside.

Add the tomatoes, onions, stock, olives, lemon juice, oregano and garlic to the frying pan; cover and cook for 3 minutes, or until the vegetables are soft.

Spoon the vegetables and their juices over the swordfish and bake at 350° for 15 minutes, or until the fish turns opaque and just begins to flake when gently pressed.

Serve the fish with the vegetables on top.

Preparation time: 5 minutes
Cooking time: 5 minutes
Baking time: 15 minutes

Per serving: 163 calories, 5.3 g. fat (30% of calories), 0.7 g. dietary fiber, 45 mg. cholesterol, 217 mg. sodium.

Baked Red Snapper

SERVES 4

*F*lavors synonymous with southern Italy and the Mediterranean—capers, olives, garlic and basil—make this fish especially good. This is delicious served with simple roasted potatoes.

2	red snapper fillets (8 ounces each)
½	cup white wine or vegetable stock
¼	cup lemon juice
½	cup canned tomatoes, drained and chopped
¼	cup chopped fresh Italian parsley
1	teaspoon chopped fresh marjoram
1	clove garlic, minced
2	imported black olives, pitted and chopped
1	teaspoon drained capers
2	tablespoons chopped fresh basil

Place the snapper, skin side down, in a shallow baking dish. Pour the wine or stock and lemon juice over the fish and let marinate for 5 minutes.

Distribute the tomatoes, parsley, marjoram and garlic evenly over the snapper. Cover the dish loosely with foil. Bake at 450° for 10 minutes, or until the fish turns opaque and just begins to flake when gently pressed. Remove from the oven and distribute the olives and capers evenly over the snapper.

To serve, spoon the pan ingredients and juices over the fish; sprinkle with the basil.

Preparation time: 10 minutes plus 5 minutes marinating time
Baking time: 10 minutes

Chef's note: You may also use halibut, cod or swordfish in this dish.

Per serving: 150 calories, 2 g. fat (12% of calories), 0.5 g. dietary fiber, 42 mg. cholesterol, 122 mg. sodium.

Lemon Sole with Asparagus

*T*his dish is light and quick. The asparagus cooks along with the sole and a touch of lemon and herbs. All is ready in 10 minutes.

  4 sole fillets (4 ounces each)
  12 asparagus spears
  4 sprigs fresh marjoram
  2 tablespoons chopped fresh parsley
  2 tablespoons grated lemon rind

Cut 4 (12″) pieces of foil or parchment paper (see note). Place a fillet in the middle of each piece of foil or parchment paper. Place 3 spears of asparagus and 1 sprig of marjoram on each fillet. Sprinkle the parsley and lemon rind over the sole. Fold the foil over the sole to create four separate packets. Or, fold the parchment over the sole and seal by folding and creasing the paper in a half circle around the sole, tucking the end piece under the packet. Place the packets on a 15″ × 10″ jelly-roll pan.

Bake at 350° for 10 minutes, or until the asparagus is tender and the sole flakes when gently pressed with a fork.

Preparation time: 5 minutes
Baking time: 10 minutes

Chef's note: The parchment paper or foil allows the sole to steam gently while being baked and helps to keep the sole and vegetables moist. The advantage of using parchment is that the individual packets may be served on plates and sliced open at the table for a dramatic presentation. The foil is not as attractive, and the sole should be removed before serving.

Per serving: 113 calories, 1.5 g. fat (12% of calories), 0.9 g. dietary fiber, 53 mg. cholesterol, 86 mg. sodium.

Halibut with Sun-Dried Tomatoes, Broccoli and Shiitakes

SERVES 4

A delicious autumn dinner that blends together the complex flavors of sun-dried tomatoes and earthy mushrooms; serve it over polenta or with risotto.

> 1 pound broccoli, cut into 2" pieces
> 4 halibut steaks (about 4 ounces each)
> 3 tablespoons lemon juice
> ½ teaspoon extra-virgin olive oil
> 2 cloves garlic, minced
> 2 cups stemmed sliced shiitake mushrooms
> ½ cup chopped reconstituted sun-dried tomatoes (page 72)
> Salt and black pepper
> Chopped fresh Italian parsley
> Lemon wedges

Blanch the broccoli in a pot of boiling water for 5 minutes, or until bright green and crisp-tender; drain. Refresh under cold running water. Set aside.

Coat a baking sheet with no-stick spray. Place the halibut on the prepared baking sheet. Sprinkle with 2 tablespoons of the lemon juice; add salt and pepper to taste. Bake at 400° for 15 minutes, or until the fish turns opaque and just begins to flake when gently pressed.

While the halibut is cooking, heat the oil in a large no-stick skillet over medium-high heat. Add the garlic and cook, stirring constantly, for 30 seconds, or until it begins to soften. Add the mushrooms and cook for 2 minutes, or until they begin to brown. Cover and cook for 5 to 7 minutes, or until the mushrooms are tender. Add the broccoli and sun-dried tomatoes and cook for 3 minutes, or until the broccoli is warmed through. Add the remaining 1 tablespoon lemon juice; add salt and pepper to taste.

To serve, spoon the vegetables and their sauce over the halibut steaks. Garnish with the parsley and lemon wedges.

Preparation time: 5 minutes
Cooking time: 18 minutes
Baking time: 15 minutes

Per serving: 263 calories, 3.8 g. fat (12% of calories), 1.3 g. dietary fiber, 36 mg. cholesterol, 120 mg. sodium.

CATCH OF THE DAY

*W*hatever your nutritional concerns, fish seem the best catch. Fish, mollusks and crustaceans are high in protein, vitamins and minerals and low in total fat. Lean fish such as cod, pollock and halibut yield about 100 calories per 4-ounce serving (uncooked). The term "fatty" fish is a misnomer; salmon, mackerel and bluefish, though higher in fat, yield only about 200 calories per serving. Mollusks (oysters, scallops, mussels, squid and clams) and crustaceans (crabs, shrimp and lobsters) generally have fewer than 100 calories per 4-ounce serving.

Seafood is also generally low in cholesterol. Even a "fatty" fish such as albacore tuna is extremely low in cholesterol, and even shrimp are far lower in cholesterol than eggs.

For the most part, fish and shellfish are delicate creatures; their flesh does not have a lot of tensile-strength protein. They are high in albumen, like eggs, and so burn or overcook quickly. The most important thing to remember when cooking fish is not to overdo it with anything—heat, sauce, herbs or seasonings. It is best fresh, but sometimes, if the "fresh" is not truly fresh and the quality not high, then flash-frozen is better.

Salmon with Lemon and Herbs

SERVES 4

Although the percentage of calories from fat is fairly high in this recipe, the "culprit," salmon, is still a healthful choice. Salmon is high in protein, vitamin A and vitamin B-complex, and the fat in salmon comes from polyunsaturated omega-3 oils, which are actually beneficial to your health.

1   *salmon fillet (12 ounces)*
2   *tablespoons lemon juice*
1   *teaspoon extra-virgin olive oil*
3   *sprigs fresh marjoram*
3   *sprigs fresh Italian parsley*
1   *teaspoon grated lemon rind*
    Lemon wedges

Rinse and dry the salmon. Remove as many bones as possible (see note). Place the salmon on a piece of foil about 2″ larger than the salmon (or on a fish-grill). In a cup, whisk together the lemon juice and oil; drizzle over the salmon. Place the marjoram and parsley on the salmon and sprinkle with the lemon rind.

Put the salmon on a medium-hot grill or broil about 5″ from the heat. Cover the grill and cook or broil for 10 minutes, or until the fish turns opaque and just begins to flake when gently pressed.

Transfer the salmon from the foil to a work surface. Remove and discard the marjoram and parsley. Remove the skin by sliding a sharp knife or spatula between the skin and the fish. To serve, garnish with lemon wedges.

Preparation time: 5 minutes
Grilling time: 10 minutes

Chef's note: To remove fish bones, use a clean needle-nosed pliers, blunt tweezers, a strawberry huller or a bone puller.

Per serving: 92 calories, 4 g. fat (40% of calories), 0.2 g. dietary fiber, 15 mg. cholesterol, 521 mg. sodium.

TROUT BAKED IN ESCAROLE

SERVES 4

*E*scarole, a variety of endive, adds flavor and keeps the trout moist through baking.

16 *large escarole leaves*
¼ *cup plus 2 tablespoons chopped fresh Italian parsley*
2 *tablespoons chopped shallots*
5 *cloves garlic, minced*
2 *teaspoons chopped fresh thyme*
  Salt and black pepper
4 *small whole trout, dressed, with heads on*
¾ *cup lemon juice*
¾ *cup orange juice*
½ *cup water*

In a large pot of rapidly boiling water, cook the escarole leaves for 5 minutes, or until pliable. Drain and set aside to cool while preparing the trout.

In a small bowl, mix together the parsley, shallots, garlic and thyme. Lightly salt and pepper the inside and outside of the trout; rub half of the herb and shallot mixture inside.

Carefully wrap each trout in 4 of the leaves, leaving the head showing. Coat a large shallow baking dish with no-stick spray. Place the fish in the prepared dish.

Mix together the lemon juice, orange juice, water and remaining half of the herb and shallot mixture and pour over the fish. Cover tightly with foil. Bake at 450° for 20 minutes, or until the fish just begins to flake when gently pressed.

Preparation time: 10 minutes
Cooking time: 5 minutes
Baking time: 20 minutes

Per serving: 137 calories, 2.9 g. fat (18% of calories), 0.8 g. dietary fiber, 45 mg. cholesterol, 28 mg. sodium.

Trout with Barley, Peppers and Pine Nuts

*B*arley is an ancient grain that predates rice as a cultivated crop. While it takes a back seat to rice and pasta in many Italian dishes, it does figure in homey soups and baked casseroles. Here it provides an unusual background to the trout, zucchini and fragrant pine nuts.

2	*cups cooked barley*
½	*cup finely diced red peppers*
2	*tablespoons chopped fresh Italian parsley*
1	*tablespoon pine nuts, toasted and chopped (page 71)*
1	*teaspoon grated orange rind*
	Dash of hot-pepper sauce
	Salt and black pepper
4	*trout fillets (about 4 ounces each)*
¼	*cup fresh orange juice*
	Chopped fresh Italian parsley

In a large bowl, stir together the barley, red peppers, parsley, pine nuts, orange rind and hot-pepper sauce; add salt and black pepper to taste.

Coat a medium baking dish with no-stick spray. Spread the barley mixture evenly in the prepared baking dish, patting it down to make an even base. Season the trout with salt and black pepper to taste and place on the barley. Drizzle with the orange juice. Cover. Bake at 400° for 8 to 12 minutes, or until the fish turns opaque and just begins to flake when gently pressed. Sprinkle the parsley over the trout.

Preparation time: 5 minutes
Baking time: 12 minutes

Per serving: 254 calories, 5.4 g. fat (19% of calories), 4.9 g. dietary fiber, 65 mg. cholesterol, 35 mg. sodium.

STUFFED FLOUNDER FLORENTINE

SERVES 4

*F*lounder is a flatfish prized for its fine texture and delicate flavor. It is sometimes mislabeled "fillet of sole." All of the fish called "sole" (except for the imported British "Dover sole") are actually varieties of flounder.

1	package (10 ounces) frozen chopped spinach, thawed
½	cup nonfat ricotta cheese
¼	cup toasted bread crumbs (page 14)
2	tablespoons nonfat sour cream
2	tablespoons chopped onions
¼	teaspoon ground nutmeg
	Dash of hot-pepper sauce
	Salt and black pepper
4	flounder fillets (about 4 ounces each)
2	tablespoons orange juice

Squeeze the spinach dry with paper towels. In a medium bowl, mix together the spinach, ricotta, bread crumbs, sour cream, onions, nutmeg and hot-pepper sauce; add salt and black pepper to taste.

Coat a medium baking dish with no-stick spray. Spread the spinach mixture over the fillets to about ½″ from the edge. Starting at the tail, roll up the fillets. Secure with toothpicks and place, spiral side down, in the prepared baking dish. Drizzle the orange juice over the fillets.

Bake the fish at 350° for 15 minutes, or until the fish turns opaque and just begins to flake when gently pressed.

Preparation time: 10 minutes
Baking time: 15 minutes

Per serving: 153 calories, 1.5 g. fat (9% of calories), 1.8 g. dietary fiber, 56 mg. cholesterol, 183 mg. sodium.

SEARED BASS WITH BRAISED ONIONS, GARLIC AND EGGPLANT

SERVES 4

*H*ere, firm fish steaks are quickly seared on the stove, then finished in the oven while the onions, garlic and eggplant cook into a smooth and mellow stew to be served on top of the fish. Halibut works well if you don't have sea bass.

1	*pound sea bass steaks*
1	*lemon, thinly sliced*
1	*teaspoon extra-virgin olive oil*
1	*cup chopped onions*
5	*cloves garlic, minced*
1	*cup diced eggplant*
¼	*cup white wine or ¼ cup orange juice with 1 tablespoon lemon juice*
2	*tablespoons lemon juice*
2	*tablespoons drained capers*

Coat a baking sheet with no-stick spray and set in a 400° oven.

Coat a large no-stick frying pan with no-stick spray and set over high heat. Sear the bass in the prepared pan for 2 minutes per side, or until brown on both sides.

Transfer the bass to the prepared baking sheet; lay the lemon slices over the fish. Bake at 400° for 5 to 8 minutes, or until the fish turns opaque and just begins to flake when lightly pressed.

While the bass is cooking, heat the oil in the same frying pan over medium-high heat; add the onions and garlic and sauté for 5 minutes, or until brown and soft. Add the eggplant and cook for 3 minutes, stirring occasionally. Add the wine or the orange juice and and lemon juice mixture, lemon juice and capers. Lower the heat and simmer for 5 minutes, or until the liquid is absorbed.

To serve, remove the lemon slices from the bass and set beside the bass as garnish. Divide the stew and spoon over each portion of fish.

Preparation time: 10 minutes
Cooking time: 17 minutes
Baking time: 8 minutes

Per serving: 176 calories, 3.6 g. fat (18% of calories), 0.8 g. dietary fiber, 47 mg. cholesterol, 143 mg. sodium.

BLUEFISH WITH GARLIC AND SAGE

SERVES 4

*S*age is a bold herb, not often used with fish. Here it has met its match—the distinctive, full-flavored, almost meaty-tasting bluefish, the closest fish available in the U.S. to fresh sardines.

1	*bluefish fillet (about 12 ounces)*
1	*clove garlic, cut into slivers*
12	*medium fresh sage leaves*
2	*tablespoons lemon juice*
	Salt and black pepper
	Lemon wedges

Line a 15″ × 10″ jelly-roll pan with foil; coat the foil with no-stick spray. Place the bluefish, skin side down, in the prepared pan. Dot with the garlic and sage. Drizzle with the lemon juice; add salt and pepper to taste.

Bake at 425° for 10 to 15 minutes, or until the fish turns opaque and just begins to flake when gently pressed.

To serve, cut the bluefish into 4 pieces and lift the pieces from the pan, leaving the skin. Garnish with the lemon wedges.

Preparation time: 10 minutes
Baking time: 15 minutes

Chef's note: If bluefish is not available, substitute another dark, rich fish such as tuna or mackerel.

Per serving: 137 calories, 4.6 g. fat (31% of calories), 0.2 g. dietary fiber, 35 mg. cholesterol,

COD BRAISED WITH TOMATOES, FENNEL AND OLIVES

SERVES 4

*I*n this recipe, the vegetables are first baked with the fish and then finished on the stove to become a flavorful sauce.

1   *cup chopped fennel (page 100)*
1   *cup chopped tomatoes*
¼   *cup white wine or clam juice*
1   *bay leaf*
4   *cod fillets (5 ounces each)*
1   *tablespoon lemon juice*
1   *teaspoon extra-virgin olive oil*
¼   *cup chopped fresh basil*
2   *tablespoons pitted and chopped imported black olives*

In a 13″ × 9″ flame-proof baking dish, combine the fennel, tomatoes, wine or clam juice and bay leaf. Place the cod on top of the vegetables. Cover with foil. Bake at 450° for 15 minutes, or until the cod turns opaque and just begins to flake when gently pressed. Transfer the fillets to a plate; cover with foil and keep warm.

Put the baking dish of vegetables on the stove over medium-high heat and bring to a boil. Cook for 7 to 10 minutes, or until the liquid is reduced by half. Stir in the lemon juice and oil. Remove the bay leaf.

To serve, top the cod with the vegetable sauce; sprinkle with the basil and olives.

Preparation time: 5 minutes
Baking time: 15 minutes
Cooking time: 10 minutes

Per serving: 147 calories, 2.6 g. fat (16% of calories), 0.6 g. dietary fiber, 56 mg. cholesterol, 133 mg. sodium.

TUNA WITH BROCCOLI AND PASTA

SERVES 4

*T*una and broccoli are natural partners, playing off each other's bold and interesting flavors.

8	*ounces penne or rigatoni*
3	*cups broccoli florets*
1½	*cups cubed tomatoes*
½	*cup sliced scallions*
2	*tablespoons lemon juice*
2	*tablespoons chopped fresh basil*
1	*tablespoon extra-virgin olive oil*
2	*teaspoons ground black pepper*
1	*clove garlic, minced*
2	*tuna steaks (about 6 ounces each) or*
	1 can (12 ounces) water-packed tuna, drained
½	*cup pitted and sliced imported black olives*
2	*tablespoons chopped fresh Italian parsley*

Cook the pasta in a large pot of boiling water for 7 minutes. Add the broccoli and continue cooking for another 3 minutes, or until the broccoli is bright green and the pasta is tender; drain well.

In a large bowl, mix together the tomatoes, scallions, lemon juice, basil, oil, pepper and garlic. Set aside.

Grill or broil the tuna about 5″ from the heat for 3 to 7 minutes per side, or until the fish turns opaque and is no longer pink when cut with a knife. Remove from the heat and cut into 1″ cubes.

To serve, add the pasta, broccoli, olives and parsley to the tomato mixture and toss together. Add the tuna and toss gently.

Preparation time: 15 minutes
Cooking time: 10 minutes
Grilling time: 14 minutes

Per serving: 408 calories, 11.3 g. fat (25% of calories), 3.5 g. dietary fiber, 84 mg. cholesterol, 109 mg. sodium.

Marinated Tuna on Broccoli Rabe

*B*roccoli rabe, also known as broccoli raab, rape, *brocoletti di rape* and *rapini*, is broccoli's assertive cousin. Its slightly bitter flavor works nicely with the rich-tasting tuna.

Marinated Tuna

2 *tablespoons white wine vinegar*

2 *tablespoons chopped fresh oregano*

1 *tablespoon lemon juice*

1 *teaspoon extra-virgin olive oil*

2 *cloves garlic, minced*

Dash of hot-pepper sauce

4 *tuna steaks (about 4 ounces each)*

Broccoli Rabe

½ *teaspoon extra-virgin olive oil*

½ *cup thinly sliced red onions*

1 *pound fresh broccoli rabe, sliced into narrow, even strips (see note)*

½ *teaspoon sugar*

Lemon wedges

To make the marinated tuna: In a small bowl, combine the vinegar, oregano, lemon juice, oil, garlic and hot-pepper sauce. Pour over the tuna and let marinate for 10 minutes at room temperature.

Remove the tuna from the marinade, reserving ¼ cup of the marinade. Place the tuna on a hot grill or broil about 5″ from the heat for 3 to 5 minutes per side, basting twice with the reserved marinade, until the tuna is no longer pink when cut with a knife. Transfer to a plate and tent with foil to keep warm.

To make the broccoli rabe: In a large no-stick frying pan over medium heat, heat the oil and sauté the onions for 1 to 2 minutes, or until soft. Add the broccoli rabe, sugar and remaining reserved marinade. Cook, stirring occasionally, for 1 to 2 minutes, or until the broccoli rabe is bright green.

Serve the tuna on the broccoli rabe, garnished with the lemon wedges.

Preparation time: 5 minutes plus 10 minutes marinating time
Grilling time: 10 minutes
Cooking time: 4 minutes

Chef's notes: Broccoli rabe has more stem and fewer florets than conventional broccoli. The stem is also less woody, so the cook can use more of it. To prepare, slice off 1″ of the stem end, then chop or slice the entire plant.

If broccoli rabe is not available, substitute sliced spinach, collard greens or kale.

Per serving: 240 calories, 8.2 g. fat (30% of calories), 3.5 g. dietary fiber, 47 mg. cholesterol, 80 mg. sodium.

FISH COOKING PRIMER

*G*enerally, the less fish cooks, the better. Here are some additional tips:

- Keep the fish or shellfish in the refrigerator until you're ready to cook it. Don't leave it out while preparing the rest of the meal.

- Whenever possible, cook fish with the skin on. It helps the fish hold its shape and retain moisture. Make a few shallow slashes across the skin of the fillet or whole fish to prevent curling.

- When baking fish fillets that taper, tuck the thin ends under so they don't overcook.

- Turn the fish just once during cooking so there is less risk of it falling apart.

- Wash the knives and cutting boards with soap and hot water immediately after working with fish and before working with other foods.

SARDINES WITH PAN-FRIED POTATOES AND TOMATOES

SERVES 4

In Italy, small fresh fish such as anchovies and sardines are most often quickly sautéed in garlic-scented olive oil, finished with a dash of lemon juice and eaten whole—bones, head and all—a great source of omega-3 fatty acids.

In the U.S., fresh sardines are almost impossible to come by. A few Italian, Portuguese and Spanish specialty stores may stock frozen sardines. Good quality canned sardines packed in water make an acceptable alternative. They are delicious in this speedy recipe.

> 2 *cups thinly sliced new potatoes*
> 2 *cups cubed plum tomatoes*
> ¼ *cup white wine or water*
> 2 *tablespoons lemon juice*
> 2 *tablespoons chopped fresh sage*
> 1 *tablespoon capers*
> 8 *ounces fresh or canned, water-packed sardines, drained (see note)*

Coat a large no-stick frying pan with no-stick spray. Layer the potatoes in the pan and brown for about 5 minutes, turning the potatoes so they cook evenly.

Add the tomatoes, wine or water, lemon juice, sage and capers. Cook for 3 minutes, or until the tomatoes are wilted and the liquid is reduced slightly. Add the sardines and gently heat through.

Preparation time: 5 minutes
Cooking time: 8 minutes

Chef's note: If you are lucky enough to find fresh or frozen sardines, clean and pre-cook them for this recipe. To clean each sardine, snap off the head and pull away with it the intestines. Remove the center back fin. Split the sardine in half and remove the spine. Wash the sardines under cold running water. Cook the sardines over high heat for about 2 to 3 minutes per side. Proceed with the recipe.

Per serving: 183 calories, 5.5 g. fat (27% of calories), 1.9 g. dietary fiber, 34 mg. cholesterol, 94 mg. sodium.

Poached Scallops
in Orange Tomato Cream Sauce

*Z*esty and tender scallops are bathed in a light creamy orange sauce in this luscious dish. Serve on a bed of rice, with a side of risotto or over pasta or polenta.

> 1 cup orange juice
> 1 pound scallops
> 2 teaspoons grated orange rind
> 1 small tomato, chopped
> 1 teaspoon chopped fresh marjoram
> 2 tablespoons nonfat sour cream
> Cracked black pepper

In a large no-stick frying pan over medium heat, bring the orange juice to a boil. Reduce the heat and add the scallops and orange rind. Cover and simmer for 5 minutes, or until the scallops are opaque and tender. Remove the scallops with a slotted spoon and transfer to a plate; tent with foil to keep warm.

Add the tomatoes and marjoram to the pan; simmer for 2 minutes, or until the liquid is reduced by half. Stir in the sour cream; cook until the sauce is thick enough to coat the back of a spoon. Season with pepper. Put the scallops back in the frying pan to heat through.

Preparation time: 5 minutes
Cooking time: 10 minutes

Per serving: 143 calories, 1.5 g. fat (9% of calories), 0.9 g. dietary fiber, 48 mg. cholesterol, 254 mg. sodium.

SCALLOPS IN SWEET-AND-SOUR SAUCE

SERVES 4

*T*his dish reflects the flavors of Venice, a city known for its spiritual mosaics and poetic tinted marbles, and the ancient home of painters Bellini and Titian. It is best served at room temperature or chilled.

> 1   *teaspoon extra-virgin olive oil*
> 1   *cup finely chopped onions*
> 1   *cup orange juice*
> 1   *cup water*
> 2   *tablespoons lemon juice*
> 2   *tablespoons white wine vinegar*
> 2   *tablespoons raisins*
> 2   *teaspoons honey*
> 1   *pound fresh bay scallops*
> 1   *tablespoon pine nuts, toasted (page 71)*

In a large no-stick frying pan over medium-high heat, heat the oil and sauté the onions for 10 minutes, or until the onions are very soft and lightly browned.

Add the orange juice, water, lemon juice, vinegar, raisins and honey. Simmer for 10 minutes, or until the liquid is reduced by half.

Add the scallops; cover and steam for 5 minutes, or until opaque.

Transfer the scallops and sauce to a large bowl. Let cool for about 10 minutes to room temperature, or cover and refrigerate overnight. Sprinkle with the pine nuts before serving.

Preparation time: 5 minutes
Cooking time: 25 minutes
Cooling time: 10 minutes

Chef's note: Try fish fillets poached in this interesting, delicious sauce.

Per serving: 194 calories, 3.8 g. fat (17% of calories), 1.5 g. dietary fiber, 48 mg. cholesterol, 244 mg. sodium.

SHRIMP WITH PEPPERS, FENNEL AND TOMATOES

SERVES 4

This simple, beautiful dish is typical of the seafood specialties found in the casual waterside *trattorias* of Venice. Serve this over rice or pasta for a main dish or as an antipasto with plenty of crusty bread for dipping up the flavorful garlicky sauce.

1   *pound fresh or frozen shrimp, thawed*
1   *teaspoon extra-virgin olive oil*
1   *yellow pepper, diced*
3   *plum tomatoes, diced*
1   *fennel bulb, diced (page 100)*
¼   *cup chopped onions*
4   *cloves garlic, minced*
2   *tablespoons lemon juice*
1   *tablespoon chopped fresh marjoram*
1   *teaspoon grated lemon rind*
     Dash of hot-pepper sauce
3   *tablespoons chopped fresh basil*

In a large no-stick frying pan over medium heat, sauté the shrimp in the oil for 1 minute.

Add the peppers, tomatoes, fennel, onions and garlic; sauté for 1 minute, or until the vegetables begin to soften. Add the lemon juice, marjoram, lemon rind and hot-pepper sauce. Cover and continue cooking for 2 to 3 minutes, or until the shrimp turn pink. Sprinkle with the basil.

Preparation time: 5 minutes
Cooking time: 5 minutes

Per serving: 140 calories, 2.6 g. fat (16% of calories), 1.7 g. dietary fiber, 174 mg. cholesterol, 248 mg. sodium.

GRILLED SHRIMP WITH POTATOES, PEAS AND BASIL

SERVES 4

*J*ust right for languid summer appetites, this dish may be made ahead or tossed together minutes before serving.

1 *pound fresh jumbo shrimp, unpeeled*

½ *cup orange juice*

1 *tablespoon lemon juice*

1 *tablespoon white wine vinegar*

1 *teaspoon extra-virgin olive oil*

½ *teaspoon drained green peppercorns in brine (see note)*

¼ *teaspoon sugar*

   Dash of hot-pepper sauce

8 *new red potatoes, steamed until tender and quartered*

1 *cup fresh or frozen peas, cooked until tender*

1 *sweet red pepper, diced*

¼ *cup chopped scallions*

2 *tablespoons finely chopped fresh basil*

   Salt and black pepper

   Lemon wedges

Lightly coat the shrimp with no-stick spray. Grill over a high flame or broil about 5″ from the heat for 3 to 5 minutes per side, or until the shrimp turn pink. Remove the shells and devein. Set aside.

In a large bowl, whisk together the orange juice, lemon juice, vinegar, oil, peppercorns, sugar and hot-pepper sauce.

Add the potatoes, peas, red peppers, scallions, basil and shrimp. Toss gently to combine. Add salt and black pepper to taste. Serve garnished with lemon wedges.

Preparation time: 5 minutes
Grilling time: 10 minutes

Chef's note: Green peppercorns in brine are deliciously peppery and salty-sour. They may be omitted or replaced with capers.

Per serving: 348 calories, 2.5 g. fat (6% of calories), 0.7 g. dietary fiber, 174 mg. cholesterol, 218 mg. sodium.

SPICY JUMBO SHRIMP

SERVES 4

*S*hrimp abound off the southern coast of Italy. Especially in Sardinia, where those who fish the coast are of mixed ethnic ancestry, fresh seafood is prepared in myriad ways reflecting the Spanish and Arabic influences. This spicy shrimp dish is traditionally fried in olive oil, then finished with a hot-pepper sauce. In this recipe, the frying is eliminated, but the sauce remains piquant as ever.

> 1 *pound fresh jumbo shrimp, peeled and deveined*
> 1 *teaspoon extra-virgin olive oil*
> ½ *cup white wine or ½ cup water with 3 tablespoons lemon juice*
> 1 *hot chili pepper, chopped (wear plastic gloves when handling)*
> 1 *tablespoon lemon juice*
> *Dash of hot-pepper sauce*

In a large no-stick frying pan over medium-high heat, sauté the shrimp in the oil for 1 minute. Add the wine or water with lemon juice, chili peppers, lemon juice and hot-pepper sauce. Cover and cook for 3 minutes, or until the shrimp turn pink.

Remove the shrimp to a serving bowl. Cook the sauce over high heat for 3 minutes, or until it is slightly reduced. Pour the sauce over the shrimp. Serve warm or cold.

Preparation time: 10 minutes
Cooking time: 7 minutes

Per serving: 123 calories, 2.1 g. fat (16% of calories), 0.1 g. dietary fiber, 174 mg. cholesterol, 201 mg. sodium.

CLASSIC SHELLFISH STEW

SERVES 6

*E*very village along Italy's coastline makes a version of this hearty, simple one-dish meal. Choose a variety of shellfish that is in season and fresh. The stew is traditionally served on toasty Crostini (page 31) but is equally good over rice or pasta.

1	*teaspoon extra-virgin olive oil*
½	*cup finely chopped onions*
1	*clove garlic, minced*
1	*cup diced fresh or canned plum tomatoes, drained*
1	*cup dry white wine or clam juice*
¼	*cup chopped fresh Italian parsley*
	Dash of hot-pepper sauce
	Salt and black pepper
1	*pound littleneck clams, scrubbed (page 42)*
1	*pound mussels, scrubbed and debearded (page 41)*
8	*ounces fresh medium shrimp, peeled and deveined (see note)*

Coat a large saucepan with no-stick spray; add the oil over medium-high heat. Add the onions and sauté for 1 minute. Add the garlic and continue cooking for 3 minutes, or until the onions and garlic become very soft. Add the tomatoes, wine or clam juice, parsley and hot-pepper sauce; add salt and black pepper to taste. Lower the heat, cover and simmer for about 20 minutes. Uncover and continue cooking for 5 minutes, or until the liquid is slightly reduced.

Add the clams and mussels. (Discard any that are already open or have broken shells.) Cover and cook for 3 minutes. Check to see if they are beginning to open. If not, cover and cook another minute. If so, add the shrimp and continue cooking, uncovered, for another 2 to 3 minutes, or until the shellfish have opened and the shrimp are pink. Discard any mussels or clams that have not opened.

Preparation time: 15 minutes
Cooking time: 36 minutes

Chef's note: To prepare the shrimp, remove the shells and pull out the dark vein that runs the length of the spine. Wash in cold water. If larger than medium shrimp, cut in half lengthwise.

Per serving: 139 calories, 2.4 g. fat (16% of calories), 0.7 g. dietary fiber, 92 mg. cholesterol, 202 mg. sodium.

CRAB RISO SALAD WITH BASIL AND MINT

SERVES 4

*L*ight and refreshing, this crab and pasta salad may be made several hours ahead and kept in the refrigerator until ready to serve. *Riso* is another name for *orzo*, the rice-shaped pasta. You may substitute other small pasta.

⅓ *cup nonfat plain yogurt*

¼ *cup nonfat mayonnaise*

2 *tablespoons lemon juice*

2 *tablespoons chopped fresh basil*

2 *tablespoons chopped fresh mint*

2 *cups cooked riso, drained*

12 *ounces cooked crabmeat, drained*

½ *cup finely chopped sweet red peppers*

¼ *cup chopped scallions*

  Salt and black pepper

2 *tablespoons pine nuts, toasted (page 71)*

In a large bowl, whisk together the yogurt, mayonnaise, lemon juice, basil and mint. Add the riso, crabmeat, red peppers and scallions; add salt and black pepper to taste.

To serve, sprinkle with the pine nuts.

Preparation time: 15 minutes

Chef's note: This is especially bright and attractive served in hollowed-out sweet red, yellow and orange peppers.

Per serving: 227 calories, 4.2 g. fat (17% of calories), 1.5 g. dietary fiber, 81 mg. cholesterol, 434 mg. sodium.

CHAPTER 7

HEART
SMART
AND EASY

POULTRY AND MEAT

here is little room on the healthful Italian table for huge cuts of meat or fowl. Vegetables with risotto, pasta or polenta, plus loaves of steaming rustic bread and salads of beans and greens compete for space in the weekly menu. Chicken, turkey, pork and beef dishes augment but never dominate this healthful fare. Portions are small and preparation is simple. These days, "stretching" the quantity of meat served by adding vegetables and pasta does much to enrich the nutritional quality of a meal. It also makes for colorful, fresh and interesting fare.

ROASTED CHICKEN WITH LEMON AND GARLIC

SERVES 4

*G*reat hot or cold, take this lemony chicken on a picnic or tote it to a pot-luck supper. The lemon juices bake into the chicken so that it remains moist without additional fat. Be sure to remove the skin before serving. Leftovers (if there are any) are delicious in salad.

> 1 *fryer chicken (about 3–3½ pounds)*
> 3 *whole lemons*
> 5 *cloves garlic*
> 2 *sprigs fresh rosemary*

Using a sharp knife, butterfly the chicken by cutting it in half along the top of the breast through the bone. Open the chicken up so that it lies flat and place, cut side down, in a baking pan. Thinly slice 2 of the lemons. Using your fingers, gently lift the skin up from the breast and work half of the lemon slices under the skin along the breast meat. Tuck the garlic and rosemary under the chicken. Lay the remaining lemon slices on top of the chicken. Slice the remaining lemon in half. Squeeze the juice of both halves over the chicken.

Roast the chicken at 375° for 10 minutes. Reduce the heat to 350° and continue roasting for 25 minutes, or until the juices run clear when poked with a knife. Remove the skin before serving the chicken.

Preparation time: 10 minutes
Baking time: 35 minutes

Per serving: 149 calories, 3.1 g. fat (19% of calories), no dietary fiber, 72 mg. cholesterol, 63 mg. sodium.

POACHED CHICKEN BREASTS IN BALSAMIC VINEGAR

SERVES 4

*A*ged balsamic vinegar's rich nature forms the basis for this robust rosemary sauce. Serve the chicken on pasta or polenta to absorb the flavorful sauce. You may also serve the chicken on a bed of dark greens.

1   *cup defatted chicken stock*
4   *boneless, skinless chicken breast halves*
    (4 ounces each)
½   *cup orange juice*
⅓   *cup balsamic vinegar*
2   *tablespoons grated orange rind*
1   *large sprig fresh rosemary*

In a large frying pan, bring the stock to a boil. Add the chicken; lower the heat and poach for 7 to 9 minutes, or until the inside is no longer pink when cut with a knife. Transfer the chicken to a plate and tent with foil to keep warm.

Increase the heat to high; add the orange juice, vinegar, orange rind and rosemary. Boil for 8 to 10 minutes, or until the liquid is reduced by half. Slice the chicken into 2″ strips and return to the pan to heat through. Remove and discard the rosemary.

Preparation time: 5 minutes
Cooking time: 20 minutes

Chef's note: The longer the chicken sits in its sauce, the richer and more flavorful it will taste. This recipe may be prepared a day ahead and stored, covered, in the refrigerator. To serve, bring the chicken and sauce to room temperature or heat through.

Per serving: 133 calories, 2 g. fat (14% of calories), 0.2 g. dietary fiber, 46 mg. cholesterol, 162 mg. sodium.

CHICKEN BREASTS WITH FRESH TOMATOES

SERVES 4

*E*specially nice on *orzo* or rice, this flavorful chicken can be served warm or at room temperature.

4 boneless, skinless chicken breast halves
   (4 ounces each)
1 cup defatted chicken stock
½ cup sliced scallions
½ cup chopped plum tomatoes
2 teaspoons red wine vinegar
1 teaspoon brown sugar

In a no-stick frying pan over medium-high heat, sauté the chicken breasts for 1 to 2 minutes per side, or until browned on both sides. Add the stock, scallions, tomatoes, vinegar and brown sugar. Cover the pan, reduce the heat and simmer for 5 to 8 minutes, or until the inside of the chicken is no longer pink when cut with a knife. Transfer the chicken to a plate and tent with foil to keep warm.

Increase the heat and boil the stock mixture for 10 minutes, or until the liquid is reduced to a sauce.

To serve, spoon the sauce with the tomatoes and scallions over the chicken.

Preparation time: 5 minutes
Cooking time: 22 minutes

Chef's note: To make the sauce richer-tasting, omit the vinegar, brown sugar and ½ cup of the stock; substitute ½ cup dry sherry.

Per serving: 138 calories, 2 g. fat (14% of calories), 0.5 g. dietary fiber, 46 mg. cholesterol, 101 mg. sodium.

GRILLED CHICKEN BREASTS
IN SAGE VINAIGRETTE

SERVES 4

*I*ntense and slightly sweet, this marinade turns the chicken breast meat a golden caramel color.

¼ *cup balsamic vinegar*
1 *tablespoon extra-virgin olive oil*
2 *teaspoons chopped fresh sage*
4 *boneless, skinless chicken breast halves*
  (4 ounces each)

In a small bowl, whisk together the vinegar, oil and sage. Brush over the chicken; let marinate for 15 minutes at room temperature.

Remove the chicken from the marinade; cook over a medium-hot grill or broil about 5″ from the heat for 6 to 8 minutes, or until the chicken is cooked through, turning once and basting occasionally with the marinade.

Preparation time: 2 minutes plus 15 minutes marinating time
Grilling time: 8 minutes

Chef's note: To make a light sauce for the chicken, double the marinade ingredients. After the chicken has marinated and while it is cooking, pour the marinade into a saucepan over medium-low heat. Bring to a boil; reduce the heat to low and simmer for 2 minutes, whisking constantly. Drizzle over the chicken or serve alongside.

Per serving: 112 calories, 3.6 g. fat (31% of calories), no dietary fiber, 46 mg. cholesterol, 41 mg. sodium.

LEMON-HERB CHICKEN BREASTS

SERVES 4

*T*his fresh-tasting chicken is best served over pasta, rice or polenta that will soak up the lemony juices.

- 2   tablespoons unbleached flour
     Salt and black pepper
- 4   boneless, skinless chicken breasts halves
     (4 ounces each)
- 1   clove garlic, minced
- ¼   cup defatted chicken stock
- 2   tablespoons lemon juice
- 12 thin strips lemon rind
- 1   teaspoon chopped fresh oregano
- 1   tablespoon chopped fresh basil

Season the flour with salt and pepper to taste. Dredge the chicken in the seasoned flour.

In a large no-stick frying pan over medium-high heat, sauté the garlic for 1 minute, or until soft. Add the chicken breasts and sauté for 5 minutes per side, or until cooked through and no longer pink when cut with a knife. Transfer the chicken to a plate and tent with foil to keep warm.

Add the stock, lemon juice, lemon rind and oregano to the pan and bring the mixture to a boil. Reduce the heat and simmer for 5 minutes, or until the liquid is reduced by half.

To serve, spoon the sauce with the lemon rind over the chicken breasts and sprinkle with the basil.

Preparation time: 5 minutes
Cooking time: 16 minutes

Per serving 110 calories, 2 g. fat (17% of calories), 0.1 g. dietary fiber, 46 mg. cholesterol, 69 mg. sodium.

CHICKEN WITH TOMATOES AND ARTICHOKES

SERVES 4

*S*erve the chicken over pasta or *orzo*. It is also good as a warm salad over bitter greens.

2	*teaspoons virgin olive oil*
4	*boneless, skinless chicken breast halves (4 ounces each)*
1	*can (14 ounces) artichoke hearts, drained and quartered*
1	*cup sliced plum tomatoes*
½	*cup sliced red onions*
¼	*cup defatted chicken stock*
¼	*cup orange juice*
6	*imported black olives, pitted and sliced*
2	*tablespoons chopped fresh parsley*
2	*teaspoons chopped fresh rosemary*
2	*teaspoons grated orange rind*
2	*cloves garlic, minced*
	Salt and black pepper

In a large no-stick frying pan over medium heat, heat the oil and sauté the chicken for 4 minutes per side, or until lightly browned.

Add the artichoke hearts, tomatoes, onions, stock, orange juice, olives, parsley, rosemary, orange rind and garlic. Reduce the heat, cover and simmer for 7 to 10 minutes, or until the vegetables are hot and the chicken is no longer pink when cut with a knife. Add salt and pepper to taste.

Preparation time: 5 minutes
Cooking time: 18 minutes

Per serving: 194 calories, 5.8 g. fat (25% of calories), 1.2 g. dietary fiber, 46 mg. cholesterol, 198 mg. sodium.

ITALIAN CHICKEN AND PEPPER STIR-FRY

SERVES 4

*V*ary the vegetables in this dish with the season. Make sure they are cut the same size so that they cook evenly.

- 1 *pound boneless, skinless chicken breasts, cut into 1" strips*
- 1 *sweet red pepper, cut into 1" strips*
- 1 *yellow pepper, cut into 1" strips*
- 1 *green pepper, cut into 1" strips*
- ¼ *cup chopped onions*
- 1 *clove garlic, minced*
- ½ *cup defatted chicken stock*
- 1 *tablespoon lemon juice*
- 1 *tablespoon chopped fresh oregano*
- 2 *tablespoons chopped fresh basil*

In a large no-stick frying pan over medium-high heat, sauté the chicken, red peppers, yellow peppers, green peppers, onions and garlic for 1 minute, or until the chicken strips are browned on both sides.

Add the stock, lemon juice and oregano to the pan. Reduce the heat, cover and cook for 1 minute. Uncover and continue cooking for 3 to 4 minutes, or until the chicken is no longer pink, the peppers are tender and the liquid is reduced by half. Stir in the basil.

Preparation time: 5 minutes
Cooking time: 6 minutes

Chef's note: Serve this light but flavorful chicken over cooked pasta, brown rice or polenta to absorb the juices.

Per serving: 113 calories, 2.1 g. fat (17% of calories), 1.1 g. dietary fiber, 46 mg. cholesterol, 100 mg. sodium.

Herbed Chicken Thighs

*T*his dish plays on the distinct flavor of dark-meat chicken. The chicken thighs are seasoned with herbs and sautéed with lots of garlic. They're finished in a sauce made rich-tasting with balsamic vinegar and served over pasta.

- 4   *chicken thighs (1¼ pounds)*
- 1   *tablespoon chopped fresh sage*
- 1   *tablespoon chopped fresh parsley*
- ¼   *teaspoon ground black pepper*
- 1   *cup defatted chicken stock*
- ¼   *cup balsamic vinegar*
- ¼   *cup coarsely minced garlic*
- 2   *cups hot cooked pasta*

Remove the skin and any excess fat from the chicken. In a small dish, mix together the sage, parsley and pepper. Rub the chicken with the herb mixture.

Coat a large no-stick frying pan with no-stick spray. Cook the chicken over medium heat for 2 minutes per side, or until brown. Add the stock, vinegar and garlic; cover, lower the heat and simmer for 10 to 12 minutes, or until the chicken is cooked and no longer pink when cut with a knife. Transfer the chicken to a platter and tent with foil to keep warm.

Increase the heat and cook the liquid for 3 minutes, or until it is reduced by half. Return the chicken to the pan and heat through. Serve the chicken and sauce over the pasta.

Preparation time: 10 minutes
Cooking time: 20 minutes

Per serving: 314 calories, 8.6 g. fat (25% of calories), 1.2 g. dietary fiber, 89 mg. cholesterol, 209 mg. sodium.

CHICKEN CACCIATORE

SERVES 4

Cacciatore means "hunter," and this chicken dish, made with dark-meat thighs, is reminiscent of the game dishes of the Italian countryside—fragrant stews of tomatoes, onions and herbs. Serve this over rice to absorb the sauce.

4	chicken thighs (1¼ pounds)
3	cloves garlic, minced
2	cups chopped canned tomatoes, drained
1	cup chopped mushrooms (see note)
¼	cup red wine or defatted chicken stock
¼	cup chopped fresh parsley
4	imported black olives, pitted and chopped
2	cups hot cooked brown rice

Remove the skin and any excess fat from the chicken.

Coat a large no-stick frying pan with no-stick spray. Sauté the chicken and the garlic over medium heat for 5 minutes, or until the chicken is browned on all sides.

Add the tomatoes, mushrooms, wine or stock and parsley. Lower the heat and simmer for 20 minutes, or until the chicken is tender and the sauce is reduced.

Stir in the olives. Serve over the rice.

Preparation time: 10 minutes
Cooking time: 25 minutes

Chef's note: Use a combination of different mushrooms for the most flavor. Good choices include portobello, shiitake, cremini and button mushrooms.

Per serving: 350 calories, 9 g. fat (24% of calories), 2.5 g. dietary fiber, 89 mg. cholesterol, 297 mg. sodium.

Turkey Scaloppine with Zucchini

*Y*ou'll only need one frying pan for this simple, quick dish of turkey, zucchini and mushrooms.

2   *tablespoons lemon juice*
2   *cloves garlic, minced*
2   *teaspoons chopped fresh oregano*
2   *teaspoons chopped fresh Italian parsley*
4   *turkey breast slices (4 ounces each)*
½   *teaspoon extra-virgin olive oil*
2   *cups sliced zucchini*
1   *cup sliced mushrooms*
¼   *cup sliced scallions*
   Salt and black pepper

Mix the lemon juice, garlic, oregano and parsley together in a small dish. Brush the mixture over the turkey.

In a large no-stick frying pan over medium-high heat, heat the oil and sauté the turkey for 2 minutes per side, or until no longer pink. Transfer to a platter and tent with foil to keep warm.

Add the zucchini, mushrooms and scallions; cook over medium-low heat, stirring constantly, for 3 minutes, or until the vegetables are tender. Add salt and pepper to taste. Serve the vegetables over the turkey.

Preparation time: 5 minutes
Cooking time: 7 minutes

Per serving: 146 calories, 1.4 g. fat (9% of calories), 1.4 g. dietary fiber, 74 mg. cholesterol, 50 mg. sodium.

Turkey Scaloppine in Wild Mushroom Sauce

SERVES 4

A dark, rich-tasting sauce that boasts earthy portobello mushrooms, leeks and sun-dried tomatoes. Finished with balsamic vinegar, it is complex and wonderful with light white turkey meat.

4	*turkey breast slices (4 ounces each)*
1	*teaspoon extra-virgin olive oil*
1	*cup finely sliced leeks (page 83)*
1	*pound portobello mushrooms, thinly sliced*
2	*cups defatted chicken stock*
¼	*cup sliced reconstituted sun-dried tomatoes (page 72)*
1	*tablespoon balsamic vinegar*
2	*sprigs fresh thyme*
1	*sprig fresh oregano*
¼	*cup nonfat sour cream*
	Salt and black pepper

In a large no-stick frying pan over medium-high heat, sear the turkey for about 2 minutes per side. Transfer to a plate and tent with foil to keep warm.

Add the oil to the pan and sauté the leeks for 5 minutes, or until very soft. Add the mushrooms and sauté for 5 minutes, or until the mushrooms are soft and the leeks are browned. Add the stock, tomatoes, vinegar, thyme and oregano. Cover and cook for 10 minutes, or until the mushrooms are very soft. Uncover and cook for 10 minutes, or until the liquid is reduced by half.

Stir in the sour cream. Add the turkey and cook for 1 minute, or until the turkey is no longer pink when sliced with a knife.

Remove and discard the thyme and oregano; add salt and pepper to taste. Serve the sauce over the turkey.

Preparation time: 5 minutes
Cooking time: 35 minutes

Per serving: 274 calories, 2.6 g. fat (8% of calories), 2.1 g. dietary fiber, 74 mg. cholesterol, 339 mg. sodium.

TURKEY: THE SUM OF ITS PARTS

*F*resh cuts of turkey offer a meaty, low-calorie, low-fat low-cost alternative to red meat. Trimmed of excess fat and bone, fresh cuts of breast meat are available in several different varieties. Here is a quick guide to the different cuts with suggestions on how to use them.

- **Turkey Breast Roast:** Cut from the turkey breast, these 2- to 3-pound bone-in roasts bake in just over 1 hour. Some include pop-up thermometers to indicate doneness. Allow about 40 minutes per pound at 325° and cook until the meat thermometer reads 165°, not 185° as specified in older cookbooks. The lower cooking temperature and shortened cooking time yield a juicier roast. The leftovers from a turkey roast make wonderful sandwiches, salads and pastas.

- **Turkey Breast Tenderloins:** Cut from the prime, most tender section of the turkey breast, tenderloins are fillets of white meat. They make flavorful replacements for chicken breasts. Poach these meaty, boneless skinless tenderloins for use in salads, soups and pasta dishes. They also may be baked, broiled, grilled or sautéed.

- **Fresh Turkey Breast Slices:** A low-cost alternative to veal, these prime breast meat crosscuts are perfect for scaloppine dishes, sautés and pastas.

- **Fresh Ground Turkey:** Packages of ground turkey can contain a mixture of white and dark meat or white meat only. Ground white turkey is lower in fat and calories; the dark and white meat mixture has more flavor. Ground turkey can stand in for higher-calorie ground beef but may require more seasoning to enhance the subtle flavor. Try mixing ground turkey with turkey sausage for use in your favorite casserole and meatloaf recipes.

STUFFED TURKEY TENDERLOINS

SERVES 4

The tenderloin is the most succulent cut of the turkey breast, absolutely lean. Here it is braised then served with a rich sauce made from the cooking juices. Delicious on pasta or with risotto.

2	*turkey breast tenderloins (about 8 to 12 ounces each)*
¼	*cup nonfat ricotta cheese*
2	*tablespoons nonfat cream cheese*
2	*tablespoons diced sweet red peppers*
1	*tablespoon grated Parmesan cheese*
1	*tablespoon chopped fresh oregano*
1	*tablespoon drained capers*
	Salt and black pepper
1	*cup defatted chicken stock*
2	*tablespoons nonfat sour cream*
2	*teaspoons lemon juice*

Cut a 3″ wide horizontal slit into the center of each tenderloin. In a small bowl, mix together the ricotta, cream cheese, red peppers, Parmesan, oregano and capers; add salt and black pepper to taste. Stuff into the slit pockets.

In a large no-stick frying pan over medium heat, brown the turkey for about 2 minutes per side. Add the stock; cover, reduce the heat and simmer for 15 minutes, or until the turkey is cooked through and the meat is no longer pink when cut with a knife.

Transfer the turkey to a plate and tent with foil to keep warm. Increase the heat and cook the stock for 3 minutes, or until the liquid is reduced by half. Whisk in the sour cream and lemon juice. To serve, slice each tenderloin in half crosswise and drizzle with the sauce.

Preparation time: 10 minutes
Cooking time: 22 minutes

Per serving: 164 calories, 1.2 g. fat (7% of calories), no dietary fiber, 78 mg. cholesterol, 285 mg. sodium.

MEDITERRANEAN TURKEY IN APRICOT SAUCE

SERVES 4

*T*he apricots and pine nuts in this interesting, sweet and tart-tasting sauce originated with Italy's Mediterranean neighbors.

> 4   *turkey breast slices (4 ounces each)*
> 1   *cup defatted chicken stock*
> 1   *cup orange juice*
> ¼   *cup coarsely chopped dried apricots*
> 1   *tablespoon white wine vinegar*
> 1   *teaspoon honey*
> 2   *cups hot cooked rice*
> 2   *tablespoons pine nuts, toasted (page 71)*

In a large no-stick frying pan over medium-high heat, sear the turkey for 2 minutes per side. Transfer to a plate and tent with foil to keep warm.

Add the stock, orange juice, apricots, vinegar and honey to the pan. Simmer for 10 minutes, or until the liquid is reduced by half.

Return the turkey to the pan and simmer for 2 to 3 minutes, or until the meat is no longer pink when sliced with a knife.

Serve the turkey and the sauce over the cooked rice. Sprinkle with the pine nuts.

Preparation time: 5 minutes
Cooking time: 17 minutes

Per serving: 334 calories, 3.4 g. fat (9% of calories), 2.4 g. dietary fiber, 74 mg. cholesterol, 170 mg. sodium.

POACHED TURKEY
WITH LEMON-CAPER MAYONNAISE

SERVES 4

*G*reat for summer entertaining, this light, cool dish is lovely served on a bed of dark greens or lettuce leaves and garnished with lemon wedges.

Turkey

2	*turkey breast tenderloins (about 8 ounces each)*
8	*cups defatted chicken stock*
2	*stalks celery, cut in half crosswise*
2	*carrots, cut in half crosswise*
1	*small onion, studded with 15 cloves*
2	*cloves garlic*

Mayonnaise

½	*cup nonfat mayonnaise*
½	*cup nonfat plain yogurt*
1	*tablespoon lemon juice*
1	*tablespoon chopped fresh tarragon*
1	*teaspoon chopped fresh oregano*
1	*teaspoon drained capers*
	Salt and black pepper

To make the turkey: In a large saucepan, cover the turkey with the stock (adding water if necessary so that the meat is covered with liquid). Add the celery, carrots, onion and garlic. Bring to a boil. Cover, reduce the heat and simmer for 20 to 25 minutes, or until the meat is no longer pink when sliced with a knife.

Remove the turkey and let cool for 15 minutes, or until near room temperature; save the stock for another use. Or, if preparing this dish ahead, let the turkey stay in the stock, cool to room temperature and refrigerate, covered, until ready to use.

To make the mayonnaise: In a small bowl, stir together the mayonnaise, yogurt, lemon juice, tarragon, oregano and capers; add salt and pepper to taste.

To serve, slice the turkey; spoon the mayonnaise evenly over the slices.

Preparation time: 5 minutes
Cooking time: 25 minutes
Cooling time: 15 minutes

Per serving: 171 calories, 0.8 g. fat (4% of calories), 0.2 g. dietary fiber, 75 mg. cholesterol, 556 mg. sodium.

STUFFED PEPPERS

SERVES 4

*S*weet red and yellow peppers make festive containers for this simple meal, served over a bed of rice.

2 *sweet red peppers*
2 *yellow or orange peppers*
4 *ounces turkey sausage patties*
1 *cup chopped onions*
1 *cup chopped mushrooms*
1 *clove garlic, minced*
1 *cup bread crumbs*
1 *tablespoon grated Parmesan cheese*
2 *cups hot cooked white rice*

Cut the tops off the peppers, about 1″ down. Remove the seeds and veins, being careful not to tear or rip the peppers. Put the peppers on a microwave-safe plate and set aside.

Crumble the sausage patties into a no-stick frying pan over medium-high heat; brown for 5 minutes, or until no longer pink, stirring occasionally. Remove the sausage and set aside. Drain the fat and juices from the pan and wipe it clean.

Set the pan over medium-high heat and sauté the onions, mushrooms and garlic for 1 minute. Cover and cook for 3 minutes, or until very soft. Add the sausage and mix with the onions and mushrooms. Remove the pan from the heat and stir in the bread crumbs.

Stuff the peppers with the sausage mixture; sprinkle with the Parmesan. Cover with plastic wrap and microwave for 2 to 5 minutes on high, or until heated through. Serve over the rice.

Preparation time: 5 minutes
Cooking time: 9 minutes
Microwaving time: 5 minutes

Per serving: 407 calories, 12.3 g. fat (27% of calories), 4 g. dietary fiber, 1 mg. cholesterol, 219 mg. sodium.

SPAGHETTI AND SPICY TURKEY MEATBALLS

SERVES 4

*E*asy to make, these ground turkey meatballs are also wonderful served in hollowed-out Italian bread rolls instead of over spaghetti.

1 *pound spaghetti*
1 *pound ground turkey*
½ *cup dry bread crumbs*
¼ *cup finely chopped fresh Italian parsley*
1 *tablespoon finely chopped fresh oregano*
1 *tablespoon grated Parmesan cheese*
1 *egg white*
5 *dashes of hot-pepper sauce*
4 *cups no-salt-added spaghetti sauce*

In a large pot, cook the spaghetti in boiling water for 10 to 12 minutes, or until tender; drain well.

While the spaghetti is cooking, prepare the meatballs. In a large bowl, mix together the turkey, bread crumbs, parsley, oregano, Parmesan, egg white and hot-pepper sauce. Shape into 2″ balls.

In a large no-stick frying pan over medium-high heat, cook the meatballs for 5 minutes, or until brown on all sides. Add the sauce and simmer for 5 minutes, or until the meatballs are cooked and no longer pink when sliced with a knife.

Serve the meatballs and sauce over the spaghetti.

Preparation time: 5 minutes
Cooking time: 10 minutes

Per serving: 851 calories, 22.5 g. fat (24% of calories), 0.6 g. dietary fiber, 43 mg. cholesterol, 231 mg. sodium.

TURKEY SAUSAGE WITH PEPPERS AND ONIONS

SERVES 4

This lively medley is great sandwiched in crusty Italian bread or served over soft polenta. It tastes even better the next day.

8   ounces spaghetti
8   ounces Italian-style turkey sausage links
1   green pepper, sliced
1   sweet red pepper, sliced
1   small onion, sliced
1   clove garlic, sliced
¼   cup red wine or defatted chicken stock
1   teaspoon chopped fresh sage

In a large pot, cook the spaghetti in boiling water for 10 to 12 minutes, or until tender; drain well.

While the spaghetti is cooking, heat a large no-stick frying pan over medium heat. Brown the sausages for 1 to 2 minutes; cover, lower the heat and cook for 5 minutes, or until no longer pink when sliced with a knife. Transfer the sausages to a plate.

Drain the fat from the pan and wipe it clean with a paper towel. Add the green peppers, red peppers, onions, garlic, wine or stock and sage. Cover and cook over medium heat for 3 minutes, or until the vegetables are soft.

Slice the sausages and return to the pan. Cook, uncovered, for 1 to 2 minutes, or until the liquid is reduced and the sausages are heated through.

Turn the spaghetti into the frying pan and toss with the sausages and vegetables.

Preparation time: 5 minutes
Cooking time: 12 minutes

Per serving: 327 calories, 9.6 g. fat (26% of calories), 0.9 g. dietary fiber, 49 mg. cholesterol, 11 mg. sodium.

Roasted Cornish Hens
with Rosemary and Tomato

*F*resh rosemary is tucked under the skin of these plump little birds set to roast on beds of herbed fresh tomatoes, then served over pasta.

> 2 *Cornish hens*
> 5 *tablespoons chopped fresh rosemary*
> 4 *cups cubed plum tomatoes*
> ½ *cup orange juice*
>   *Salt and black pepper*
> 2 *cups hot cooked pasta*

Split the hens in half. Using your fingers, gently work 1 tablespoon of the rosemary under the skin of each breast half.

Coat a large baking pan with no-stick spray. Lay 4 "beds" of tomatoes (1 cup each) in the prepared pan; sprinkle the remaining 1 tablespoon rosemary over all. Set a half-hen on top of each bed. Drizzle the orange juice over the hens; add salt and pepper to taste.

Roast the hens at 400° for 40 minutes, basting every 10 minutes with the pan juices, until the hens are brown and crisp and their juices run clear. Serve the hens with the tomatoes over the pasta.

Preparation time: 5 minutes
Roasting time: 40 minutes

Per serving: 440 calories, 14.1 g. fat (29% of calories), 4 g. dietary fiber, 93 mg. cholesterol, 71 mg. sodium.

MARINATED TUSCAN STEAK

SERVES 4

A simple marinade complements the rich flavors of flank steak, a lean and inexpensive cut of meat. It is just right served alongside baked potatoes. Leftovers are delicious in a salad or sandwich with sharp mustard.

2   *cups orange juice*
2   *tablespoons grated orange rind*
2   *tablespoons chopped fresh sage*
2   *tablespoons red wine vinegar*
3   *cloves garlic, minced*
1   *teaspoon Dijon mustard*
1   *teaspoon ground black pepper*
1   *pound flank steak*

To make the marinade, in a large glass bowl, mix together the orange juice, orange rind, sage, vinegar, garlic, mustard and pepper.

Add the steak to the marinade and turn to coat. Allow to marinate at room temperature for 15 minutes, or cover and refrigerate overnight.

Grill the steak on a hot grill or broil about 5″ from the heat for 5 minutes per side, or until the meat is light pink when cut with a knife for medium-rare. Baste twice with the marinade while grilling.

Transfer the steak to a carving board, cover with foil and allow to rest for about 5 minutes; slice thinly across the grain and on an angle.

Preparation time: 5 minutes plus 15 minutes marinating time
Cooking time: 10 minutes
Grilling time: 10 minutes plus 5 minutes resting time

Chef's note: This marinade is also good with chicken breasts and turkey tenderloins.

Per serving: 183 calories, 8 g. fat (40% of calories), 0.4 g. dietary fiber, 52 mg. cholesterol, 71 mg. sodium.

PEPPERY MINUTE STEAKS
WITH SUN-DRIED TOMATOES

SERVES 4

*N*eed a quick dinner? These simple steaks are ready in a flash. Serve them over pasta or rice.

4   cube steaks (about 3 ounces each)
    Black pepper
½   cup chopped reconstituted sun-dried tomatoes (page 72)
¾   cup defatted chicken or beef stock
1   tablespoon balsamic vinegar

Sprinkle the steaks with the pepper. In a large no-stick frying pan over high heat, sear the steaks for about 1 minute per side. Transfer to a plate and tent with foil to keep warm.

Add the tomatoes, stock and vinegar to the pan and cook for 3 to 5 minutes, or until the liquid is reduced by half. Return the steaks to the pan and heat through. Serve the steaks with the pan juices and tomatoes.

Preparation time: 5 minutes
Cooking time: 10 minutes

Per serving: 234 calories, 7 g. fat (26% of calories), 1.3 g. dietary fiber, 73 mg. cholesterol, 170 mg. sodium.

HERBED BEEF TENDERLOIN

A wonderful dish for entertaining; the potatoes roast along with the meat. All you need is a tossed salad. Be sure to trim any fat from the meat.

1	pound new potatoes, cut into 1" pieces
2	tablespoons minced shallots
2	tablespoons minced fresh rosemary
2	tablespoons minced fresh oregano
2	tablespoons minced fresh parsley
2	tablespoon cracked blacked peppercorns
1	tablespoon minced fresh garlic
1	teaspoon extra-virgin olive oil
1	pound lean beef tenderloin

Coat a medium baking dish with no-stick spray. Scatter the potatoes over the prepared dish. Roast at 375° for 10 minutes. While the potatoes are roasting, prepare the meat.

In a small bowl, mix together the shallots, rosemary, oregano, parsley, peppercorns, garlic and oil. Rub the mixture over the meat until well coated.

Heat a large no-stick frying pan over medium-high heat. Sear the beef very quickly for 2 minutes, turning to brown it evenly on all sides.

Remove the baking dish from the oven and shake or stir the potatoes to prevent them from sticking to the dish. Put the beef on top of the potatoes and bake at 375° for 15 minutes. Reduce the heat to 350° and bake for 10 minutes, or until the internal temperature reads 130° on a meat thermometer for rare, or 140° for medium.

Remove the beef from the oven and let it rest for at least 10 minutes before carving. If the potatoes are not brown enough, return them to the oven while the beef is resting.

Preparation time: 10 minutes
Cooking time: 2 minutes
Roasting time: 35 minutes plus 10 minutes resting time

Per serving: 276 calories, 8.5 g. fat (28% of calories), 0.4 g. dietary fiber, 64 mg. cholesterol, 56 mg. sodium.

BRAISED ROSEMARY PORK TENDERLOINS

SERVES 4

*O*ne trick to cooking this extremely lean cut of meat is not to overcook it, pulling it from the heat just before it's done.

> 4 *pieces pork tenderloin (about 3 ounces each)*
> 1 *orange, peeled and sectioned*
> ½ *cup defatted chicken stock*
> ½ *cup sliced reconstituted sun-dried tomatoes (page 72)*
> ½ *cup orange juice*
> 1 *tablespoon balsamic vinegar*
> 1 *sprig fresh rosemary*

In a large no-stick frying pan over high heat, sear the pork for 2 minutes per side, or until it is lightly browned all over.

Add the oranges, stock, tomatoes, orange juice, vinegar and rosemary. Reduce the heat to medium-low; cover and cook for 8 to 10 minutes, or until the pork is no longer bright pink when sliced with a knife (pale pink indicates a tender medium-rare meat).

Uncover and continue cooking for 1 minute, or until the liquid is reduced. Remove and discard the rosemary. Serve the pork with the tomatoes, oranges and sauce spooned over it.

Preparation time: 5 minutes
Cooking time: 15 minutes

Per serving: 207 calories, 3.3 g. fat (14% of calories), 2.4 dietary fiber, 60 mg. cholesterol, 129 mg. sodium.

PORK WITH BALSAMIC VINEGAR AND PEARS

SERVES 4

*P*ork tenderloin stays tender in a light sauce of balsamic vinegar and sliced pears. This tastes far richer than it is.

1 *pound pork tenderloin*
2 *teaspoons whole-wheat flour*
1 *cup defatted chicken stock*
½ *cup sliced scallions*
1 *tablespoon balsamic vinegar*
1 *medium pear, sliced*

Cut the pork into 4 pieces and pound with a wooden mallet to flatten slightly. Lightly dust the pork with the flour, shaking off any excess.

Coat a large no-stick frying pan with no-stick spray. Brown the pork over high heat for 2 to 3 minutes per side, or until just cooked through.

Transfer the pork to a plate and tent with foil to keep warm. Add the stock, scallions and vinegar to the pan; cover, reduce the heat and simmer for 2 minutes, or until the scallions are soft. Uncover and cook for 1 to 2 minutes, or until the stock is reduced to a thin glaze.

Stir in the pears. Return the pork to the pan and heat through. Serve the pears and sauce over the pork.

Preparation time: 5 minutes
Cooking time: 10 minutes

Chef's note: An apple will also work well in this dish.

Per serving: 172 calories, 3.5 g. fat (18% of calories), 2.6 g. dietary fiber, 60 mg. cholesterol, 162 mg. sodium.

LAMB CHOPS WITH CUCUMBERS AND TOMATOES

SERVES 4

*G*resh rosemary and mint, crisp cucumbers, sweet tomatoes and a splash of orange play off the distinct flavor of quickly seared lamb chops.

1 *cup thinly sliced tomatoes*
1 *cup thinly sliced cucumber*
2 *tablespoons orange juice*
2 *tablespoons chopped fresh mint*
1 *tablespoon chopped fresh rosemary*
1 *teaspoon grated orange rind*
  Salt and black pepper
4 *loin lamb chops (about 4 ounces each)*

In a medium bowl, combine the tomatoes, cucumbers, orange juice, mint, rosemary and orange rind; add salt and pepper to taste.

Heat a large no-stick frying pan over medium-high heat; add the lamb and sauté for 3 to 7 minutes per side, or until medium-rare. Serve the lamb on a bed of the tomato-cucumber mixture.

Preparation time: 10 minutes
Cooking time: 14 minutes

Per serving: 63 calories, 2.3 g. fat (32% of calories), 0.9 g. dietary fiber, 20 mg. cholesterol, 22 mg. sodium.

CHAPTER 8

NOT JUST
MINESTRONE

SOUPS AND STEWS

A soup can tell you where you are in Italy, almost more precisely than a map. The soups of the south rely on tomatoes and garlic, often rounded out with pasta. In Tuscany and other central regions, soups are thick with beans and sometimes bread. Rice gives northern soups their hearty, warming substance. Along the Riviera, lettuces, tender vegetables and fresh herbs become cooling first courses or satisfying entrées. Here is a collection of Italian soups, both light and hearty, all simple and delicious.

BASIC CHICKEN STOCK

MAKES 2 QUARTS

4–5 *pounds skinless chicken pieces (including breasts, thighs and drumsticks)*
2 *quarts cold water*
1 *large carrot, unpeeled*
1 *small onion, studded with 3 cloves*
3 *cloves garlic, unpeeled*
5 *sprigs fresh Italian parsley*
1 *bay leaf*

In a large stock pot, cover the chicken with the cold water. Bring to a boil, skim the foam from the top, and reduce the heat to low. Add the carrot, onion, garlic, parsley and bay leaf. Simmer, partially covered, for 3 hours, or until the liquid is slightly reduced and has a rich chicken flavor. Remove the chicken and reserve for another use.

Pour the stock through a fine sieve or strainer lined with 1 layer of cheesecloth. Cool to room temperature and then refrigerate overnight—the fat will solidify into a pliable layer that should be lifted off.

Preparation time: 5 minutes
Cooking time: 3 hours

Chef's note: The stock may be refrigerated for up to 2 days or frozen in small containers for up to 6 months.

Per cup: 35 calories, 1.6 g. fat (27% of calories), 0.4 g. dietary fiber, 9 mg. cholesterol, 8 mg. sodium.

ITALIAN BARLEY SOUP

SERVES 4

*W*arming and hearty, this soup is the essence of Italian home cooking—comforting, effortless and full of good things. It is reliable and sure to please. Serve it with lots of crusty bread or Focaccia (page 246) and call it a meal.

> 1 *teaspoon olive oil*
> ½ *cup chopped onions*
> 1 *ounce prosciutto, diced*
> 1 *tablespoon chopped fresh rosemary*
> 1 *tablespoon chopped fresh Italian parsley*
> 4 *cups defatted chicken stock*
> 1 *medium potato, peeled and diced*
> 2 *small carrots, diced*
> ½ *cup quick-cooking barley (see note)*
> 2 *teaspoons grated Parmesan cheese*

In a large saucepan over medium-high heat, heat the oil and sauté the onions for 3 to 4 minutes, or until golden. Stir in the prosciutto, rosemary and Italian parsley.

Add the stock, potatoes, carrots and barley. Bring the liquid to a boil; reduce the heat and simmer for 10 to 15 minutes, or until the potatoes, carrots and barley are tender. To serve, sprinkle with the Parmesan.

Preparation time: 10 minutes
Cooking time: 19 minutes

Chef's note: The two most common varieties of barley available are quick-cooking barley and pearl barley. Cooked pearl barley has a firmer, chewier texture than the quick-cooking variety but takes about 40 minutes to cook. Quick-cooking barley is ready in 10 minutes.

To substitute pearl barley for quick-cooking barley in this recipe, increase the stock to 5 cups. Add ½ cup pearl barley to the stock;

bring to a boil, reduce the heat, cover and simmer for 30 minutes. Continue with the recipe.

Per serving: 318 calories, 5.6 g. fat (15% of calories), 10.3 g. dietary fiber, 1 mg. cholesterol, 585 mg. sodium.

ITALIAN SPRING VEGETABLE SOUP

SERVES 4

*B*ig on taste, this *minestrina* ("little soup") of spring vegetables was inspired by a centuries-old recipe from the Emilia-Romagna area of northern Italy. It makes a lovely first course to an elegant meal.

4½ *cups defatted chicken stock*
1½ *cups frozen artichoke hearts, thawed and cut into 1" pieces*
6 *ounces asparagus, cut into 1" pieces*
¾ *cup sliced fresh spinach*
1 *egg*
2 *tablespoons lemon juice*
   Salt and black pepper

In a large saucepan, bring the stock to a boil. Add the artichoke hearts and asparagus and cook for 3 minutes, or until the asparagus is almost tender. Add the spinach and cook for 1 minute, or until it turns soft and bright green.

In a small cup, beat the egg. Slowly and gently stir the egg into the soup, cooking just until thin threads form (see note). Stir in the lemon juice; add salt and pepper to taste. Serve immediately.

Preparation time: 10 minutes
Cooking time: 5 minutes

Chef's note: Watch closely when adding the egg; the threads form within seconds. It's important that the soup not overcook.

Per serving: 82 calories, 1.6 g. fat (16% of calories), 0.3 g. dietary fiber, 53 mg. cholesterol, 614 mg. sodium.

White Bean Soup with Basil and Tomatoes

SERVES 4

*A*surprisingly light yet satisfying soup, this is best in the summer when fresh basil and tomatoes are at their peak.

½ teaspoon extra-virgin olive oil
¼ cup chopped onions
1 clove garlic, minced
2 cups defatted chicken stock
2 cups water
1 can (15 ounces) white navy or cannellini beans, rinsed and drained
1 large potato, peeled and diced
1 teaspoon chopped fresh oregano
Salt and black pepper
¼ cup chopped fresh tomatoes
2 tablespoons chopped fresh basil

In a large no-stick stock pot over medium heat, heat the oil and sauté the onions and garlic for 1 minute, or until tender. Add the stock, water, beans, potatoes and oregano. Cover, reduce the heat and simmer for 15 minutes, or until the potatoes are tender.

Transfer three-fourths of the soup to a blender or food processor fitted with the steel blade; puree. Pour the puree back into the pot with the remaining soup and heat through. Add salt and pepper to taste. Stir in the tomatoes and basil just before serving.

Preparation time: 5 minutes
Cooking time: 20 minutes

Chef's note: In the winter, substitute chopped reconstituted sun-dried tomatoes (page 72) for the fresh tomatoes and fresh parsley for the fresh basil.

Per serving: 165 calories, 0.6 g. fat (3% of calories), 0.7 g. dietary fiber, no cholesterol, 571 mg. sodium.

ASPARAGUS, POTATO AND LEEK SOUP

SERVES 4

A flavorful and satisfying soup of mild leeks and sweet tender asparagus sparked by a touch of lemon.

1	teaspoon extra-virgin olive oil
¾	cup chopped leeks, white part only (page 83)
3	cups defatted chicken stock
1½	cups water
2	medium potatoes, peeled and chopped
8	ounces asparagus, cut into 1" pieces, tips reserved
½	teaspoon grated lemon rind
	Salt and black pepper
8	mushrooms, stemmed and quartered

Coat a large saucepan with no-stick spray; heat ½ teaspoon of the oil over low heat. Add the leeks; sauté for 5 minutes, or until soft. Add the stock, water, potatoes, asparagus (except the tips) and lemon rind. Increase the heat and simmer for 15 minutes, or until the vegetables are tender.

Pour the soup into a blender or a food processor fitted with the steel blade. Puree; add salt and pepper to taste.

In a small no-stick frying pan, heat the remaining ½ teaspoon oil; sauté the reserved asparagus tips and the mushrooms for 3 to 5 minutes, or until crisp-tender.

To serve, garnish the soup with the asparagus tips and mushrooms.

Preparation time: 10 minutes
Cooking time: 20 minutes

Per serving: 118 calories, 1.6 g. fat (11% of calories), 1.9 g. dietary fiber, no cholesterol, 364 mg. sodium.

MINESTRONE

SERVES 4

*I*n Italy, *minestrone* ("big soup") means just about any kind of soup made with chicken or beef stock, whatever vegetables are growing in the garden, pasta and beans. In winter, it's made with canned tomatoes and root vegetables. As with most soups, reheating heightens the flavors. This recipe is easily doubled so you can have extra to freeze.

½   *teaspoon olive oil*
1   *cup chopped onions*
1   *clove garlic, minced*
1   *cup chopped carrots*
½   *cup chopped celery*
2   *cups shredded cabbage*
1   *cup chopped spinach*
½   *cup chopped fresh parsley*
2   *bay leaves*
2   *teaspoons chopped fresh rosemary*
1   *teaspoon chopped fresh sage*
2   *cups defatted chicken stock (see note)*
2   *cups water*
1   *can (15 ounces) no-salt-added stewed tomatoes, chopped (with juice)*
1   *can (16 ounces) chick-peas, rinsed and drained*
½   *cup small pasta, such as elbows or shells*
     Salt and black pepper

In a large soup pot over medium-high heat, heat the oil and sauté the onions and garlic for 1 minute, or until tender. Add the carrots, celery, cabbage, spinach, parsley, bay leaves, rosemary and sage; sauté for 3 minutes, or until the vegetables begin to wilt. Add the stock, water, tomatoes (with juice), chick-peas and pasta. Bring to a boil; lower the heat, cover and simmer for 20 minutes. Uncover and cook for 10 minutes longer. Remove and discard the bay leaves. Add salt and pepper to taste.

Preparation time: 15 minutes
Cooking time: 34 minutes

Chef's note: For a thinner soup, add up to 4 cups stock.

Per serving: 240 calories, 3.4 g. fat (12% of calories), 9.4 g. dietary fiber, no cholesterol, 609 mg. sodium.

SCALLOP AND SPRING PEA SOUP

SERVES 4

*D*elicate sweet scallops and tender spring peas come together in a soup as quick and fresh as spring itself.

4   cups water
2   cups bottled clam juice
1   cup fresh or frozen peas
8   ounces bay scallops
⅔   cup cooked white rice
3   tablespoons lemon juice
1   tablespoon chopped fresh Italian parsley
1   teaspoon chopped fresh basil
    Salt and black pepper

In a large saucepan over high heat, bring the water and clam juice to a boil. Add the peas, scallops and rice; reduce the heat and simmer for 1 to 2 minutes, or until the peas are cooked and the scallops are opaque. Add the lemon juice, parsley and basil; add salt and pepper to taste.

Preparation time: 5 minutes
Cooking time: 2 minutes

Per serving: 134 calories, 0.6 g. fat (4% of calories), 0.4 g. dietary fiber, 19 mg. cholesterol, 352 mg. sodium.

MILAN-STYLE TURKEY STEW

SERVES 4

This light, lemony stew was inspired by *osso bucco*, a Milanese dish that slow-cooks vegetables and veal shanks until meltingly tender. It is traditionally served with *gremolada*, an aromatic mixture of lemon peel, garlic and parsley.

½ *cup finely chopped onions*

½ *cup finely chopped carrots*

½ *cup finely chopped celery*

1 *tablespoon grated lemon rind*

1 *clove garlic, finely minced*

1 *pound boneless, skinless turkey thighs, cut into 2" cubes*

1 *can (14½ ounces) no-salt-added tomatoes, chopped (with juice)*

1 *cup white wine or defatted chicken stock*

2 *tablespoons lemon juice*

1 *teaspoon dried oregano*

3 *sprigs fresh parsley*

1 *bay leaf*

Salt and black pepper

Gremolada (see note)

In a large saucepan over medium heat, combine the onions, carrots, celery, lemon rind and garlic; sauté for 2 minutes, or until soft. Add the turkey and continue to cook, stirring constantly, for 2 minutes, or until the turkey begins to brown. Add the tomatoes (with juice), wine or stock, lemon juice, oregano, parsley and bay leaf. Cover, lower the heat and cook for 5 minutes. Uncover and simmer for 15 minutes, or until the sauce thickens. Add salt and pepper to taste. Remove and discard the parsley and bay leaf. Serve sprinkled with the *gremolada*.

Preparation time: 5 minutes
Cooking time: 24 minutes

Chef's note: *Gremolada* is an aromatic mixture that's added to *osso buco* and other braised meats and fish just before the dish is finished cooking. Simply mix together 1 tablespoon finely chopped fresh parsley, 1 teaspoon grated lemon rind and ½ teaspoon minced garlic. Sprinkle over the meat or fish just before it's finished cooking, so that the *gremolada* cooks no longer than 2 minutes, or add it at serving time.

Per serving: 237 calories, 6.3 g. fat (24% of calories), 1.9 g. dietary fiber, 70 mg. cholesterol, 101 mg. sodium.

STOCKING UP

A good stock is hard to find (but very easy to make). Many of the canned varieties are loaded with salt and are seasoned with a heavy hand, making them difficult to cook with. Fortunately, there are currently more varieties of reduced-fat, low-sodium stock available on the market. Still, nothing beats the clean, pure flavor of homemade stock—especially in the health-conscious kitchen. In these recipes, stock is often used in place of oil for sautéing and making sauces, and it plays a critical role in their success.

SICILIAN SAUSAGE STEW

*M*ain-dish soups don't come any heartier than this. Double the recipe so you'll have some to freeze. It reheats beautifully.

8   *ounces Italian-style turkey sausage (hot, sweet or a mix of both)*

2   *cups defatted chicken stock*

1   *can (16 ounces) no-salt-added tomatoes (with juice)*

2   *large potatoes, cut into ½" cubes*

1   *small yellow summer squash or zucchini, diced*

1   *can (15 ounces) kidney beans*

1   *can (15 ounces) white navy or cannellini beans*

½   *cup diced onions*

1   *stalk celery, diced*

2   *tablespoons pitted and sliced imported black olives*

2   *tablespoons chopped fresh parsley*

1   *tablespoon chopped fresh oregano*

2   *cloves garlic, minced*

1   *teaspoon anise seeds*

   Salt and black pepper

Crumble the sausage into a large saucepan and sauté over medium heat until brown, about 5 minutes. Drain the fat.

Add the stock and stir to loosen any brown bits stuck to the pan. Add the tomatoes (with juice), potatoes, squash or zucchini, kidney beans (with liquid), white beans (with liquid), onions, celery, olives, parsley, oregano, garlic and anise seeds. Bring to a boil. Reduce heat to low; cover and simmer for 25 minutes, or until the vegetables are tender. Add salt and pepper to taste.

Preparation time: 5 minutes
Cooking time: 30 minutes

Per serving: 271 calories, 7.8 g. fat (25% of calories), 5.3 g. dietary fiber, no cholesterol, 414 mg. sodium.

BASIC VEGETABLE STOCK

*I*f you have odds and ends of fresh vegetables you are not sure what to do with, throw them into the stock. You may vary your vegetable choices with the season but avoid broccoli, cauliflower, cabbage and other strong-tasting vegetables that will dominate the flavor of the stock. This is a wonderful stock to have on hand.

2 *carrots, chopped*
2 *onions, chopped (see note)*
3 *scallions*
2 *stalks celery*
5 *mushrooms*
1 *tomato, cut into 8 pieces*
5 *sprigs fresh Italian parsley*
1 *bay leaf*
2 *quarts cold water*

In a large stock pot, combine the carrots, onions, scallions, celery, mushrooms, tomatoes, parsley and bay leaf; cover with the water. Bring to a boil; reduce the heat and simmer for 30 to 40 minutes, or until the liquid has a rich vegetable flavor; skim off any foam that rises to the surface with a spoon.

Pour the stock through a fine sieve or strainer lined with 1 layer of cheesecloth. Discard the vegetables.

Preparation time: 5 minutes
Cooking time: 40 minutes

Chef's notes: For a richer color, leave the onion skins on.

The stock may be refrigerated for up to 2 days or frozen for up to 6 months. Freeze it in small containers to use in soups and stews and for braising meat and poultry.

Per cup: 3 calories, 0.2 g. fat (6% of calories), 0.2 g. dietary fiber, no cholesterol, 2 mg. sodium.

TOMATO-BASIL SOUP

SERVES 4

*B*right and refreshing, this soup makes great use of summer tomatoes.

2½	teaspoons extra-virgin olive oil
4	shallots, minced
3	cloves garlic, minced
2	pounds tomatoes, chopped
3	cups vegetable stock or water
10	large fresh basil leaves
⅓	cup cooked white rice
	Salt and black pepper

In a large no-stick frying pan over medium heat, heat the oil and sauté 2 of the shallots and 1 clove of the garlic for 2 minutes, or until soft. Add the tomatoes and the remaining 2 shallots and 2 cloves garlic. Cook for 10 minutes, stirring frequently.

Add the stock or water, basil and rice; add salt and pepper to taste. Simmer for 15 minutes.

Preparation time: 5 minutes
Cooking time: 27 minutes

Chef's note: This soup is refreshing and delicious served cold. Simply chill it in the refrigerator and add 1 tablespoon fresh lemon juice before serving.

Per serving: 112 calories, 3.6 g. fat (27% of calories), 3.2 g. dietary fiber, no cholesterol, 374 mg. sodium.

TOMATO-ORANGE SOUP

SERVES 4

*M*ake this refreshing cold soup on one of those dog-days of summer. It comes together quickly and may be made ahead and chilled early in the day, before you can't stand the heat in the kitchen.

½ *cup chopped onions*

1 *teaspoon olive oil*

1¼ *cups vegetable stock*

1 *can (12 ounces) no-salt-added tomatoes, chopped (with juice)*

1 *tablespoon quick-cooking tapioca*

1 *cup water*

¼ *cup orange juice*

¼ *cup 2% fat milk*

 Salt and black pepper

Coat a large saucepan with no-stick spray and set over medium-high heat. Sauté the onions in the oil for 2 minutes, or until soft. Add ¾ cup of the stock, tomatoes (with juice) and tapioca. Simmer for 20 minutes, or until the soup begins to thicken.

Pour the soup into a blender and puree. Add the remaining ½ cup stock, water, orange juice and milk. Process to blend. Add salt and pepper to taste. Chill in the refrigerator for at least 15 minutes, or overnight, before serving.

Preparation time: 5 minutes
Cooking time: 22 minutes
Chilling time: 15 minutes

Per serving: 62 calories, 1.7 g. fat (23% of calories), 1 g. dietary fiber, 1 mg. cholesterol, 166 mg. sodium.

Soup Savvy

The good soups of Italy span the spectrum from heroic country stew-like *pasta e fagioli* ("pasta and beans") to the sprightly compotes of roasted vegetables and light broths. Some are meant to start the meal, others to be the meal itself.

Many soups taste even better left to sit a few hours or overnight so their flavors have a chance to "marry." Others, of garden-fresh vegetables and herbs, are best served right as they are made. When made with attention to flavor and ingredients, soups are among the healthiest dishes in a smart diet. Here's how:

• **Skim!** Discard the fat from a soup as it simmers away on the back of the stove. Place a quarter of the pot on a high flame so that some of the liquid continues to boil and the rest is still. The fat and scum will travel to the cooler area of the pot, where they may be spooned off. Or, chill the soup so that the fat becomes a pliable layer that may simply be lifted off. Skimming works just as well when there isn't time to wait.

• **Choose the right stock:** The best substitutes for home-made stocks are those canned stocks made without additional salt, spices or herbs that will interfere with a recipe's flavor. Several commercial varieties are labeled "low sodium, reduced fat" or look for the organic brands of stock in health-food stores.

• **Use the Crock-Pot:** Many a long-cooking soup tastes even better made in a Crock-Pot or other slow-cooker, which uses very low steady heat to keep the liquid at the most gentle simmer. To convert your favorite recipes, and those in this book, follow the instructions for sautéing or braising first, then turn the ingredients that are to be cooked the longest into the slow-cooker set on low. Most soups will be ready after 4 hours of cooking. Add those ingredients that need a short time to cook last, such as pasta, fresh vegetables and canned beans, using the original recipe as a guide. Then, turn the Crock-Pot to high and cook those ingredients according to the original recipe's instructions. For example, cook the pasta for 8 to 10 minutes, or until tender; the fresh vegetables for 5 to 10 minutes, or until crisp-tender; the canned beans for a minute or two, or until just heated through.

Squash Stew with Tomatoes, Garlic and Olives

SERVES 4

Tomatoes, garlic and olives give character to this mellow vegetarian stew of sweet winter squash. This comforting meal is characteristic of home-style Italian cooking.

1	tablespoon extra-virgin olive oil
½	cup chopped onions
2	cloves garlic, chopped
1½	pounds hubbard or butternut squash, peeled, seeded and cut into 1" cubes
1	cup nonfat tomato sauce
¼	cup vegetable stock or water
4	imported black olives, pitted and sliced in half
1	teaspoon chopped fresh sage
	Pinch of ground nutmeg
	Dash of hot-pepper sauce
1	cup cooked or canned white navy or cannellini beans, rinsed and drained
	Salt and black pepper

In a large, heavy saucepan over medium heat, heat the oil and sauté the onions and garlic for 2 minutes, or until soft.

Add the squash, tomato sauce, stock or water, olives, sage, nutmeg and hot-pepper sauce. Cover and simmer gently for 25 minutes, or until the squash is tender.

Add the beans; add salt and pepper to taste.

Preparation time: 10 minutes
Cooking time: 27 minutes

Chef's note: This stew keeps well in the refrigerator for up to 3 days. The flavors seem to mellow and become richer over time.

Per serving: 195 calories, 4.6 g. fat (20% of calories), 0.4 g. dietary fiber, no cholesterol, 216 mg. sodium.

ZUCCHINI ROSEMARY SOUP

SERVES 4

*P*iney rosemary gives a surprising edge to light, delicate-tasting zucchini. This summery soup is ready in minutes.

> 1 *teaspoon olive oil*
> ¾ *cup chopped onions*
> 1 *pound zucchini, sliced*
> 5 *cups vegetable stock*
> 2 *sprigs fresh rosemary*
> ½ *cup 2% fat milk*
> *Salt and black pepper*

In a large saucepan over medium-high heat, heat the oil and sauté the onions for 2 minutes, or until transparent and soft.

Add the zucchini; cook, turning occasionally, for 3 minutes. Add the stock and rosemary; simmer for 5 minutes, or until the zucchini is soft. Stir in the milk; add salt and pepper to taste. Remove and discard the rosemary before serving.

Preparation time: 5 minutes
Cooking time: 10 minutes

Chef's note: This light soup becomes a robust entrée when served with Bruschetta (page 30) or Crostini (page 31) that has been topped with fresh tomatoes, dusted with grated cheese and broiled until hot and bubbly.

Per serving: 61 calories, 1.9 g. fat (26% of calories), 1.7 g. dietary fiber, 2 mg. cholesterol, 606 mg. sodiu

MINTED PEA SOUP

SERVES 4

*M*inty and luscious, this lovely green soup is the essence of spring itself. It's wonderful hot or cold.

 4   *cups water*
12   *ounces fresh or frozen peas*
 2   *cups vegetable stock*
10   *ounces frozen chopped spinach*
 1   *tablespoon chopped fresh mint*
¼   *cup 2% fat milk*
     Salt and black pepper
     Fresh mint sprigs

In a large saucepan over high heat, bring the water to a boil. Add the peas and cook for 1 minute. Add the stock, spinach and mint; lower the heat and simmer for 20 minutes. Stir in the milk; add salt and pepper to taste.

Pour the soup into a blender and puree. Serve hot or cold; garnish with sprigs of fresh mint.

Preparation time: 5 minutes
Cooking time: 21 minutes

Chef's note: This may be made a day ahead and kept in the refrigerator overnight.

Per serving: 99 calories, 0.6 fat (5% of calories), 1 g. dietary fiber, 1 mg. cholesterol, 281 mg. sodium.

CHILLED CUCUMBER AND BASIL SOUP

SERVES 4

*A*n eye-catching soup of pale green garnished with bright radishes, this is delicious on a hot summer's day.

3   medium cucumbers, peeled, cut in half lengthwise, seeded and diced

2   tablespoons nonfat plain yogurt

1   tablespoon chopped fresh basil

1   teaspoon Dijon mustard

1   teaspoon lemon juice

    Salt and black pepper

10   red radishes, trimmed and thinly sliced

Put the cucumbers into a blender or a food processor fitted with the steel blade. Process for 1 minute. Add the yogurt, basil, mustard and lemon juice. Puree until completely smooth. Add salt and pepper to taste.

To serve, top the soup with the radishes.

Preparation time: 5 minutes

Per serving: 37 calories, 0.5 g. fat (10% of calories), 2.5 g. dietary fiber, 1 mg. cholesterol, 30 mg. sodium.

CHICK-PEA, LENTIL AND GREEN PEA STEW

SERVES 4

This glorious stew is a satisfying meatless main course. The dried legumes are loaded with protein and B vitamins.

1   medium onion, chopped
1   teaspoon olive oil
2   cups water
1   can (15 ounces) tomatoes, drained and chopped
½   cup lentils
½   cup sliced leeks (page 83)
2   cloves garlic, minced
2   sprigs fresh thyme
    Salt and black pepper
1   cup cooked or canned chick-peas, rinsed
    and drained
4   teaspoons chopped fresh mint
¾   cup pasta shells
¾   cup fresh or frozen peas

In a large soup pot over medium heat, sauté the onions in the oil for 3 to 5 minutes, or until the onions begin to brown.

Add the water, tomatoes, lentils, leeks, garlic and thyme; add salt and pepper to taste. Bring to a boil; reduce the heat and simmer for 25 minutes, or until the lentils begin to soften.

Add the chick-peas and mint and cook for 15 minutes.

Meanwhile, cook the pasta in a large pot of boiling water for 10 to 12 minutes, or until just tender; drain well.

Stir the peas into the stew; cook for 5 minutes, or until the peas are just cooked. Remove and discard the thyme. Serve over the pasta.

Preparation time: 10 minutes
Cooking time: 50 minutes

Per serving: 261 calories, 2.8 g. fat (9% of calories), 5.8 g. dietary fiber, no cholesterol, 159 mg. sodium.

Marinated Tuscan Steak (page 174)

Pork with Balsamic Vinegar and Pears (page 178)

Lamb Chops with Cucumbers and Tomatoes (page 179)

White Bean Soup with Basil and Tomatoes (page 184), Panzanella (page 216)

Milan-Style Turkey Stew (page 188)

Tomato-Orange Soup (page 193), Minted Pea Soup (page 198)

Roasted Red Pepper Pasta Salad (page 222)

Couscous Salad with Oranges and Olives (page 223)

CHAPTER 9

THE BEST
OF FIELD
AND GARDEN

SALADS OF GRAINS
AND GREENS

alads offer the cook infinite variety and surprise. Consider

the wealth of ingredients: tender and bitter greens,

brilliant vegetables, lean meats and poultry, fish and shellfish,

cooked pasta, couscous and rice, nuts and legumes, and those

Italian elixirs—extra-virgin olive oil and fine vinegar. It's the best

of Italy served up as antipasto, first course, last course or entrée.

Here is a collection of fine Italian salads, deliciously low in calories

and fat, ready in 20 minutes or less.

Basic Balsamic Vinaigrette

MAKES ½ CUP

This versatile vinaigrette is a must in the well-stocked Italian kitchen. Delicious on tossed greens or drizzled over sliced tomatoes, it also makes a wonderful marinade and a fine basting sauce while grilling or roasting chicken, turkey, pork or beef. It keeps indefinitely in the refrigerator. Bring to room temperature and whisk the ingredients or shake briskly in a small jar to distribute the oil before serving.

½ *cup balsamic vinegar*
1 *teaspoon extra-virgin olive oil*
½ *teaspoon honey*
½ *teaspoon Dijon mustard*
   Salt and black pepper

In a small bowl, whisk together the vinegar, oil, honey and mustard; add salt and pepper to taste.

Preparation time: 2 minutes

Chef's note: Try adding the following ingredients, alone or in combination, for variations on the basic theme:

• 2 tablespoons orange juice

• 2 tablespoons nonfat plain yogurt or sour cream

• 2 tablespoons tomato juice

• 1 teaspoon lemon juice

Per tablespoon: 22 calories, 0.6 g. fat (25% of calories), trace of dietary fiber, no cholesterol, 7 mg. sodium.

BALSAMIC VINEGAR

$\mathcal{A}$ staple for centuries, balsamic vinegar may be the most versatile and valuable ingredient in the low-fat pantry. This luscious, sweet-tart, aged and heady elixir transcends the term vinegar and is used more as a condiment than a partner to oil.

The name "balsamic" is derived from the word "balm"; earliest records show that it was used primarily for its curative, not culinary, prowess. Doctors prescribed it for everything from the head cold to a heart condition. It was thought to purify the air, aid in childbirth, lift the spirits, soothe sore throats. Today, it can doctor-up a low-fat, salt-free, low-calorie dish that needs "a dash of something," adding its deep, rich flavor to nonfat sauces and sparking up any number of dishes from antipasti to desserts. In Reggio and Modena, balsamic vinegar is used as a seasoning, often in lieu of salt, pepper or sugar. Here are a few suggestions for enjoying its unique flavor:

• Sprinkle over grilled meat, fish, poultry and vegetables instead of salt and pepper.

• Sprinkle over baked potatoes in place of sour cream or butter.

• Drizzle into bean and vegetables soups (especially those that taste flat).

• Sprinkle over polenta or toss with pasta before serving as a side dish.

• Sprinkle over poultry, meat or fish before broiling or baking.

• Add to nonfat mayonnaise before making a sandwich or potato salad.

• Add a little to nonfat yogurt for a light dip for raw vegetables.

• Sprinkle on sliced tomatoes and finish with chopped basil.

• Sprinkle over fresh berries or sliced pears for a luscious dessert.

SHRIMP AND FENNEL SALAD

SERVES 4

Crunchy, licorice-scented fennel is delicious with shrimp. This makes a hearty main-dish salad.

12 small red potatoes
⅓ cup red wine vinegar
2 tablespoons extra-virgin olive oil
¼ cup chopped scallions
1 tablespoon chopped fresh marjoram
1 clove garlic, minced
   Salt and black pepper
1 pound cooked shrimp
1 fennel bulb, cut into ¼" slices (page 100)
1 tomato, cut into 2" pieces
7 cups mixed greens (romaine, baby spinach, Bibb lettuce)
1 cup torn radicchio

Put the potatoes in a large saucepan and cover with water; bring to a boil. Reduce the heat and simmer for 15 minutes, or until tender. Drain and set aside.

In a large bowl, whisk together the vinegar and oil. Add the scallions, marjoram and garlic; add salt and pepper to taste. Reserve ¼ cup of the dressing; set aside. Add the potatoes, shrimp, fennel and tomatoes to the remaining dressing; toss gently to coat. Cover and chill for 15 minutes.

Toss the reserved ¼ cup dressing with the greens and radicchio. Serve the potato mixture on the greens and radicchio.

Preparation time: 10 minutes
Cooking time: 15 minutes
Chilling time: 15 minutes

Per serving: 352 calories, 8.6 g. fat (22% of calories), 2.6 g. dietary fiber, 221 mg. cholesterol, 331 mg. sodium.

Warm Scallop and Spinach Salad

*W*arm scallops are tossed with baby spinach, wilting the greens just enough to make them tender and flavorful. This makes an elegant meal served with crusty bread.

Dressing

2	*shallots, minced*
2	*tablespoons defatted chicken stock*
1	*tablespoon lemon juice*
2	*teaspoons extra-virgin olive oil*

Salad

2	*teaspoons extra-virgin olive oil*
1½	*pounds scallops*
2	*tablespoons defatted chicken stock*
1	*tablespoon balsamic vinegar*
8	*cups baby spinach leaves*

To make the dressing: In a small bowl, whisk together the the shallots, stock and lemon juice. Gradually whisk in the oil.

To make the salad: Heat the oil in a large no-stick frying pan over medium heat. Add the scallops and cook for 1 to 2 minutes, or until golden and just cooked through. Transfer the scallops to a platter. Add the stock and boil for 1 minute. Add the vinegar and boil until the liquid is reduced to a glaze, about 30 seconds. Return the scallops to the frying pan and stir to coat with the glaze.

Toss the spinach with enough dressing to coat the leaves; top with the scallops. Pass the remaining dressing.

Preparation time: 5 minutes
Cooking time: 4 minutes

Chef's note: The dressing may be made 1 day ahead and kept in the refrigerator. Whisk before using.

Per serving: 272 calories, 9.3 g. fat (31% of calories), 0.4 g. dietary fiber, 96 mg. cholesterol, 519 mg. sodium.

CHICKEN AND LENTIL SALAD

SERVES 4

This is a light yet substantial summer salad. Substitute leftover cooked chicken or turkey for the chicken breasts if you already have some on hand. This salad may be made a day ahead.

⅔ cup dried lentils (see note)

1 teaspoon plus 1 tablespoon extra-virgin olive oil

2 boneless, skinless chicken breast halves
(4 ounces each)

¼ cup orange juice

2 tablespoons nonfat plain yogurt

1 tablespoon grated orange rind

1 tablespoon chopped fresh rosemary

1 tomato, diced

½ cup cooked fresh or frozen peas

3 scallions, thinly sliced

¼ cup chopped fresh basil
Salt and black pepper

2 large bunches watercress, trimmed

In a large pot of boiling water, cook the lentils for 15 minutes, or until tender but firm. Drain well.

While the lentils are cooking, heat 1 teaspoon of the oil in a no-stick frying pan over medium-high heat. Sauté the chicken breasts for 5 minutes per side, or until golden brown. Put the chicken on a plate, cover with plastic wrap and refrigerate.

In a large bowl, whisk together the orange juice, yogurt, orange rind and rosemary. Whisk in the remaining 1 tablespoon oil. Add the cooked lentils, tomatoes, peas and scallions to the bowl and gently toss together.

Cut the chicken into ½″ cubes and add to the lentils along with any juices. Add the basil; add salt and pepper to taste. Mix well. Chill in the refrigerator for at least 20 minutes, or overnight.

Serve the salad on the watercress.

Preparation time: 10 minutes
Cooking time: 15 minutes
Chilling time: 20 minutes

Chef's note: For color and variety, try red lentils or the bright green organic lentils.

Per serving: 237 calories, 6.1 g. fat (22% of calories), 5.7 g. dietary fiber, 23 mg. cholesterol, 34 mg. sodium.

PEAR BALSAMIC SALAD

SERVES 4

*S*erve this very simple and elegant salad after the entrée. If you like, add a little Gorgonzola cheese on the side.

8   *leaves romaine lettuce*
2   *ripe pears, cored and thinly sliced*
     Balsamic vinegar
     Coarse black pepper

Line 4 individual salad plates or a large platter with the romaine. Arrange the pear slices over the romaine. Sprinkle with the vinegar. Lightly dust with the pepper.

Preparation time: 5 minutes

Per serving: 51 calories, 0.4 g. fat (6% of calories), 2.3 g. dietary fiber no cholesterol, 1 mg. sodium.

PANZANELLA

SERVES 4

*A*n unusual but classic Florentine bread salad, first recorded by Bronzino, a pupil of Michelangelo. It is a sunny combination of summer flavors.

Salad

1	*loaf stale rustic country bread (see note)*
4	*plum tomatoes, seeded and chopped*
¼	*cup chopped red onions*
¼	*cup chopped celery*
¼	*cup chopped scallions*
¼	*cup torn fresh basil leaves*
1	*tablespoon chopped fresh oregano*

Dressing

4	*teaspoons extra-virgin olive oil*
1	*tablespoon balsamic vinegar*
	Pinch of sugar
	Salt and black pepper

To make the salad: Cut the top off the loaf of bread and pull out all the bread inside, leaving the crust as a shell. Set the bread "bowl" aside. Sprinkle the bread pieces and the removed top crust with water and let stand for about 15 minutes, then squeeze out the moisture with a paper towel. Tear the bread into bite-size pieces.

In a medium bowl, toss together the bread, tomatoes, onions, celery, scallions, basil and oregano.

To make the dressing: In a small cup, whisk together the oil, vinegar and sugar. Pour over the salad and toss to coat. Add salt and pepper to taste.

Serve the salad in the bread "bowl" or on 4 individual salad plates lined with lettuce.

Preparation time: 10 minutes plus 15 minutes standing time

Chef's note: The bread must be sturdy, coarse and quite stale, or the salad will be soggy and tasteless.

Per serving: 388 calories, 9.5 g. fat (22% of calories), 4.5 g. dietary fiber, no cholesterol, 601 mg. sodium.

FENNEL AND TOMATO SALAD

SERVES 4

Crunchy, flavorful fennel is a classic partner to the sweet, light and tart tomatoes. Fennel is remarkably tasty and low in calories. The ancient Greeks called it *marathon*, from their verb *maraino*—to grow thin.

5   teaspoons red wine vinegar
1   teaspoon extra-virgin olive oil
1   large fennel bulb, cut into ½" slices (page 100)
4   medium tomatoes, cut into ½" slices
2   cups arugula leaves
    Salt and black pepper

In a large bowl, whisk together the vinegar and oil. Add the fennel and tomatoes; toss to coat. Add the arugula leaves and toss again. Add salt and pepper to taste.

Preparation time: 5 minutes

Per serving: 49 calories, 1.7 g. fat (27% of calories), 1.6 g. dietary fiber, no cholesterol, 55 mg. sodium.

DRESSING UP SALAD DAYS

*T*hose guilt-free tender lettuces, fresh bright vegetables and fragrant herbs that compose salads are naturally low in fat and calories; their dressings and accompaniments are often not.

Here are some fresh ideas for dressing up salads the low-fat way:

• **Smart Vinaigrette:** Most vinaigrette recipes call for 2 parts oil to 1 part acid (vinegar or lemon juice). To lower the amount of oil, replace half the amount called for with nonfat plain yogurt, nonfat buttermilk, nonfat sour cream or tomato juice.

• **The Right Mayo:** Use nonfat mayonnaise in all of your dressing and salad recipes; for a fresh, tart flavor, add a few tablespoons nonfat plain yogurt, too.

• **Zesting:** The rind of oranges, lemons and limes is loaded with aromatic oils that add lots of zip to dressings. Be sure to use only the *zest*, or top layer of the rind, grating just down to, but not into, the bitter white *pith*. If possible, grate over the ingredients you are using in order to capture the oil, too.

• **Vary the Vinegars:** Herb and fruit vinegars add wonderful flavors to dressings. Mix them with nonfat plain yogurt or non-fat sour cream for fat-free dressings. Specialty vinegars are available prebottled, or you can make your own: Combine 1 cup cut fruit or berries or 1 cup crushed herbs with 1 quart warmed vinegar. Cover and allow to steep 1 week, then strain off into bottles; seal or store in the refrigerator. These also make lovely gifts.

• **Go Greens:** The darker the greens in the salad bowl, the better. Dark greens—such as spinach, chard, collards, mustard greens, watercress and dandelion greens—have the most beta-carotene. They are all loaded with vitamin A and are very low in calories.

Fava Bean, Fennel and Apple Salad

SERVES 4

Fava beans are also called broad beans and horse beans because of their broad flat shape and dark color. They look like brown lima beans and have a very soft, velvety texture and dark, earthy flavor. This salad is an interesting combination of flavors—mellow, tart and crisp.

1 *large tart apple, chopped*

1 *cup canned fava beans, rinsed and drained (see note)*

1 *cup chopped celery or fennel (page 100)*

¼ *cup chopped red onions*

2 *tablespoons orange juice*

1 *tablespoon balsamic vinegar*

1 *teaspoon extra-virgin olive oil*

1 *teaspoon chopped fresh oregano*

1 *teaspoon grated orange rind*

Salt and black pepper

In a large bowl, combine the apples, fava beans, celery or fennel, onions, orange juice, vinegar, oil, oregano and orange rind; add salt and pepper to taste. Toss well. Cover the bowl and allow to marinate for 15 minutes.

Preparation time: 5 minutes plus 15 minutes marinating time

Chef's note: Fava beans can be purchased dried, cooked in cans and, infrequently, fresh. The dried beans need to be soaked in water, then cooked as you do other dried legumes (page 20). Fresh fava beans are sometimes available at farmers' markets and food co-ops. If you find them, choose those with pods that aren't bulging with beans, which indicates age. Remove the beans from the pods, then blanch in boiling water for 1 to 2 minutes to make removal of their tough skins easier. Cook as you would other fresh beans.

Per serving: 93 calories, 1.7 g. fat (15% of calories), 2.7 g. dietary fiber, no cholesterol, 156 mg. sodium.

LENTILS WITH MINTED CUCUMBERS
AND BASIL TOMATOES

SERVES 4

A cooling salad of garden-fresh vegetables arranged on a bed of lentils. It may be prepared ahead and kept chilled.

⅔ *cup lentils (see note)*
¼ *cup sliced scallions*
2 *tablespoons orange juice*
½ *cup nonfat plain yogurt*
2 *tablespoons lemon juice*
2 *tablespoons chopped fresh mint*
1 *tablespoon chopped fresh basil*
½ *cup peeled, seeded and chopped cucumbers*
 Salt and black pepper
 Lettuce leaves
½ *cup quartered cherry tomatoes*

In a large pot of boiling water, cook the lentils for 15 minutes, or until tender but firm. Drain; rinse in cold water. Drain well.

In a medium bowl, combine the lentils, scallions and orange juice; toss gently.

In another medium bowl, stir together the yogurt, lemon juice, mint and basil. Add the cucumbers; add salt and pepper to taste. Gently toss to coat the cucumbers with the yogurt mixture.

Arrange the lettuce leaves on a large platter or on 4 individual salad plates; top with the lentils. Spoon the cucumber mixture onto the lentils; top with the tomatoes. Sprinkle with additional chopped basil, if desired. Serve at room temperature or chilled.

Preparation time: 15 minutes
Cooking time: 15 minutes

Chef's note: Red lentils (actually an orange-pink color), available in health food stores and co-ops, make the most interesting base for this salad. They turn a salmon color when cooked.

Per serving: 145 calories, 0.5 g. fat (3% of calories), 5.5 g. dietary fiber, 1 mg. cholesterol, 26 mg. sodium.

ORANGE AND PEPPER SALAD

SERVES 4

A clean-tasting, colorful salad with lots of fresh herbs, this is especially nice served on a bed of fresh watercress after an entrée.

> 1 *sweet red pepper, cut into ½" pieces*
> 1 *small orange, peeled and cut into ¼" slices*
> 1 *imported black olive, pitted and chopped*
> ¼ *cup orange juice*
> 1 *tablespoon chopped fresh parsley*
> 1 *teaspoon chopped fresh rosemary*
> 1 *teaspoon honey*
> ½ *teaspoon grated orange rind*
> *Pinch of coarse black pepper*

In a medium bowl, combine the red peppers, oranges and olives.

In a small bowl, whisk together the orange juice, parsley, rosemary, honey, orange rind and black pepper. Pour the dressing over the salad and toss to coat.

Preparation time: 5 minutes

Chef's note: The salad may be made several hours ahead and held in the refrigerator.

Per serving: 41 calories, 0.3 g. fat (6% of calories), 1.4 g. dietary fiber, no cholesterol, 6 mg. sodium.

ROASTED RED PEPPER PASTA SALAD

SERVES 4

Sweet and slightly smoky roasted peppers are pureed into a pretty dressing for this light pasta salad.

10	*ounces angel hair pasta*
4	*sweet red peppers, roasted (page 124)*
¼	*cup white wine vinegar*
3	*tablespoons defatted chicken stock*
2	*tablespoons chopped fresh parsley*
1	*tablespoon lemon juice*
1	*tablespoon extra-virgin olive oil*
1	*tablespoon chopped fresh oregano*
1	*teaspoon grated lemon rind*
	Salt and black pepper

Cook the pasta in a large pot of boiling water for 4 to 6 minutes, or until just tender; drain well. Turn into a large bowl.

While the pasta is cooking, in a food processor fitted with the steel blade, puree the peppers, vinegar, stock, parsley, lemon juice, oil, oregano and lemon rind; add salt and pepper to taste. Pour over the pasta and toss to coat. Cover with plastic wrap and allow to marinate for at least 10 minutes before serving, or cover and refrigerate overnight.

Preparation time: 15 minutes
Cooking time: 6 minutes plus 10 minutes marinating time

Chef's note: This dish may also be served hot, sprinkled with grated Parmesan cheese. For a light entrée, add grilled, sautéed or poached chicken or turkey breasts.

Per serving: 299 calories, 5.5 g. fat (16% of calories), 1.3 g. dietary fiber, 62 mg. cholesterol, 36 mg. sodium.

Couscous Salad with Oranges and Olives

SERVES 4

*T*his zesty salad reflects the Moroccan influences so prevalent along the Mediterranean shores of Italy. This makes a refreshing side dish. It may be prepared several hours ahead.

¾ *cup couscous (see note)*
2 *tablespoons frozen orange juice concentrate, thawed*
1 *tablespoon lemon juice*
1 *teaspoon Dijon mustard*
1 *teaspoon extra-virgin olive oil*
1 *teaspoon chopped fresh oregano*
1 *teaspoon grated orange rind*
1 *cup boiling water*
1 *orange, peeled, sectioned and diced*
½ *cup chopped fresh parsley*
¼ *cup chopped scallions*
2 *tablespoons pitted and sliced imported black olives*
Salt and black pepper

In a large bowl, combine the couscous, juice concentrate, lemon juice, mustard, oil, oregano and orange rind. Stir in the boiling water. Cover and set aside for 5 minutes, or until the liquid has been absorbed.

Fluff the couscous mixture with a fork. Add the oranges, parsley, scallions and olives; toss to blend. Add salt and pepper to taste.

Preparation time: 10 minutes
Cooking time: 5 minutes

Chef's note: Couscous is granular semolina that is sold in the grain and pasta sections of the supermarket. It is ready in just 5 minutes and makes a quick stand-in for pasta and polenta.

Per serving: 181 calories, 1.9 g. fat (9% of calories), 6.8 g. dietary fiber, no cholesterol, 34 mg. sodium.

RISO ALL'INSALADA

SERVES 4

*R*ice and colorful vegetables combine to make a satisfying side dish or, with the addition of leftover chicken or canned tuna, a light meal. It may be made several hours ahead and travels well to an outdoor picnic or summer barbecue.

Rice Salad

2	*cups water*
1	*cup long-grain white rice*
1	*cup shredded carrots*
1	*cup chopped tomatoes*
¼	*cup drained capers*
¼	*cup chopped fresh Italian parsley*
2	*tablespoons chopped fresh basil*
1	*teaspoon grated orange rind*

Dressing

3	*tablespoons orange juice*
1	*tablespoon lemon juice*
1	*tablespoon white wine vinegar*
1	*teaspoon Dijon mustard*
1	*teaspoon extra-virgin olive oil*
	Salt and black pepper

To make the rice salad: In a large saucepan over high heat, bring the water to a boil . Stir in the rice and return the water to a boil. Reduce the heat to very low; cover and cook for 20 minutes, or until the rice is just tender but not too soft. Place the rice in a large colander and rinse under cold water; drain well. In a large bowl, combine the rice, carrots, tomatoes, capers, parsley, basil and orange rind.

To make the dressing: In a small bowl, whisk together the orange juice, lemon juice, vinegar and mustard. Whisk in the oil.

Pour the dressing over the salad and toss gently to combine. Add salt and pepper to taste.

Preparation time: 10 minutes
Cooking time: 20 minutes

Chef's note: To make this truly authentic, add 2 tablespoons chopped anchovies to the dressing.

Per serving: 226 calories, 1.8 g. fat (7% of calories), 2.1 g. dietary fiber, no cholesterol, 158 mg. sodium.

TUSCAN TUNA AND WHITE BEAN SALAD

SERVES 4

High in protein, low in fat, this makes a wonderful starter salad. With the addition of more tuna, it turns into a hearty main course.

2	*tablespoons lemon juice*
1	*tablespoon extra-virgin olive oil*
1¼	*teaspoons finely chopped fresh rosemary*
1	*teaspoon white wine vinegar*
1	*clove garlic, minced*
1	*can (15 ounces) white navy or cannellini beans, rinsed and drained*
1½	*cups chopped plum tomatoes*
1	*can (9 ounces) water-packed canned tuna, drained and flaked*
3	*tablespoons chopped fresh parsley*
	Salt and black pepper

In a large bowl, whisk together the lemon juice, oil, rosemary, vinegar and garlic. Add the beans, tomatoes, tuna and parsley. Toss gently to combine. Add salt and pepper to taste.

Preparation time: 10 minutes

Per serving: 172 calories, 5.3 g. fat (23% of calories), 7.2 g. dietary fiber, 15 mg. cholesterol, 355 mg. sodium.

ROASTED POTATO AND CHERRY TOMATO SALAD

*W*hile roasting, the potatoes become crispy and the tomatoes meltingly sweet. This is a robust salad, great for a hearty winter first course or side dish.

> 2 *cups diced potatoes*
> 2 *cups halved cherry tomatoes*
> 1 *tablespoon chopped fresh rosemary*
> *Coarse salt (see note)*
> *Lettuce leaves*
> 1 *tablespoon balsamic vinegar*

Coat a baking sheet with no-stick spray. Spread the potatoes and tomatoes over the prepared baking sheet and coat lightly with no-stick spray. Sprinkle with the rosemary and coarse salt.

Bake at 400° for 40 to 50 minutes, shaking the baking sheet once or twice to keep the vegetables from sticking, until the potatoes are browned and the tomatoes are very tender and have a dark sweet crust.

Arrange the lettuce leaves on a serving platter or on 4 individual salad plates. Sprinkle the roasted vegetables with the vinegar and serve on top of the lettuce leaves.

Preparation time: 10 minutes
Roasting time: 50 minutes

Chef's note: A little salt will help draw the moisture from the potatoes and tomatoes as well as add flavor. It may be omitted.

Per serving: 102 calories, 0.4 g. fat (3% of calories), 3.1 g. dietary fiber, no cholesterol, 13 mg. sodium.

BEET AND POTATO SALAD

SERVES 4

*M*agenta beets are especially beautiful in this bright salad served on lovely green escarole.

1¼	*pounds beets*
8	*ounces potatoes*
2	*tablespoons red wine vinegar*
1	*tablespoon extra-virgin olive oil*
2	*teaspoons chopped fresh Italian parsley*
¾	*teaspoon Dijon mustard*
¼	*teaspoon chopped fresh tarragon*
4	*cups torn escarole*
¾	*cup thinly sliced onions*
	Salt and black pepper

In separate pots, cover the beets and potatoes with water; bring both to a boil. Depending upon their size, cook the beets for 15 to 25 minutes and the potatoes for 15 to 20 minutes, or until just tender (easily pierced with a knife but still firm). Cool to room temperature. Peel and slice the beets; slice the potatoes. Set aside.

In a large bowl, whisk together the vinegar, oil, parsley, mustard and tarragon. Remove 1 tablespoon of the dressing and toss with the escarole; arrange on a serving platter or on 4 individual salad plates.

Add the beets, potatoes and onions to the remaining dressing and toss to combine. Add salt and pepper to taste. Arrange on the escarole.

Preparation time: 10 minutes
Cooking time: 25 minutes

Per serving: 131 calories, 3.7 g. fat (24% of calories), 1.1 g. dietary fiber, no cholesterol, 77 mg. sodium.

POTATO SALAD WITH GARLIC AND HERBS

SERVES 8

*I*n Italy, this is sometimes called "Russian Salad" because the Russians are known for growing potatoes.

Dressing

2	*tablespoons extra-virgin olive oil*
2	*tablespoons red wine vinegar*
2	*tablespoons chopped fresh marjoram*
2	*tablespoons chopped fresh parsley*
1	*tablespoon nonfat plain yogurt*
2	*cloves garlic, minced*
	Pinch of sugar

Salad

1	*pound new potatoes, quartered*
10	*carrots, thinly sliced*
8	*ounces green beans, ends removed, cut into 1" lengths*
1	*zucchini, cut into ½" chunks*
½	*cup chopped scallions*
2	*tablespoons chopped fresh basil*
	Salt and black pepper

To make the dressing: In a large salad bowl, whisk together the oil, vinegar, marjoram, parsley, yogurt, garlic and sugar.

To make the salad: Bring a large pot of water to a rolling boil. Add the potatoes and cook for 5 minutes. Add the carrots and beans and cook for 3 minutes. Add the zucchini and cook for 2 minutes, or until all the vegetables are just crisp-tender. Turn the vegetables into a large colander; drain well.

Add the hot vegetables, scallions and basil to the dressing; toss to combine. Add salt and pepper to taste. Chill for at least 10 minutes.

Preparation time: 10 minutes
Cooking time: 10 minutes
Chilling time: 10 minutes

Per serving: 134 calories, 3.7 g. fat (24% of calories), 3.8 g. dietary fiber, trace of cholesterol, 38 mg. sodium.

TOMATOES WITH BASIL AND MINT

SERVES 4

*V*ine-ripened tomatoes bursting with sweet flavor have no equals. This dish is a classic antipasto, served throughout Italy in *trattorias* as well as in homes. Often, slices of fresh buffalo mozzarella are sandwiched between the layers of sliced tomato. In the U.S., fresh buffalo mozzarella is available in Italian specialty stores. It is pale and very delicate with a mild, almost lightly sweet taste, much like fresh whole milk—far different from the packaged mozzarella. If it is available, try adding it to this dish.

> 2 *very ripe garden tomatoes, sliced ¼" to ½" thick*
>
> 1 *cup fresh basil leaves*
>
> ¼ *cup fresh mint leaves*
>
> 1 *tablespoon balsamic vinegar*
>
> ¼ *teaspoon extra-virgin olive oil*
>
> *Salt and black pepper*

· Arrange the tomatoes, basil and mint on a serving platter or on 4 individual salad plates.

In a small jar, shake the vinegar and oil until well mixed. Drizzle over the tomatoes. Add salt and pepper to taste. Let stand for about 10 minutes to allow the flavors to "marry."

Preparation time: 5 minutes plus 10 minutes standing time

Per serving: 22 calories, 0.5 g. fat (18% of calories), 0.8 g. dietary fiber, no cholesterol, 6 mg. sodium.

Sicilian Tuna and Potato Salad

SERVES 4

*A*lthough this recipe calls for canned tuna, if you have leftover cooked fresh tuna, by all means use it. The salad tastes better after the flavors have had a chance to blend awhile.

3   *new potatoes, boiled, peeled and thinly sliced*
1   *large tomato, cut into chunks*
1   *can (6 ounces) water-packed tuna, drained*
2   *tablespoons pitted and chopped imported black olives*
2   *tablespoons drained capers*
2   *tablespoons chopped scallions*
2   *tablespoons extra-virgin olive oil*
2   *tablespoons lemon juice*
1   *tablespoon chopped fresh basil*
    Salt and black pepper

In a large bowl, combine the potatoes, tomatoes, tuna, olives, capers and scallions.

In a cup, whisk together the oil and lemon juice. Pour over the tuna mixture and gently toss with the basil; add salt and pepper to taste.

Let marinate 20 minutes to 1 hour before serving.

Preparation time: 5 minutes plus 20 minutes marinating time

Per serving: 196 calories, 5 g. fat (22% of calories), 1.6 g. dietary fiber, 18 mg. cholesterol, 246 mg. sodium.

ROASTED EGGPLANT, PEPPER AND ONION SALAD

SERVES 4

*R*oasting intensifies the flavors of the vegetables in this colorful salad. It will keep several days, covered, in the refrigerator.

3	*small eggplants, cut in half lengthwise*
2	*large sweet red peppers*
1	*large green pepper*
2	*small onions, unpeeled and halved*
1	*tablespoon extra-virgin olive oil*
1	*tablespoon white wine vinegar*
1½	*teaspoons balsamic vinegar*
1	*teaspoon minced garlic*
¾	*teaspoon drained capers*
	Salt and black pepper
2	*tablespoons chopped fresh parsley*

Coat a baking sheet with no-stick spray. Place the eggplants, red peppers, green pepper and onions on the prepared sheet. Roast at 400°, turning the vegetables once, for 20 to 30 minutes, or until they are soft and beginning to brown.

Wrap the red peppers and green pepper in damp paper towels and allow to cool for about 5 minutes. Peel, halve, remove the seeds and stems and cut into 1″ strips. Cut the eggplants into 1″ strips. Peel and dice the onions.

In a large bowl, whisk together the oil, wine vinegar, balsamic vinegar, garlic and capers. Add the roasted vegetables and gently toss to coat. Add salt and black pepper to taste. Sprinkle with the parsley. Serve at room temperature or chilled.

Preparation time: 5 minutes
Baking time: 30 minutes plus 5 minutes cooling time

Per serving: 103 calories, 3.9 g. fat (31% of calories), 1.6 g. dietary fiber, no cholesterol, 15 mg. sodium.

GREEN AND WHITE BEAN SALAD

SERVES 4

This festive, satisfying salad makes a lovely first course or a light lunch. It will keep several days, covered, in the refrigerator.

8   ounces green beans

2¾ cups canned white navy or cannellini beans, rinsed and drained

¾   cup canned sweet red peppers, drained

¾   cup tomatoes cut into 1" cubes

5   teaspoons olive oil

1   tablespoon lemon juice

2   scallions, thinly sliced

1¾ teaspoons chopped fresh thyme

1½ teaspoons chopped fresh Italian parsley

Salt and black pepper

In a medium saucepan, blanch the green beans in rapidly boiling water for 5 minutes, or until bright green and crisp-tender. Drain; immediately plunge into ice water. Drain and place in a large bowl. Add the white beans, peppers and tomatoes.

In a small bowl, whisk together the oil and lemon juice; drizzle over the vegetables. Add the scallions, thyme and parsley; mix well. Add salt and pepper to taste.

Preparation time: 10 minutes
Cooking time: 5 minutes

Chef's note: White navy or cannellini beans add flavor and protein to this dish. The canned variety work nicely, or you may choose to soak and cook beans from scratch. Cannellini beans are just a little bigger than white navy beans.

Per serving: 169 calories, 6.3 g. fat (26% of calories), 9.2 g. dietary fiber, no cholesterol, 256 mg. sodium.

COUNTRY-STYLE BREADS

In Italy, man or woman could easily (and happily) live by bread alone. There the breads are varied and whimsical, nourishing and delicious. Pizzas are created of thin, moist, flavorful dough, topped frugally and simply with the finest cheeses and freshest vegetables. Rustic round and long thin loaves are hollowed out and filled with savory vegetable and meat stuffings, wrapped in butcher paper and sliced into thick portions for quick lunches and picnic fare. Such light and casual food makes healthy living easy, especially for the cook.

QUICK PIZZA DOUGH

*T*hese quick-rising crusts are ready in less than half the time it takes traditional crusts. The rye flour and cornmeal give the dough a wholesome flavor and chewy texture.

1¾   *cups unbleached flour*
1   *tablespoon rye flour*
1   *tablespoon cornmeal*
1   *package quick-rise yeast*
½   *teaspoon salt*
½   *teaspoon sugar*
¾   *cup water*
1½   *teaspoons olive oil*

Put the unbleached flour, rye flour, cornmeal, yeast, salt and sugar in a food processor fitted with the steel blade; combine with on/off pulses.

In a small saucepan, mix the water with the oil. Heat until warm to the touch (125° to 130°). With the motor running, gradually add the hot liquid through the feed tube. Process until the dough forms a ball, then process for 1 minute to knead the dough. Turn the dough out onto a lightly floured surface; cover with plastic wrap and let rest for 10 minutes before shaping into crusts.

Preparation time: 5 minutes plus 10 minutes resting time

Chef's note: The dough can be made ahead, punched down, enclosed in a large plastic bag and stored in the refrigerator overnight. Bring to room temperature before shaping into crusts.

Per crust: 237 calories, 2.4 g. fat (9% of calories), 2.5 g. dietary fiber, no cholesterol, 268 mg sodium.

PIZZA MARGUERITA

*L*egend has it that this pizza was a favorite of Margaret of Savoy; the garlic was left out so that its odor wouldn't linger on the Queen's breath.

> *1* recipe Quick Pizza Dough (page 234)
> *Cornmeal*
> *1* cup nonfat spaghetti sauce
> *1* cup shredded part-skim mozzarella cheese
> *Salt and black pepper*
> *½* cup chopped fresh basil
> *¼* cup grated Parmesan cheese

Coat a baking sheet with no-stick spray; place on the lowest rack of the oven. Preheat the oven to 500°.

Dust another baking sheet with cornmeal. Divide the dough into 4 pieces; form into 6″ rounds. Place the rounds on the cornmeal-dusted baking sheet.

Spread the sauce evenly over the rounds to within ½″ of the edges. Sprinkle the mozzarella evenly over the rounds; add salt and pepper to taste. Distribute the basil evenly over the rounds; sprinkle with the Parmesan.

Carefully slide the pizzas onto the prepared, preheated baking sheet and bake for 10 to 14 minutes, or until the bottoms are crisp and brown.

Preparation time: 10 minutes
Baking time: 14 minutes

Per pizza: 356 calories, 8.8 g. fat (22% of calories), 3.4 g. dietary fiber, 21 mg. cholesterol, 887 mg. sodium.

MUSHROOM AND SAGE PIZZAS

MAKES 4 (6″) PIZZAS

*H*ere, the earthy flavor of mushrooms is nicely balanced with pungent sage.

1½ *tablespoons olive oil*
8 *ounces mushrooms, sliced*
1 *cup sliced onions*
   Salt and black pepper
1 *recipe Quick Pizza Dough (page 234)*
   Cornmeal
½ *cup shredded part-skim mozzarella cheese*
¼ *cup grated Parmesan cheese*
4 *teaspoons chopped fresh sage*

In a small no-stick frying pan, heat the oil over medium heat. Add the mushrooms and onions and sauté for 3 minutes, or until tender. Let cool. Add salt and pepper to taste.

Coat a baking sheet with no-stick spray; place on the lowest rack of the oven. Preheat the oven to 500°. Dust another baking sheet with cornmeal. Divide the dough into 4 pieces; form into 6″ rounds. Place the rounds on the cornmeal-dusted baking sheet.

Sprinkle the mozzarella evenly over the rounds of dough. Divide the mushroom-onion mixture among the rounds. Sprinkle with the Parmesan and sage.

Carefully slide the pizzas onto the prepared, preheated baking sheet. Bake for 10 to 14 minutes, or until the bottoms are crisp and brown.

Preparation time: 10 minutes
Cooking time: 3 minutes
Baking time: 14 minutes

Per pizza: 376 calories, 11.9 g. fat (28% of calories), 3.1 g. dietary fiber, 13 mg. cholesterol, 453 mg. sodium.

PIZZA PUTTANESCA

MAKES 4 (6″) PIZZAS

*T*his flavorful pizza borrows from the bold *puttanesca* sauce of capers, anchovies and chilies.

> 1 recipe Quick Pizza Dough (page 234)
> Cornmeal
> 2 cups thinly sliced plum tomatoes
> 1 can (10 ounces) clams, drained
> ¼ cup drained capers
> ¼ cup chopped fresh oregano
> 2 tablespoons rinsed and chopped anchovies
> 2 tablespoons pitted and chopped imported black olives
> ½ teaspoon red-pepper flakes
> 2 tablespoons grated Parmesan cheese

Coat a baking sheet with no-stick spray; place on the lowest rack of the oven. Preheat the oven to 500°.

Dust another baking sheet with cornmeal. Divide the dough into 4 pieces; form into 6″ rounds. Place the rounds on the cornmeal-dusted baking sheet.

Arrange the tomatoes, clams, capers, oregano, anchovies, olives and pepper flakes evenly over the rounds. Sprinkle with the Parmesan.

Carefully slide the pizzas onto the prepared, preheated baking sheet. Bake for 12 to 14 minutes, or until the bottoms are crisp and brown.

Preparation time: 10 minutes
Baking time: 14 minutes

Per pizza: 416 calories, 6 g. fat (13% of calories), 3.6 g. dietary fiber, 52 mg. cholesterol, 621 mg. sodium.

ARTICHOKE AND LEEK PIZZAS

MAKES 4 (6″) PIZZAS

*N*ative to the Mediterranean countries, the leek has been prized by gourmets for centuries. This recipe blends the leek's mellow flavor with artichoke hearts.

> 1 *ounce pancetta or 1 strip bacon, chopped*
> ½ *onion, finely chopped*
> 1 *can (14 ounces) artichoke hearts, drained and coarsely chopped*
> 1 *large leek, thinly sliced (page 83)*
> *Salt and black pepper*
> *Cornmeal*
> 1 *recipe Quick Pizza Dough (page 234)*
> ¼ *cup shredded part-skim mozzarella cheese*
> 2 *tablespoons grated Parmesan cheese*

Coat a baking sheet with no-stick spray; place on the lowest rack of the oven. Preheat the oven to 500°.

In a large no-stick frying pan, cook the pancetta or bacon for 3 minutes, or until golden; drain on paper towels. Blot the fat from the pan with a paper towel. Add the onions to the pan and cook, stirring occasionally, for 3 minutes, or until soft but not brown. Add the artichokes and stir to mix well. Add the leeks and stir in the pancetta or bacon. Add salt and pepper to taste.

Dust another baking sheet with cornmeal. Divide the dough into 4 pieces; form into 6″ rounds. Place the rounds on the cornmeal-dusted baking sheet.

Distribute the artichoke mixture evenly over the rounds. Sprinkle evenly with the mozzarella and Parmesan.

Carefully slide the pizzas onto the prepared, preheated baking sheet. Bake for 10 to 12 minutes, or until the bottoms are crisp and brown.

Preparation time: 10 minutes
Cooking time: 7 minutes
Baking time: 12 minutes

Per pizza: 354 calories, 5.6 g. fat (14% of calories), 3.4 g. dietary fiber, 8 mg. cholesterol, 486 mg. sodium.

TOP PIZZAS

*M*aking wholesome pizzas at home is much faster than waiting for delivery. Use no-fat pita bread, packaged pizza shells or bread shells for the base and top with your favorite nonfat pizza or pasta sauce, low-fat cheeses and any number of healthful ingredients. Some bakeries even sell fresh home-style pizza crusts in whole-wheat and white varieties. These may be kept frozen until ready to use. Here are suggestions for topping off healthful pizzas:

TOP TOPPINGS

• Roasted vegetables tossed with a little balsamic vinegar.

• Cooked and drained frozen artichoke hearts sprinkled with grated Parmesan cheese.

• Cubes of cooked chicken or turkey tossed with no-fat pizza sauce and topped with shredded low-fat mozzarella cheese.

• Cooked shrimp, clams and oysters with fresh chopped peppers, onions and garlic.

• Chopped fresh tomatoes tossed with chopped fresh oregano and shredded mozzarella; sprinkle with chopped fresh basil just as it comes from the oven.

• Blanched fresh asparagus tossed with grated Parmesan cheese.

BAKING TIMES

Pizza baking times will vary. Most of these quick pizzas are ready after baking at 350° for 10 to 12 minutes. Pizzas made from the Quick Pizza Dough (page 234) need to be baked at 500° for 10 to 14 minutes. Pizza is ready when all the ingredients are hot throughout and any cheese is bubbly.

PITA PIZZAS

When using pita bread as a base, split the pita along its seam and toast at 350° for 5 minutes, or until it starts to brown; then add any sauce or topping. This will keep the pita "crust" from becoming too soft.

RICE CRUSTS

Make wholesome crusts from cooked brown or white rice. Press the rice into a pie plate and bake for 10 minutes at 350°, or until it becomes firm; then add the toppings and bake.

GREENGROCER'S PIZZAS

MAKES 4 (6″) PIZZAS

Pizza dell Ortolano, the greengrocer's special, is a fresh, crispy salad served up in a pizza shell. Popular in *trattorias* throughout Italy and across the U.S., its success relies on a variety of fresh ingredients and the chef's imagination.

Pizza Crusts

Cornmeal

1 *recipe Quick Pizza Dough (page 234)*

¼ *cup shredded provolone cheese*

Salad Topping

2 *tablespoons extra-virgin olive oil*

2 *teaspoons chopped fresh oregano*

1 *teaspoon balsamic vinegar*

1 *teaspoon fresh lemon juice*

2 *plum tomatoes, cubed*

2 *tablespoons chopped red onions*

2 *tablespoons chopped fresh basil*

Salt and black pepper

6 *cups mixed lettuce (see note)*

To make the pizza crusts: Coat a baking sheet with no-stick spray; place on the lowest rack of the oven. Preheat the oven to 500°.

Dust another baking sheet with cornmeal. Divide the dough into 4 pieces; form into 6″ rounds.

Place the rounds on the cornmeal-dusted baking sheet. Prick the dough deeply all over with a fork.

Carefully slide the crusts onto the prepared, preheated baking sheet. Bake for 9 or 10 minutes, or until they turn golden brown. Remove the crusts from the oven. Sprinkle the provolone evenly over the crusts, except for the edges. Return the crusts to the oven and bake for 1 to 2 minutes, or until the crusts are brown and the cheese melts. Remove the crusts from the oven.

To make the salad topping: While the crusts are baking, in a large bowl whisk together the oil, oregano, vinegar and lemon juice. Add the tomatoes, onions and basil; add salt and pepper to taste. Set aside.

Just before serving, add the lettuce to the tomato mixture and toss to coat the lettuce with the oil and vinegar. Distribute the salad evenly over the crusts.

Preparation time: 10 minutes
Baking time: 12 minutes

Chef's note: Use a combination of lettuces—red leaf, green leaf, radicchio—whatever looks fresh and colorful.

Per pizza: 354 calories, 11.5 g. fat (29% of calories), 4.5 g. dietary fiber, 5 mg. cholesterol, 344 mg. sodium.

Roasted Vegetable Calzones

MAKES 4 (3″) CALZONES

*C*alzones, serving-size pizza turnovers, originated in Naples. These hearty, low-fat *calzones* may be assembled ahead of time. They are perfect for a summer picnic.

- 2 teaspoons olive oil
- 1 sweet red pepper, thinly sliced
- 1 zucchini, thinly sliced
- 1 yellow summer squash, thinly sliced
- 1 small onion, thinly sliced
- 2 cloves garlic, minced
  Salt and black pepper
- 1 recipe Quick Pizza Dough (page 234)
  Cornmeal
- 2 tablespoons crumbled Gorgonzola cheese
- 2 tablespoons shredded part-skim mozzarella cheese

In a large ovenproof frying pan over medium heat, heat the oil and sauté the red peppers, zucchini, squash, onions and garlic for 2 minutes, or until tender. Put the pan in the oven and bake at 500° for 10 minutes, stirring the vegetables occasionally. Remove from the oven; add salt and black pepper to taste. Allow to cool while shaping the dough. Do not turn off the oven.

Coat a baking sheet with no-stick spray; place on the lowest rack of the oven.

Dust another baking sheet with cornmeal. Divide the dough into 4 pieces; form into 7″ rounds. Place the rounds on the cornmeal-dusted baking sheet.

Spoon the vegetable mixture evenly over half of each round. Sprinkle the Gorgonzola and mozzarella evenly over the vegetable mixture. Brush the outside edges of the rounds with water; fold the dough over the vegetables, pinching the edges to seal.

Carefully slide the *calzones* onto the prepared, preheated baking sheet. Bake for 10 to 12 minutes, or until crisp and brown.

Preparation time: 10 minutes
Cooking time: 2 minutes
Baking time: 22 minutes

Chef's note: No time for pizza dough? Simply use this delicious filling in a hollowed-out loaf of round Italian bread. Wrap the loaf in aluminum foil and bake at 350° for 10 minutes, or until the filling is hot and bubbly. To serve, slice into wedges.

Per calzone: 302 calories, 6.4 g. fat (19% of calories), 3.9 g. dietary fiber, 5 mg. cholesterol, 337 mg. sodium.

FOCACCIA

MAKES 1 (9″) ROUND LOAF; 8 WEDGES

*F*ocaccia is the flat bread of Italy, traditionally made on bread-baking day as a treat for the children. Before being baked in a hot oven, the dough is often deeply fingerprinted to hold herbs, olive oil and any number of other ingredients. Focaccia is served in place of bread or as a one-dish meal (depending on how it is topped). It is served warm or at room temperature but never sizzling hot like pizza.

> 1   *cup warm water (130°)*
> 1   *package quick-rise yeast*
> 1   *teaspoon honey*
> 2½–3   *cups unbleached flour*
> 3   *tablespoons extra-virgin olive oil*
> 1   *tablespoon chopped fresh rosemary*
> 1   *tablespoon chopped fresh sage*
> 1½   *teaspoons salt*

In a large bowl, stir together the water, yeast and honey. Add 1 cup of the flour. Beat well with a wire whisk until smooth and creamy. Let rest at room temperature for 5 minutes.

Add 2 tablespoons of the oil, rosemary, sage, salt and a second cup of the flour. Whisk hard for 3 minutes or until smooth. Add the remaining ½ to 1 cup flour a little at a time with a wooden spoon until a soft, sticky dough is formed.

Turn the dough out onto a lightly floured surface and knead lightly for 3 minutes.

Coat a baking sheet with no-stick spray. Place the dough on the baking sheet and shape into a 9″ round that's 1″ thick. Brush with the remaining 1 tablespoon oil.

Bake at 400° for 20 to 25 minutes, or until golden brown.

Preparation time: 10 minutes plus 5 minutes resting time
Baking time: 25 minutes

Per wedge: 129 calories, 3.7 g. fat (26% of calories), 0.9 g. dietary fiber, no cholesterol, 89 mg. sodium.

FOCACCIA WITH MARINATED VEGETABLES

SERVES 4

*B*right vegetables and mellow cheese are sandwiched in focaccia, which absorbs the flavors of their marinade. This is perfect to take on a hike, a bicycle ride or a picnic.

1 *sweet red pepper, roasted (page 124) or 1 jar (3½ ounces) roasted red peppers, drained*

3 *cups thickly sliced white mushrooms*

1 *tablespoon pitted and chopped imported black olives*

1 *teaspoon drained capers*

2 *tablespoons balsamic vinegar*

1 *tablespoon extra-virgin olive oil*

1 *clove garlic, minced*
  Salt and black pepper

1 *purchased or homemade focaccia (page 246)*

2 *ounces part-skim mozzarella cheese, thinly sliced*

Slice the red peppers into ¼″ strips. In a large bowl, combine the red peppers, mushrooms, olives and capers.

In a small cup, whisk together the vinegar, oil and garlic. Pour over the vegetables and toss to coat. Add salt and black pepper to taste.

Cut the focaccia into quarters; slice each quarter horizontally. Layer the bottom slices with the vegetable mixture and mozzarella; top with the remaining focaccia slices.

Preparation time: 10 minutes

Per serving: 476 calories, 16.3 g. fat (31% of calories), 3.7 g. dietary fiber, 5 mg. cholesterol, 363 mg. sodium.

Peasant Bread

*A*ppropriately named, this is a basic and uncomplicated bread. Cornmeal and whole-wheat flour add an authentic flavor and texture.

Sponge

1	cup warm water (130°)
½	cup cornmeal
½	cup whole-wheat flour
½	cup unbleached flour
1	package quick-rise yeast
1	teaspoon honey

Dough

1	cup nonfat buttermilk
3–3½	cups unbleached flour
1	tablespoon salt
2	teaspoons olive oil

To make the sponge: In a large bowl, whisk together the water, cornmeal, whole-wheat flour, unbleached flour, yeast and honey. Beat hard until creamy and smooth. Cover loosely with plastic wrap and allow to rest at room temperature for 5 minutes.

To make the dough: Add the buttermilk, 1 cup of the flour, salt and oil to the sponge and beat until smooth. Add the remaining 2 to 2½ cups flour ½ cup at a time until a soft dough that gathers into a ball is formed. Coat a medium bowl with no-stick spray. Turn the dough into the prepared bowl. Cover with plastic wrap and let rise in a warm place for 30 minutes.

To shape the loaves, gently deflate the dough with your fist. Turn out onto a lightly floured surface and form into two oblong loaves; roll lightly in flour. Sprinkle a baking sheet with cornmeal and place the loaves on it. Let rise for 10 minutes, or until puffy. Slash the tops of the loaves with a serrated knife. Bake at 400° for 30 to 35 minutes, or until the loaves are golden brown and sound hollow when tapped.

Preparation time: 10 minutes plus 5 minutes resting time and 40 minutes rising time
Baking time: 35 minutes

Per slice: 92 calories, 0.7 g. fat (7% of calories), 1.2 g. dietary fiber, no cholesterol, 279 mg. sodium.

Peppery Rosemary Quick Bread

*F*ast and fragrant, these loaves need no time to rise, and they bake in 30 minutes. They are so flavorful the slices need no butter.

1¾ cups whole-wheat flour
1½ cups unbleached flour
2 tablespoons brown sugar
2 teaspoons baking powder
1 teaspoon baking soda
½ teaspoon salt
1 teaspoon freshly ground black pepper (see note)
1½ cups nonfat buttermilk
2 tablespoons olive oil
2 tablespoons chopped fresh rosemary

In a large mixing bowl, combine the whole-wheat flour, unbleached flour, brown sugar, baking powder, baking soda, salt and pepper.

In a small bowl, stir together the buttermilk, oil and rosemary. Make a well in the center of the dry ingredients and add the buttermilk mixture. Stir with a wooden spoon until the dough is moistened and comes together. Do not overmix.

Divide the dough in half. Pat each half into a 7″ round and place on a lightly oiled baking sheet. Slash a cross about ½″ deep into the tops of the loaves with a sharp knife, and dust the tops lightly with some additional flour.

Bake at 375° for 30 minutes, or until a toothpick inserted in the center comes out clean. Cool the loaves on wire racks for 10 minutes before serving.

Preparation time: 15 minutes
Baking time: 30 minutes
Cooling time: 10 minutes

Chef's notes: It is important in this recipe to use freshly ground black pepper for the most flavor.

These loaves may be made ahead and stored, well wrapped, in the freezer for up to 2 months. Warm the frozen loaves, wrapped in foil, at 325° for 1 hour.

Per slice: 118 calories, 2.1 g. fat (16% of calories), 2 g. dietary fiber, no cholesterol, 185 mg. sodium.

CHICKEN AND GOAT CHEESE SANDWICHES

SERVES 4

*T*his sensational blend of flavors is a delicious twist on the chicken salad sandwich.

- 4 *ounces goat cheese*
- 1 *tablespoon chopped fresh rosemary*
- 1 *tablespoon pine nuts, toasted (page 71)*
- 2 *boneless, skinless chicken breasts (4 ounces each)*
- 8 *slices sourdough bread*
- 4 *large tomato slices*
- 1 *cup mixed greens*

In a food processor fitted with the steel blade, process the goat cheese, rosemary and pine nuts until well combined but still chunky.

Heat a large no-stick frying pan over medium-high heat. Sauté the chicken for 2 to 3 minutes per side, or until the meat is no longer pink when cut with a knife. Remove from the pan and slice thinly.

Spread the goat cheese mixture evenly over 4 of the bread slices. Top with the chicken, tomatoes, greens and remaining bread. Cut in half to serve.

Preparation time: 10 minutes
Cooking time: 6 minutes

Per serving: 300 calories, 10.1 g. fat (31% of calories), 2 g. dietary fiber, 71 mg. cholesterol, 404 mg. sodium.

SHRIMP, ARTICHOKE
AND SUN-DRIED TOMATO SANDWICHES

SERVES 4

*T*hese pocket-pita sandwiches are pretty and light, wonderful for casual entertaining.

12	*medium shrimp, peeled and deveined*
1	*small tomato, cut into large chunks*
½	*cup frozen artichokes, thawed and quartered*
12	*sun-dried tomato halves, reconstituted, patted dry and cut into slivers (page 72)*
2	*tablespoons pitted and coarsely chopped imported black olives*
1	*tablespoon balsamic vinegar*
1	*tablespoon extra-virgin olive oil*
	Salt and black pepper
8	*pita breads, sliced in half*
	Fresh basil sprigs

Cook the shrimp in boiling water for 2 minutes, or until they turn pink. Drain; rinse with cold water. Cut in half lengthwise.

In a large bowl, combine the shrimp, tomatoes, artichokes, sun-dried tomatoes and olives.

In a small cup, whisk together the vinegar and oil. Pour over the shrimp mixture and toss to coat. Add salt and pepper to taste.

Spoon the mixture into the pita bread halves. Tuck a few basil sprigs into each sandwich for garnish. Secure with toothpicks.

Preparation time: 10 minutes

Chef's note: In Italy, the artichokes are small and tender and have no thorny inner choke. Unfortunately, artichokes in the U.S. are grown for size (not quality). By the time they are in our stores, they have become tough and woody. Thawed frozen artichoke hearts make an acceptable substitute for Italian artichokes.

Per serving: 337 calories, 5.3 g. fat (14% of calories), 2.9 g. dietary fiber, 33 mg. cholesterol, 526 mg. sodium.

PORTOBELLO AND TOMATO SANDWICHES

*G*rilled, dark and meaty-tasting portobello mushrooms add richness to these vegetarian sandwiches.

3	*tablespoons nonfat mayonnaise*
1	*tablespoon yogurt cheese (page 28)* *or nonfat plain yogurt*
1	*tablespoon finely chopped fresh rosemary*
2	*teaspoons orange juice*
½	*teaspoon grated orange rind*
2	*teaspoons virgin olive oil*
6	*ounces portobello mushrooms, sliced ½" thick* *Salt and black pepper*
8	*slices Italian bread*
4	*lettuce leaves*
2	*tomatoes, sliced*
½	*cup coarsely chopped fresh basil*

In a small bowl, combine the mayonnaise, yogurt cheese or yogurt, rosemary, orange juice and orange rind.

Brush the oil over the cut sides of the mushrooms. Grill or broil 5″ from the heat for 3 to 4 minutes per side, or until dark and tender. Add salt and pepper to taste.

Spread 4 slices of the bread evenly with the mayonnaise mixture. Top with the lettuce, mushrooms, tomatoes, basil and remaining bread. Cut in half and serve right away.

Preparation time: 10 minutes
Grilling time: 8 minutes

Per serving: 231 calories, 2.7 g. fat (11% of calories), 3.2 g. dietary fiber, trace of cholesterol, 459 mg. sodium.

SHRIMP CAESAR SANDWICH

SERVES 4

A creative twist on the incredibly popular Caesar salad, this luscious sandwich is great for casual entertaining.

12	*medium shrimp, peeled and deveined*
1	*small loaf unsliced Italian bread or baguette*
½	*cup nonfat plain yogurt*
1	*teaspoon lemon juice*
1	*teaspoon balsamic vinegar*
1	*teaspoon Dijon mustard*
½	*teaspoon Worcestershire sauce*
1	*clove garlic, minced*
¼	*cup grated Parmesan cheese*
	Salt and black pepper
1	*small head romaine, torn into pieces*
¼	*cup finely chopped red onions*

Cook the shrimp in boiling water for 2 minutes, or until they turn pink. Drain; rinse with cold water. Cut in half lengthwise.

Slice the loaf in half lengthwise and trim off the ends. Scoop out the inside of each half, leaving ½″ shells (see note).

In a medium bowl, whisk together the yogurt, lemon juice, vinegar, mustard, Worcestershire, garlic and 2 tablespoons of the Parmesan. Add salt and pepper to taste.

Toss the romaine and onions with the yogurt mixture. Put into the bottom half of the bread shell. Top with the shrimp, remaining 2 tablespoons Parmesan and top shell. Cut crosswise into 4 sandwiches.

Preparation time: 5 minutes
Cooking time: 2 minutes

Chef's note: Reserve the inside of the loaf to make fresh or toasted bread crumbs (page 14).

Per serving: 334 calories, 2.6 g. fat (7% of calories), 4.4 g. dietary fiber, 38 mg. cholesterol, 633 mg. sodium.

BROILED TOMATO PESTO SANDWICHES

SERVES 4

*L*ots of fresh tomatoes dressed in a zesty pesto and ricotta blend transform English muffins into terrific summer sandwiches.

 1   *cup nonfat ricotta cheese*
 2   *tablespoons pesto (see note)*
 1   *clove garlic, minced*
     Salt and black pepper
 4   *English muffins, split*
 1   *large tomato, thinly sliced*

In a small bowl, combine the ricotta, pesto and garlic; add salt and pepper to taste. Set aside.

Place the muffins, cut side up, on a baking sheet; broil about 5″ from the heat for 1 to 2 minutes, or until light brown. Distribute the ricotta mixture evenly among the muffin halves and top with a few slices of tomato. Return to the oven and broil for 1 to 2 minutes, or until hot.

Preparation time: 5 minutes
Broiling time: 4 minutes

Chef's note: You may use packaged pesto or make your own following the recipe for Basil Broccoli Pesto (page 67), which is far lower in fat and calories.

Per serving: 186 calories, 1.2 g. fat (6% of calories), 1.7 g. dietary fiber, 6 mg. cholesterol, 497 mg. sodium.

Mediterranean Summer Sandwiches

Serves 4

This is a heady blend of fresh herbs, vegetables and assertive goat cheese. Serve the sandwiches hot or at room temperature.

1   teaspoon extra-virgin olive oil
¼   cup chopped onions
1   medium Japanese eggplant (or small eggplant), cut in half lengthwise, then sliced ¾" thick
1   sweet red pepper, cut into 1" pieces
1   small yellow summer squash, cut into 1" pieces
1   small zucchini, cut into 1" pieces
2   cloves garlic, minced
¼   cup red wine or defatted chicken stock
2   teaspoons chopped fresh oregano
8   cherry tomatoes, quartered
2   tablespoons chopped fresh basil
     Salt and black pepper
4   ounces goat cheese
8   slices whole-wheat bread

In a large no-stick frying pan over medium heat, heat the oil and sauté the onions for 5 minutes, or until soft. Add the eggplant, red peppers, squash, zucchini and garlic. Sauté for 5 minutes, or until the eggplant and peppers are just tender. Add the wine or stock and oregano and cook for 5 minutes, or until the liquid evaporates. Add the tomatoes and basil. Add salt and pepper to taste.

Remove the pan from the heat. Spread the goat cheese evenly over each slice of bread. Top 4 of the slices with the vegetable mixture and top with the remaining bread. Cut each sandwich in half to serve.

Preparation time: 10 minutes
Cooking time: 15 minutes

Per serving: 249 calories, 8.7 g. fat (30% of calories), 7.3 g. dietary fiber, 25 mg. cholesterol, 418 mg. sodium.

Beet and Potato Salad (page 227)

Artichoke and Leek Pizzas (page 238)

Greengrocer's Pizzas (page 242)

Focaccia with Marinated Vegetables (page 247)

Cornmeal Blueberry Cake (page 268)

Rustic Plum-Walnut Tart (page 278)

Meringues with Lemon Sorbet and Berries (page 286)

Strawberries in Raspberry Puree (page 293), Chocolate Walnut Biscotti (page 283)

CHAPTER 11

SIMPLY
SENSATIONAL
SWEETS

*L*A DOLCE VITA

*I*n Italy, fresh fruit literally takes the cake. Fruit is often the sole choice for dessert. Italy does produce luscious, elegant pastries, but these are the work of trained pastry chefs and are offered primarily at cafes and pastry shops. On religious holidays and at family celebrations, desserts are relatively modest cakes, cookies, *gelato*, *granità* and puddings. In this chapter you'll find simple, lower-fat variations of Italian classics. But the best choice is always perfectly ripe fruit. Even following a formal meal, such natural goodness is sure to please even the most sophisticated palate.

ITALIAN PLAIN CAKES WITH STRAWBERRIES

*I*n Italy, plain cakes with fruit are usually served with coffee or tea, and often for breakfast. Each region has a variation on a plain cake, and all are distinguished by their simplicity. These simple cakes resemble our shortcakes. They may be made a day ahead and kept in an airtight container. Assemble just before serving.

Plain Cakes

1½	cups unbleached flour
¼	cup plus 1½ teaspoons sugar
1	teaspoon baking powder
½	teaspoon baking soda
	Pinch of salt
2	tablespoons cold butter, cut into small pieces
½–⅔	cup nonfat buttermilk
1	tablespoon oil
½	teaspoon vanilla
2	teaspoons skim milk

Filling

1	pint strawberries, sliced ¼" thick
1	tablespoon sugar

Assembly

1	cup nonfat vanilla yogurt

To make the plain cakes: Coat a baking sheet with no-stick spray.

In a mixing bowl, combine the flour, ¼ cup of the sugar, baking powder, baking soda and salt. Using a pastry cutter or 2 knives, cut the butter into the flour mixture until crumbly.

In a small bowl, combine ½ cup of the buttermilk, oil and vanilla. Make a well in the center of the flour mixture and add the buttermilk mixture. With a fork, stir until just combined, adding additional buttermilk as necessary to form a sticky dough. Do not overmix.

Place the dough on a floured surface and sprinkle with a little flour. With your fingertips, gently pat the dough into a 7″ circle. With a sharp knife, cut the circle into 8 wedges. Transfer to the prepared baking sheet. Brush the skim milk over the cakes and sprinkle lightly with the remaining 1½ teaspoons sugar.

Bake the cakes at 425° for 10 to 12 minutes, or until golden. Transfer to a rack and allow to cool slightly.

To make the filling: In a large bowl, toss the strawberries with the sugar. With the back of a wooden spoon, crush a few of the strawberries. Stir and allow to rest for 5 minutes, or until the strawberries have formed a light syrup.

To assemble: Split the cakes with a serrated knife. Spoon the strawberries and yogurt onto the bottom half of each cake. Crown with the tops. Serve immediately.

Preparation time: 20 minutes plus 5 minutes resting time
Baking time: 12 minutes

Chef's notes: The cake dough may be made ahead and stored, covered, in the refrigerator for up to 1 hour before baking.

Try substituting all-fruit sorbet for the frozen yogurt.

Per serving: 198 calories, 5.1 g. fat (23% of calories), 1.7 g. dietary fiber, 8 mg. cholesterol, 128 mg. sodium.

CORNMEAL BLUEBERRY CAKE

*H*ere's a dense, lemony loaf cake with a light, crunchy texture.

1½	*cups unbleached flour*
½	*cup yellow cornmeal*
1½	*teaspoons baking powder*
½	*teaspoon salt*
¼	*teaspoon baking soda*
⅔	*cup nonfat plain yogurt*
1	*tablespoon lemon juice*
1	*teaspoon vanilla*
¾	*cup sugar*
¼	*cup oil*
2	*teaspoons grated lemon rind*
1	*egg*
1	*egg white*
1	*cup blueberries*

In a small bowl, combine the flour, cornmeal, baking powder, salt and baking soda.

In another small bowl, combine the yogurt, lemon juice and vanilla.

In a medium bowl, whisk together the sugar, oil and lemon rind. Beat in the egg, then the egg white, beating well after each addition. Alternately add the dry ingredients and the yogurt mixture to the egg mixture, beginning and ending with the dry ingredients. Mix until just combined. Gently fold in the blueberries.

Coat an 8″ × 4″ loaf pan with no-stick spray. Pour the batter into the prepared loaf pan. Bake at 350° for 45 to 55 minutes, or until the cake is golden and a toothpick inserted in the center comes out clean.

Cool the cake in the pan on a rack for 10 minutes, then turn out onto the rack and cool completely.

Preparation time: 10 minutes
Baking time: 50 minutes
Cooling time: 10 minutes

Per slice: 138 calories, 4 g. fat (26% of calories), 1.1 g. dietary fiber, 13 mg. cholesterol, 127 mg. sodium.

LEMON MINT ICE

SERVES 4

*W*hat better refreshment for a scorching summer's day than cool lemon and fresh mint?

¾ *cup frozen lemonade concentrate*
½ *cup fresh mint leaves*
3 *cups crushed ice*
½ *cup cold water*

In a blender, puree the lemonade concentrate with the mint leaves. Add the ice and water and process until smooth and icy.

Pour into an 8″ × 8″ baking dish and freeze for 15 minutes, or until semifirm.

Preparation time: 5 minutes
Freezing time: 15 minutes

Per serving: 86 calories, 0.1 g. fat (1% of calories), 1.2 g. dietary fiber, no cholesterol, 2 mg. sodium.

CASSATA SICILIANA

*I*n this traditional Sicilian dessert, layers of angel food cake are dressed with a creamy filling. The cake is often served at Christmas and Easter.

¼ *cup water*
¼ *cup plus ⅓ cup sugar*
1 *teaspoon rum extract*
1 *container (15 ounces) nonfat ricotta cheese*
½ *cup chopped mixed candied fruit (citron, lemon rind, orange rind, pineapple, cherries)*
1 *ounce semisweet chocolate, chopped*
1 *tablespoon grated orange rind*
1 *(10-ounce) angel food cake*
1 *tablespoon unsweetened cocoa powder*

In a small saucepan, bring the water to a boil. Add ¼ cup of the sugar and stir to dissolve. Stir in the rum extract and turn off the heat.

Line a 9″ × 5″ loaf pan with plastic wrap.

In a medium bowl, combine the ricotta and the remaining ⅓ cup sugar. Stir in the fruit, chocolate and orange rind.

With a serrated knife, slice the angel food cake into ½″-thick slices. Line the bottom of the loaf pan with a layer of slices. Brush the slices with 2 tablespoons of the syrup. Spread with one-third of the ricotta filling. Repeat the layers twice. Arrange the remaining slices of cake over the top and brush with the remaining syrup. Cover with plastic wrap and weigh down the cake with another loaf pan and a heavy weight or can.

Refrigerate for at least 15 minutes or overnight. To serve the cassata, invert the loaf pan onto a serving dish. Remove the plastic wrap. Dust with the cocoa.

Preparation time: 15 minutes
Cooking time: 3 minutes
Chilling time: 15 minutes

Per serving: 292 calories, 1.2 g. fat (4% of calories), no dietary fiber, 6 mg. cholesterol, 342 mg. sodium.

RICOTTA COFFEE CREAM

SERVES 4

One of the easiest desserts to make, this delicious combination of ricotta and coffee takes just minutes in the food processor. It may be made a day ahead (in fact, it tastes even better once the flavors have mellowed).

1   *container (15 ounces) nonfat ricotta cheese*
½   *cup cold very strong coffee or espresso*
¼   *cup sugar*
1   *teaspoon ground nutmeg*

In a food processor fitted with the steel blade, combine the ricotta, coffee or espresso, sugar and nutmeg; process for 2 minutes, stopping once to scrape down the sides of the bowl with a rubber spatula.

Turn into 4 serving dishes or glasses and freeze for 20 minutes. If planning to store for more than 30 minutes before serving, cover and place in the refrigerator.

Preparation time: 5 minutes
Freezing time: 20 minutes

Chef's note: Try serving this topped with a few whole coffee beans or fresh strawberries, raspberries or sliced bananas.

Per serving: 131 calories, 0.2 g. fat (1% of calories), no dietary fiber, 12 mg. cholesterol, 62 mg. sodium.

Citrus Ricotta Cannoli

MAKES 20

*T*rue Italian *cannoli* are light and zesty with a creamy mascarpone filling. In this recipe, the *cannoli* shells are baked (not fried), and whipped nonfat ricotta replaces the calorie- and fat-laden mascarpone cheese. These are wonderful on a dessert platter for a buffet.

Cannoli Shells

2	tablespoons butter, melted and cooled
⅓	cup sugar
2	egg whites
½	teaspoon almond extract
½	teaspoon vanilla
⅓	cup unbleached flour

Citrus Ricotta Filling

1	container (15 ounces) nonfat ricotta cheese
¼	cup sugar
1	tablespoon grated orange rind
2	teaspoons grated lemon rind
1	teaspoon grated lime rind
1	teaspoon vanilla
1	ounce bittersweet chocolate, finely chopped

To make the cannoli shells: In a large bowl, blend the butter and sugar. Add the egg whites, almond extract and vanilla; beat to combine. Stir in the flour.

Coat 2 baking sheets with no-stick spray. Place 3 mounds of batter (1 tablespoon each) on each sheet; spread each mound into a very thin 4″ circle. Bake at 375° for 6 to 8 minutes, or until set. Using a spatula, gently lift the *cannoli* off and wrap around thick dowels, a clean broom handle or *cannoli* molds; cool, then slide off the molds. Repeat until the remaining batter is used up.

To make the citrus ricotta filling: In a medium bowl, use an electric beater to whip the ricotta with the sugar, orange rind, lemon rind, lime rind and vanilla. Stir in the chocolate.

To assemble, spoon the filling into the *cannoli* shells.

Preparation time: 10 minutes
Baking time: 32 minutes

Chef's note: The shells and filling may be made several days in advance. Store the shells in an airtight container; keep the filling in a covered container in the refrigerator. Assemble just before serving.

Per cannoli: 65 calories, 1.9 g. fat (25% of calories), trace of dietary fiber, 5 mg. cholesterol, 29 mg. sodium.

TIRAMISU

SERVES 6

A specialty of Italian *trattorias* serving simple, family-style fare, this dessert is heavenly. Appropriately enough, *tiramisu* literally means "lift me up."

36 *ladyfingers*
¼ *cup cold coffee*
1 *teaspoon rum extract*
1 *tablespoon instant espresso granules*
¾ *cup sugar*
2 *egg whites*
2 *tablespoons cold water*
   Pinch of cream of tartar
½ *cup yogurt cheese (page 28)*
½ *cup softened nonfat cream cheese*
1 *teaspoon vanilla*
2 *tablespoons unsweetened cocoa powder*

Spread the ladyfingers on a baking sheet and toast them at 350° for 6 to 8 minutes, or until dry.

In a small bowl, stir together the coffee, rum extract and espresso granules. Brush over the flat side of the ladyfingers and set aside.

Bring 1″ of water to a simmer in a large saucepan. In a heatproof mixing bowl that will fit over the saucepan, combine the sugar, egg whites, water and cream of tartar.

Set the bowl over the simmering water and beat with an electric mixer at low speed for 4 to 5 minutes, or until a candy thermometer inserted in the mixture registers 140°. Increase the speed to high and continue beating over the heat for 3 minutes, or until the mixture is thick and smooth enough that when you lift the beaters, a flat trail of egg white mixture stretches between the beaters and the bowl, like a glossy ribbon. Remove the bowl from the heat and beat for 4 minutes, or until cool and fluffy. Set aside.

In a large bowl, beat the yogurt cheese and cream cheese until creamy. Add the egg white mixture and the vanilla. Beat until smooth, occasionally scraping down the sides of the bowl.

Line the bottom and sides of a medium soufflé dish or glass bowl with some of the ladyfingers. Spoon in one-fourth of the filling and top with a layer of ladyfingers. Repeat with 2 more layers, arranging the fourth layer of ladyfingers over the top and trimming to fit if necessary. Top with the remaining filling. Cover and refrigerate for at least 30 minutes or overnight. Dust with the cocoa.

Preparation time: 20 minutes
Cooking time: 8 minutes
Chilling time: 30 minutes

Per serving: 225 calories, 1.9 g. fat (7% of calories), no dietary fiber, 4 mg. cholesterol, 168 mg. sodium.

LEMON RICOTTA CHEESECAKE

SERVES 10

Torta di ricotta is an Italian cheesecake, traditionally served at Easter celebrations, that varies from region to region. In this recipe, tart apricots and sweet golden raisins are offset against the mild and creamy background.

¼ *cup ground amaretti cookies*

⅓ *cup golden raisins*

⅓ *cup diced apricots*

⅓ *cup orange juice*

¾ *cup yogurt cheese (page 28)*

⅔ *cup sugar*

1¾ *cups nonfat ricotta cheese*

¼ *cup unbleached flour*

1 *egg*

2 *egg whites*

1 *tablespoon lemon juice*

1 *teaspoon grated lemon rind*

1 *teaspoon grated orange rind*

Coat an 8″ springform pan with no-stick spray. Place the cookies in the prepared pan; tilt and rotate the pan to coat the bottom and sides. Tap the pan on the counter so that the cookies are evenly distributed. Set aside.

In a small saucepan over low heat, combine the raisins, apricots and orange juice; cook for 2 minutes. Turn off the heat and allow the fruit to plump while preparing the filling.

In a large mixing bowl, beat the yogurt cheese and sugar until creamy. Add the ricotta, flour, egg, egg whites, lemon juice, lemon rind and orange rind; mix well. Drain the plumped fruit; stir into the batter. Pour the batter into the prepared pan.

Bake at 350° for 45 minutes, or until puffed at the edges but still slightly wobbly in the center. Turn off the oven and leave the cheesecake inside with the door closed for 15 minutes longer.

Remove the cheesecake from the oven and let it cool completely on a wire rack. Remove the springform sides. Serve at room temperature or refrigerate, covered, for up to 2 days.

Preparation time: 20 minutes
Baking time: 45 minutes plus 15 minutes resting time

Per serving: 154 calories, 0.9 g. fat (1% of calories), 0.8 g. dietary fiber, 26 mg. cholesterol, 61 mg sodium.

Rustic Plum-Walnut Tart

*T*his rustic free-form tart makes delicious use of those beautiful late-summer plums. A nutty crust absorbs the luscious plum juices, yet stays crisp and light.

Crust

1	cup unbleached flour
1	tablespoon sugar
¼	teaspoon salt
¼	teaspoon ground cinnamon
2	tablespoons vegetable oil or walnut oil (see note)
3–4	tablespoons ice water

Filling

2	tablespoons chopped walnuts
6	plums
4	tablespoons whole-grain nugget cereal or low-fat granola
⅓	cup plus 1 teaspoon sugar
2	tablespoons unbleached flour
1	tablespoon skim milk
2	tablespoons red currant jelly

To make the crust: In a medium bowl, stir together the flour, sugar, salt and cinnamon. Using a fork, slowly stir in the vegetable or walnut oil until the flour mixture becomes crumbly. Stir in enough ice water so that the dough holds together in a ball. (The dough will be wetter than traditional pastry doughs.) Press the dough into a flattened disk.

On a work surface, overlap two 14″ × 24″ pieces of plastic wrap, making a square about 24″ × 24″. Place the dough in the center and cover with 2 more identical overlapping pieces of plastic wrap. Roll the dough into a rough 12″ circle about ⅛″ thick, patching when necessary. Remove the top plastic wrap and invert the dough onto a baking sheet. Refrigerate, still covered, while preparing the filling.

To make the filling: Spread the walnuts on a pie plate and bake at 400° for 5 minutes, or until fragrant. Let cool.

Quarter the plums, discarding the pits. Place the cereal or granola, ⅓ cup of the sugar, flour and walnuts in a blender or a food processor fitted with the steel blade; pulse until finely ground.

Remove the plastic wrap and spread the nut mixture over the pastry, leaving a 1½″ border around the edge. Arrange the plums, resting on their sides, in concentric circles over the nut mixture. Fold the pastry border over the outside edge of the plums. Brush the milk over the pastry and sprinkle with the remaining 1 teaspoon sugar.

Bake at 400° for 30 to 40 minutes, or until the crust is golden and the juices are bubbling. With a long metal spatula, loosen the pastry bottom. Slide the tart onto a serving platter and let cool. Before serving, in a small saucepan over low heat, heat the jelly until melted; brush over the plums.

Preparation time: 20 minutes
Baking time: 45 minutes

Chef's note: Walnut oil adds a wonderfully nutty richness to baked goods and salads. Available at specialty food stores and food co-ops, it must be stored in the refrigerator after opening.

Per serving: 244 calories, 6.2 g. fat (22% of calories), 1.7 g. dietary fiber, no cholesterol, 123 mg. sodium.

BISCOTTI

*B*iscotti, the crunchy and not-too-sweet Italian cookie, literally means "twice baked." The dough is formed into logs and baked, then the logs are sliced and returned to the oven for a second baking. These days, however, the term *biscotti* is used generically for all kinds of cookies.

The biscotti recipes in this book are made in a pan and baked only once, to save time and trouble. These biscotti are not quite as dry as those baked twice, but they will harden after a day and be great dunkers.

To make these recipes into traditional twice-baked cookies, turn the dough onto a floured surface. Using the heels of your hands, shape it into two 12″ × 2″ logs. Place on baking sheets that have been coated with no-stick spray and bake at 350° for 20 to 25 minutes, or until firm. Reduce the oven temperature to 300°.

Cool the logs for 15 minutes; cut them diagonally into ½″ slices. Arrange the slices, cut side down, on the baking sheet and bake for 8 to 10 minutes, or until crisp.

ANISE BISCOTTI

*Z*esty orange and lemon enliven the anise flavor in this biscotti; the dried cherries are tart and moist.

> 1 *cup unbleached flour*
> ½ *cup sugar*
> 2 *teaspoons anise seeds, crushed*
> ½ *teaspoon baking powder*
> ¼ *teaspoon baking soda*
> ¼ *teaspoon salt*
> 1 *egg*
> 1 *tablespoon grated orange rind*
> 1 *tablespoon grated lemon rind*
> 1 *tablespoon lemon juice*
> ½ *cup chopped dried cherries*

In a large bowl, combine the flour, sugar, anise seeds, baking powder, baking soda and salt. In a small bowl, whisk together the egg, orange rind, lemon rind and lemon juice. Add to the dry ingredients and mix well. Stir in the cherries.

Coat an 11″ × 7″ or a 9″ × 9″ baking pan with no-stick spray. Press the dough into the prepared pan. Bake at 350° for 25 minutes, or until firm. Immediately cut into 30 fingers. Cool before serving.

Preparation time: 10 minutes
Baking time: 25 minutes

Per biscotti: 33 calories, 0.2 g. fat (7% of calories), trace of dietary fiber, 7 mg. cholesterol, 32 mg. sodium.

Black Pepper and Fig Biscotti

MAKES 30

This crunchy biscotti is a surprising blend of the hot and sweet flavors of black pepper and dried figs. It makes a great appetizer or late-afternoon snack.

½ cup whole-wheat flour
½ cup unbleached flour
2 teaspoons sugar
1 teaspoon coarsely ground black pepper
½ teaspoon baking powder
¼ teaspoon baking soda
¼ teaspoon salt
1 egg
1 egg white
2 tablespoons oil
½ cup finely chopped dried figs

In a large bowl, combine the whole-wheat flour, unbleached flour, sugar, pepper, baking powder, baking soda and salt. In a small bowl whisk together the egg, egg white and oil. Add to the dry ingredients and mix with a wooden spoon until almost smooth. Stir in the figs.

Coat an 11″ × 7″ or a 9″ × 9″ baking pan with no-stick spray. Press the dough into the prepared pan. Bake at 350° for 25 minutes, or until firm. Immediately cut into 30 fingers. Cool before serving.

Preparation time: 10 minutes
Baking time: 25 minutes

Per biscotti: 35 calories, 1.2 g. fat (29% of calories), 0.6 g. dietary fiber, 7 mg. cholesterol, 35 mg. sodium.

CHOCOLATE WALNUT BISCOTTI

*D*ark and rich-tasting, these biscotti keep well in a cookie tin or in the freezer. They are especially good dunked in espresso.

1	*cup unbleached flour*
½	*cup sugar*
¼	*cup unsweetened cocoa powder*
½	*teaspoon baking powder*
¼	*teaspoon baking soda*
¼	*teaspoon salt*
1	*egg*
1	*egg white*
1½	*teaspoons vanilla*
2	*ounces bittersweet chocolate, chopped*
¼	*cup chopped walnuts*

Spread the walnuts on a pie plate and bake at 400° for 5 minutes, or until fragrant. Let cool.

In a large bowl, combine the flour, sugar, cocoa, baking powder, baking soda and salt. In a medium bowl, whisk together the egg, egg white and vanilla. Add to the flour mixture and stir until smooth. Stir in the chocolate and walnuts.

Coat an 11″ × 7″ or a 9″ × 9″ baking pan with no-stick spray. Press the dough into the prepared pan. Bake at 350° for 25 minutes, or until firm. Immediately cut into 30 fingers. Cool before serving.

Preparation time: 10 minutes
Baking time: 25 minutes

Per biscotti: 75 calories, 2.6 g. fat (29% of calories), 0.7 g. dietary fiber, 12 mg. cholesterol, 44 mg. sodium.

MOCHA-ALMOND BISCOTTI

MAKES 30

Mild chocolate and light almond flavor come together nicely in this crunchy cookie. Great for dunking.

⅓ *cup slivered almonds*

1¼ *cups unbleached flour*

½ *cup sugar*

½ *teaspoon baking powder*

¼ *teaspoon baking soda*

¼ *teaspoon salt*

1 *egg*

1 *egg white*

1 *teaspoon vanilla*

½ *teaspoon almond extract*

1 *tablespoon instant coffee powder*

1 *tablespoon water*

1 *ounce unsweetened chocolate, melted*

Spread the almonds on a baking sheet and toast at 350° for 8 to 10 minutes, or until lightly toasted. Set aside.

In a large bowl, stir together the flour, sugar, baking powder, baking soda and salt.

In a small bowl, whisk together the egg, egg white, vanilla and almond extract. In a cup, combine the coffee and the water. Add the coffee mixture and chocolate to the egg mixture. Add to the dry ingredients and mix just until incorporated. Stir in the almonds.

Coat an 11″ × 7″ or a 9″ × 9″ baking pan with no-stick spray. Press the dough into the prepared pan. Bake at 350° for 25 minutes, or until firm. Immediately cut into 30 fingers. Cool before serving.

Preparation time: 10 minutes
Baking time: 35 minutes

Per biscotti: 73 calories, 2.2 g. fat (26% of calories), trace of dietary fiber, 11 mg. cholesterol, 52 mg. sodium.

Warm Pear Compote

SERVES 4

*J*ust right for impromptu entertaining, this simple, homey compote is easily put together at the last minute.

5   *ripe but firm pears, peeled, cored and cut into eighths*
¼   *cup dried cherries*
¾   *teaspoon ground cinnamon*
½   *teaspoon ground nutmeg*
⅔   *cup apple juice*
1   *tablespoon honey*
1   *teaspoon vanilla*
1   *teaspoon lemon juice*
    Nonfat frozen vanilla yogurt

Coat a 2-quart microwave-safe baking dish with no-stick spray. Place the pears and cherries in the prepared dish. Sprinkle the cinnamon and nutmeg over the fruit.

In a small bowl, mix together the apple juice, honey, vanilla and lemon juice. Pour over the fruit and toss to coat.

Microwave the fruit, uncovered, for 5 minutes on high. Stir. Microwave for another 5 minutes. Stir. Microwave for 2 minutes more, or until the fruit is soft and hot. Let stand for 2 minutes. Serve with a dollop of frozen yogurt.

Preparation time: 5 minutes
Microwaving time: 12 minutes plus 2 minutes standing time

Chef's note: Substitute apples for two of the pears for a delicious variation.

Per serving: 156 calories, 0.9 g. fat (5% of calories), 4.7 g. dietary fiber, no cholesterol, 3 mg. sodium.

Meringues with Lemon Sorbet and Berries

SERVES 4

*I*talian meringue, *meringa*, is crisp and dry, a heavenly contrast to the tart sorbet and sweet mixed berries. Use whatever berries are in season.

Meringue Shells

3	*egg whites, at room temperature*
¼	*teaspoon cream of tartar*
⅛	*teaspoon salt*
¾	*cup sugar*
½	*teaspoon vanilla*
½	*teaspoon lemon juice*

Filling

2	*cups sliced mixed berries (such as blackberries, raspberries, blueberries or strawberries)*
1	*tablespoon sugar*
2	*cups lemon sorbet*

To make the meringue shells: In a large bowl, combine the egg whites, cream of tartar and salt. Beat with an electric mixer until soft peaks form. Gradually beat in the sugar, 1 tablespoon at a time. Beat in the vanilla and lemon juice, stopping occasionally to scrape down the sides of the bowl, until the sugar is dissolved and the meringue is stiff and shiny.

Cover a large baking sheet with parchment paper. Drop 4 large spoonfuls of meringue, evenly spaced, on the prepared baking sheet. With the back of a spoon, form the meringue into little nests. Bake at 225° for 1 hour. Turn the oven off and let the meringues rest inside with the door closed for 1 hour. Cool the meringues on a wire rack.

To make the filling: Toss the berries with the sugar. Fill each shell with a scoop of sorbet and top with berries.

Preparation time: 10 minutes
Baking time: 1 hour plus 1 hour resting time

Chef's note: Meringues may be made ahead and stored in an airtight container for up to 2 weeks.

Per serving: 268 calories, 2.8 g. fat (9% of calories), 1.9 g. dietary fiber, no cholesterol, 143 mg. sodium.

ESPRESSO GRANITÀ

SERVES 4

*G*ranità, a sweet, frozen confection, is traditionally made without an ice cream machine. The texture is icy and the dessert, light and very refreshing.

   2   cups hot espresso
  ½ cup sugar

Pour the espresso into a large bowl. Add the sugar; stir until dissolved. Let cool to room temperature.

Pour into a 13″ × 9″ pan and place in the freezer for 30 minutes, or until completely frozen. Transfer the *granità* to a food processor fitted with the steel blade; pulse briefly until icy and fluffy.

Preparation time: 5 minutes
Freezing time: 30 minutes

Chef's note: *Granità* may be made several days ahead. Soften and process briefly just before serving.

Per serving: 184 calories, no fat (0% of calories), no dietary fiber, no cholesterol, 4 mg. sodium.

SIMPLY DELICIOUS DESSERTS

A healthy diet certainly does not mean deprivation. There are many ways to satisfy a sweet tooth, all low in calories, fat and sugar. Thanks to nonfat plain yogurt, nonfat ricotta cheese, nonfat sour cream and nonfat half-and-half, traditional Italian desserts are now within sensible reach. Here's a collection of quick and simple sweet nothings.

CREAMIEST FRUIT CREAMS

Create a compote of your favorite fruits and top with yogurt cream. Mix 1 cup nonfat plain yogurt with 2 tablespoons nonfat sour cream and add these ingredients for extra flavor:

• **Lemon Mint Cream:** Whisk in ¼ cup chopped fresh mint, 1 tablespoon lemon juice, 1 teaspoon grated lemon rind and 1 teaspoon sugar.

• **Orange Cream:** Whisk in 1 tablespoon frozen orange juice concentrate, 1 teaspoon grated orange rind and 1 teaspoon honey.

• **Spice Cream:** Whisk in 1 teaspoon brown sugar, ¼ teaspoon ground cinnamon and a pinch of ground nutmeg.

LUSCIOUS ICED DRINKS

With a blender and fresh fruit, nonfat plain yogurt, a little ice and some imagination, you can whip up smooth, refreshing "after-dinner" drinks that are also great after school or even midmorning. Each recipe makes 2 cups.

• **Iced Cappuccino:** In a blender, combine 1 cup skim milk, ½ cup regular or decaf espresso, 1 tablespoon sugar and a pinch of ground nutmeg. Process until frothy.

• **Very Berry:** In a blender, combine 1 cup skim milk and 1 cup frozen raspberries, blueberries, cherries or sliced strawberries. Process until frothy.

• **Peach Express:** In a blender, combine 1 cup skim milk, 1 cup frozen sliced peaches, a pinch of ground nutmeg and a pinch of ground cinnamon.

SEMIFREDDO AL LAMPONE

SERVES 4

A classic *semifreddo* is a partially frozen confection made of heavy cream and eggs. In this recipe, nonfat ricotta provides a lush flavor to a lighter dessert that does not need to be frozen but has the creamy texture of the original.

> 1   *container (15 ounces) nonfat ricotta cheese*
> ⅓   *cup plus 2 tablespoons sugar*
> 1   *tablespoon orange juice*
> 2   *cups raspberries*
>   *Mint leaves*

In a food processor fitted with the steel blade, combine the ricotta, ⅓ cup of the sugar and orange juice; process for 30 seconds, or until creamy and smooth. Transfer the ricotta mixture to a large bowl and refrigerate.

Rinse and dry the food processor bowl; puree the raspberries with the remaining 2 tablespoons sugar. Dollop over the ricotta mixture. Using a small knife, cut the raspberry puree through the ricotta mixture to create swirls. Cover and refrigerate for at least 4 hours. Serve garnished with the mint leaves.

Preparation time: 5 minutes
Chilling time: 4 hours

Chef's notes: If the raspberries seem very seedy, you may want to sieve the seeds out. After pureeing the berries with the sugar, turn them into a fine sieve set over a bowl and press with the back of a spoon or rubber spatula.

If fresh raspberries are not available, use half of a 12-ounce package of frozen berries. Thaw and drain them well before pureeing.

Per serving: 202 calories, 0.4 g. fat (1% of calories), 2.8 g. dietary fiber, 12 mg. cholesterol, 58 mg. sodium.

BROILED PEACHES WITH AMARETTI COOKIES

SERVES 4

*S*weet, toothsome fresh peaches are topped with crunchy, almond-scented amaretti cookies in a healthful fruit crisp.

4   *ripe peaches, peeled, pitted and cut into ¼" slices*
1   *tablespoon lemon juice*
1   *teaspoon almond extract*
1   *teaspoon vanilla*
½   *cup ground amaretti cookies*
1   *teaspoon ground cinnamon*

In a medium bowl, toss together the peaches, lemon juice, almond extract and vanilla. Set aside.

In a small bowl, toss together the cookies and cinnamon.

Spread the peaches on a baking sheet and broil about 5" from the heat for 5 to 7 minutes, or until tender. Leave the broiler on. Sprinkle the cookies over the peaches and return to the broiler. Broil for 1 to 2 minutes, or until the topping is golden brown.

Preparation time: 5 minutes
Broiling time: 9 minutes

Chef's note: Serve the peaches with a dollop of nonfat frozen vanilla yogurt or plain nonfat yogurt.

Per serving: 155 calories, 1.8 g. fat (1% of calories), 5.4 g. dietary fiber, no cholesterol, 18 mg. sodium.

CANTALOUPE IN CINNAMON HONEY

*R*ipe cantaloupe's fruity sweetness is highlighted by the richness of cinnamon-scented honey.

1   *cup water*
2   *cinnamon sticks*
2   *tablespoons honey (see note)*
2   *tablespoons sugar*
½   *cantaloupe, seeded and chilled*

In a heavy medium saucepan, combine the water, cinnamon sticks, honey and sugar. Bring to a boil over high heat; boil for 2 minutes. Turn off the heat and skim off the foam. Transfer the syrup to a bowl; chill in the freezer or refrigerator for 20 minutes.

Cut the rind from the cantaloupe and quarter it. Then cut each quarter into ½" slices. Discard the cinnamon sticks. Pour the syrup over the slices just before serving.

Preparation time: 5 minutes
Cooking time: 2 minutes
Chilling time: 20 minutes

Chef's note: Choose a fairly mild honey so it won't overpower the cantaloupe flavor.

Per serving: 112 calories, 0.5 g. fat (3% of calories), 1.3 g. dietary fiber, no cholesterol, 15 mg. sodium.

MIXED BERRY AMBROSIA

SERVES 4

Several different kinds of berries make for a colorful presentation, but you may choose to make a single-berry ambrosia, too.

2 *tablespoons honey*

2 *tablespoons lemon juice*

2 *tablespoons orange juice*

2 *large sprigs fresh mint*

4 *cups mixed fresh berries (such as red or golden raspberries, blueberries or strawberries)*

1 *cup chilled champagne or nonalcoholic champagne*

In a small saucepan, combine the honey, lemon juice, orange juice and mint; stir over low heat until the honey melts. Remove from the heat and allow to steep for 5 minutes. Discard the mint.

In a large bowl, combine the berries and honey mixture; stir gently to combine. Chill for 15 minutes or up to 1 hour. Just before serving, stir in the champagne.

Preparation time: 5 minutes
Cooking time: 5 minutes
Chilling time: 15 minutes

Per serving: 148 calories, 0.6 g. fat (3% of calories), 4.5 g. dietary fiber, no cholesterol, 5 mg. sodium.

STRAWBERRIES IN RASPBERRY PUREE

SERVES 4

*P*lump, juicy strawberries are drenched in a brilliant raspberry sauce. Serve this beautiful combination in long-stemmed goblets, garnished with mint leaves.

2 *cups raspberries (see note)*
2 *tablespoons sugar*
¼ *teaspoon almond extract*
1 *pint strawberries, hulled*

In a food processor fitted with the steel blade, puree the raspberries, sugar and almond extract. Pour into a sieve set over a bowl; with the back of a spoon or rubber spatula, press the puree through the sieve to remove the seeds.

Put the strawberries into 4 long-stemmed goblets or a serving dish. Pour the puree over the strawberries. Chill in the refrigerator for 15 minutes.

Preparation time: 5 minutes
Chilling time: 15 minutes

Chef's note: You may use fresh or frozen raspberries in this puree. If you use frozen berries, thaw them before putting them in the food processor.

Per serving: 76 calories, 0.6 g. fat (7% of calories), 4.7 g. dietary fiber, no cholesterol, 1 mg. sodium.

CHAPTER 12

MENUS
SERVING
A FAMILY OF
FOUR—OR
MANY MORE

CELEBRATING— ITALIAN STYLE

Whether you're hosting a full-blown feast, entertaining friends alfresco or simply preparing a weekday supper, here's a harvest of menus to help you in planning. The "Farmhouse Kitchen Supper" menu provides an easy family meal everyone will enjoy. The "Elegant Dinner Party" menu is as easy on the cook as it is on the waistline. The "Antipasti Repast" and "Pizza Party" menus are great casual entertaining.

Influenced by traditional Italian feast days, regional festivals and the wealth of fresh produce and specialty Italian ingredients now available in the U.S., these 20 easy, low-fat and healthy menus will help you celebrate your life—Italian style.

TRATTORIA SUPPER

Cannellini Bean Dip* with
  whole-wheat crackers
Chicken Cacciatore*
Spinach Risotto*

Peasant Bread*
Pear Balsamic Salad*
Rustic Plum Walnut Tart*

MEDITERRANEAN SEAFOOD PARTY FEAST

Mussels Marinara*
Grilled Shrimp with Potatoes,
  Peas and Basil*
Mediterranean Cauliflower*

Marinated Tuna on Broccoli Rabe*
Peppery Rosemary Quick Bread*
Orange and Pepper Salad*
Lemon Mint Ice*

ANTIPASTI REPAST

Roasted Eggplant Spread* with
  fresh vegetables and whole-
  wheat crackers
Roasted Ceci Nuts*
Bruschetta variations:

Tomato and Watercress*; Cucumber,
  Sun-Dried Tomato and Olive*
Chicken and Artichoke Kabobs*
Sicilian Tuna and Potato Salad*
Peperonata*
Citrus Ricotta Cannoli*

PICNIC IN THE TUSCANY HILLS FOR EIGHT

Mediterranean Summer
  Sandwiches*
Shrimp Caesar Sandwich

Marinated Vegetables*
Cornmeal Blueberry Cake*

PIZZA PARTY! (FOR EIGHT KIDS OF ALL AGES)

Mini-Pita Pizzas*
Roasted Vegetable Calzones*
Pizza Puttanesca*

Mushroom and Sage Pizzas*
Chocolate Walnut Biscotti*

INTIMATE FAMILY CHRISTMAS EVE

Roasted Clams with Zesty Fresh
  Tomatoes*
Poached Chicken Breasts in
  Balsamic Vinegar*

Saffron Risotto with Vegetables*
Baked Fennel*
Cassata Siciliana*

PASTA PARTY BUFFET

Basic Balsamic Vinaigrette*
  tossed with bitter greens
Lemon, Asparagus and Mushroom
  Fettuccine*
Scallops with Garlic and Parsley
  on Linguine*

Tuscan Fettuccine*
Riso All' Insalada*
Semifreddo al Lampone*

*See recipe.

SOUP SAMPLER FOR TEN
Chilled Cucumber and Basil Soup*
Asparagus, Potato and Leek Soup*
Sicilian Sausage Stew*

Broiled Tomato Pesto Sandwiches*
Lemon Ricotta Cheesecake*

EASTER DINNER
Italian Spring Vegetable Soup*
Lamb Chops with Cucumbers
   and Tomatoes*
Roasted Rosemary Potatoes*

Parsleyed Carrots with Garlic
   and Capers*
Meringues with Lemon Sorbet
   and Berries*

MID-MORNING CAPPUCCINO FOR EIGHT
Mixed Berry Ambrosia*
Black Pepper and Fig Biscotti*

Yogurt Cheese* on whole wheat
   toast with honey
Cappuccino

SPA LUNCH
Artichoke-Herb Spread* with
   sweet red pepper strips
Swordfish with Tomatoes, Onions
   and Olives*

Lemon and Herb Riso*
Sugar Snap Peas with Mint*
Strawberries in Raspberry Puree*

FARMHOUSE KITCHEN SUPPER
(Not) Fried Zucchini*
Lemon-Pepper Polenta with Baked
   Fish and Peppers*

Asparagus with Roasted Peppers
   and Olives*
Warm Pear Compote*

AN ELEGANT DINNER PARTY
Minted Pea Soup*
Turkey Scaloppine in Wild
   Mushroom Sauce*
Focaccia*

Baked Radicchio*
Anise Biscotti*
Espresso

A MEATLESS MEAL
Stuffed Cherry Tomatoes*
Chick-Pea, Lentil and Green
   Pea Stew*
Asparagus Risotto*

Lemony Green Beans with
   Sunchokes*
Broiled Peaches with Amaretti
   Cookies*

*See recipe.

SIMPLE WORKDAY SUPPER

*Pasta Primavera**
*Lemon-Herb Chicken Breasts**

*Green and White Bean Salad**
*Ricotta Coffee Cream**

SUNDAY BRUNCH FOR EIGHT

*Broccoli-Red Pepper Frittata**
*Spaghetti Carbonara**

*Poached Turkey Breast with
Lemon-Caper Mayonnaise**
*Cantaloupe in Cinnamon Honey**

SUMMER GRILL

*Grilled Chicken Breasts
in Sage Vinaigrette**
*Roasted Eggplant, Pepper and
Onion Salad**

*Grilled Polenta with Roasted
Onions and Raisins**
*Tomatoes with Basil and Mint**
*Italian Plain Cakes with
Strawberries*

FALL HARVEST DINNER

*Garlicky Spinach Dip** with fresh
vegetables and crackers
*Herbed Chicken Thighs**
*Sun-Dried Tomato Pesto** tossed
with pasta

*Fava Bean, Fennel and Apple
Salad**
*Tiramisu**

SUNDAY SUPPER

*Panzanella**
*Roasted Chicken with Lemon and
Garlic**
*Sicilian Stuffed Eggplant**

*Garden Asparagus with Lemon
and Garlic**
*Espresso Granità**

EASY SATURDAY LUNCH

*Herb-Pickled Mushrooms**
*Greengrocer's Pizzas**

*Mocha-Almond Biscotti**

*See recipe.

Index

Note: Underscored page references indicate boxed text. **Boldface** references indicate photographs.